Red Channels
The Bible of Blacklisting

By Jason Hill

RED CHANNELS: THE BIBLE OF BLACKLISING

Red Channels: The Bible of Blacklisting by Jason Hill
© 2016, ALL RIGHTS RESERVED
No part of this book may be reproduced in any form or by any means, electronic, mechanical, digital, photocopying, or recording, except for inclusion of a review, without permission in writing from the publisher or Jason Hill.

Published in the USA by:
BearManor Media
P O Box 71426
Albany, Georgia 31708
www.bearmanormedia.com

ISBN: 978-1-59393-916-8
BearManor Media, Albany, Georgia
Printed in the United States of America
Book design by Robbie Adkins, www.adkinsconsult.com

Dedication

To the 151 unjust victims of *Red Channels*,
who suffered so long and lost so much.

Table of Contents

Acknowledgements..................................iv
Foreword..vii
Prologue..ix

Book One — The Accusers..........................1
Chapter One — Overview..............................2
Chapter Two — The Publication.......................4
Chapter Three — Kirkpatrick, Bierly, and Keenan.....7
Chapter Four — Laurence A. Johnson.................12
Chapter Five — Hartnett, McNamara, and Aware, Inc..17
Chapter Six — The Fronts...........................23
Chapter Seven — Clearance..........................30
Chapter Eight— Loyalty Oaths.......................34
Chapter Nine— Friendlies...........................38
Chapter Ten — The House Un-American Activities Committee..42

Book Two — The Accused..........................47
Chapter Eleven - Jean Muir.........................48
Chapter Twelve — Ireene Wicker.....................53
Chapter Thirteen — Philip Loeb.....................57
Chapter Fourteen — Walter Bernstein................62
Chapter Fifteen — Zero Mostel......................68
Chapter Sixteen — Pete Seeger......................74
Chapter Seventeen — Millard Lampell................82
Chapter Eighteen — Marc Blitzstein.................89
Chapter Nineteen — Artie Shaw......................98
Chapter Twenty — Hazel Scott......................104
Chapter Twenty-One — Lena Horne...................109
Chapter Twenty-Two — Leonard Bernstein............115
Chapter Twenty-Three — William N. Robson..........121
Chapter Twenty-Four — Norman Corwin...............126

Chapter Twenty-Five – Arthur Miller 132
Chapter Twenty-Six – Dorothy Parker 140
Chapter Twenty-Seven – Lillian Hellman 146
Chapter Twenty-Eight – Dashiell Hammett 156
Chapter Twenty-Nine – Henry Morgan 163
Chapter Thirty – Howard Duff 167
Chapter Thirty-One – Lionel Stander 172
Chapter Thirty-Two – Marsha Hunt 178
Chapter Thirty-Three – Jose Ferrer 183
Chapter Thirty-Four – John Garfield 190
Chapter Thirty-Five – Orson Welles 199
Chapter Thirty-Six – Edward G. Robinson 206
Chapter Thirty-Seven – Langston Hughes 212
Chapter Thirty-Eight – The Others 222

Book Three – Nearing the End 231
Chapter Thirty-Nine – John Henry Faulk 232
   Part One - The Filing
Chapter Forty – John Henry Faulk 237
   Part Two - The Pre-Trial
Chapter Forty-One –John Henry Faulk 241
   Part Three - The Trial
Chapter Forty-Two – John Henry Faulk 258
   Part Four - The Summation and Verdict
Chapter Forty-Three –John Henry Faulk 265
   Part Five - The Aftermath
Afterword - The Story of *The Front* 267
Source Notes 270
Bibliography 275
Index 278
About the Author 287

Acknowledgements

No book can ever be completed for publication by just that one person who is called the author. It is always a team effort. Without that team it would never reach the market place. My team consists of three wonderful women to whom I owe immense gratitude.

First and foremost there is Michaela Nelson, who is truly my right arm. She is responsible for hours and days of work on the final editing and assembly of my sometimes disjointed work.

Next is Robbie Adkins for her marvelous layout and formatting work on the final copy for print, and the third is Paula Slade. Her vast knowledge of the publishing industry has given me moral support for each and every one of my literary efforts.

Of course, I must also thank my publisher, Ben Ohmart, for having faith in my work, and his assistant, David W. Menefee, for his editing and promotional work.

Lastly, I am grateful to the many people who allowed me to interview them, and thus, by doing so, added credence to the subject matter. –Jason Hill

Foreword

Before you read this book, I want to make my intentions in writing it perfectly clear. I will not deny that during the 1940s and 1950s, the Communist Party USA and other groups were responsible for a great deal of unrest on the home front. Had it not been for the work of agencies such as the Federal Bureau of Investigation (FBI) and the wartime intelligence agency Office of Strategic Services (OSS, which was later changed to the CIA), our whole existence might be different today. This book is not about the genuine problems that were confronted at that time. No, this book is about the over-zealous and often misguided efforts put forth by many red-baiters who, for reasons of their own, decided to take it upon themselves to punish people in the world of entertainment for their ability to think.

Those persecutors had a one-track approach to everything. Subversion was subversion in their minds, even when it only existed due to innuendo and presumption of guilt gained from scurrilous, unproven sources. The end result was the ruin of many lives—at least temporarily—but, in some cases, permanently.

Lists were created, although most of those in power denied that fact. There were blacklists, there were graylists and there were also whitelists. All three were extremely detrimental to those included.

Of course, the blacklist was the worst. If you were on it, you could not get hired to work in your chosen profession. The graylist was nearly as bad. It meant that you had been partially cleared, but that you were still under suspicion. The result was very similar. The third one, the whitelist, was something used by the witch-hunters to try to justify their theories. It was a list of far-right anti-Communists, who claimed that they, too, could not find work in what they alleged to be the red-infiltrated media. This all became an intriguing conundrum. People from all sides of the question were constantly at each other's throats. Friends turned on friends with no good basis for doing so. All it took was a small germ of third party misinformation.

There were many blacklists, far too complicated a subject to tackle in one book. There were blacklists of government employees including the military. There were blacklists of educators. There were blacklists of members of the clergy. There were blacklists of unionists.

The only blacklist I will be speaking of is one that was created by a publication called *Red Channels: The Report of Communist Iinfluence in Radio and Television*. It came to be known as "The Bible of Blacklisting." Its effects were devastating for the mostly innocent victims it claimed.

I only hope that you, the reader, will keep in mind the words written by Spanish philosopher George Santayana so long ago. He said, "Those who cannot remember the past are condemned to repeat it."

Prologue

Red Channels
The Bible of Blacklisting

What was it all about?

It was about a witch hunt that made 1692 in Salem seem like a tea party.

It was about a national scandal that affected the lives of all of us in one way or another.

It was about a small segment of our population who lost many millions of dollars in earning power and in some cases, their very lives.

It was about a period in our national history during which each and every one of us had to maintain extreme caution when talking with strangers or even friends, lest some minuscule bit of the conversation be misconstrued or misinterpreted.

It was about a publisher, who was willing to accept tidbits of information, not necessarily documented, as gospel and make this data available to those who could use it to create devastating aftershocks.

It was about a US Congress that countermanded most of the measures put forth by their Commander-in-Chief, crippling and at times nearly canceling the powers of the Executive branch of our governmental system.

It was about the impotence of any defense put forth against this reign of terror, but most of all, it was about the sheer mayhem of misguided public opinion.

What kind of time was it?

It was a time of anger and fear and complacency and agony.

It was a time when the American populous was suffering the confusion of trying to relate to two wars and their differences because the recently concluded World War II was a struggle that allied some of the same forces that had become deadly foes in Korea.

It was a time when every person who preferred to do his or her own thinking and sort out the surrounding environment individually, was considered suspect.

It was a time when the words "Friend" or "Fellow Traveler" were derogatory terms.

It was a time when many of the provisions of the American judicial system flew out the window, becoming only glowing expressions from the casebook of democracy.

It was a time when the best known McCarthy of the airwaves was not a little wooden fellow named Charlie.

It was good times and bad times intermingled in an olio of frustration.

Who were the instigators?

They were the participators in an insidious type of warfare that took no prisoners, a practice called "Blacklisting."

They were both hardened professionals and very efficient amateurs.

They were people such as Theodore Kirkpatrick, Jack Keenan, and Ken Bierly, who co-founded an organization called American Business Consultants, whose sole purpose was to ferret out small bits of information, some based on fact, some mere supposition. Their regularly published newsletter called *Counterattack* went many leagues toward the ruination of the performing careers of many actors, writers, directors, producers, and musicians of all types.

They were people such as Frank McNamara, who edited *Counterattack* and later became director of anti-communist activities for the Veterans of Foreign Wars.

They were people such as Jack Wren, formerly with naval intelligence, who became the middle man between *Counterattack* and the advertising agencies that held the reins controlling most of the radio and television money sources.

They were people such as Vincent Hartnett and Paul Milton, who set up *Aware, Inc.* in 1952 for the sole purpose of disseminating often unproved information to their more than 600 members in key positions. Milton also served as a constant link between

Aware and a group of "Red Baiters" within the Writers Guild who dubbed themselves, "We, the Underground."

They were also people with no professional background but who proved that the wrong words dropped in the right places can be effective; people such as Laurence Johnson, a Syracuse supermarket proprietor, who made a crusade of walking up and down Madison Avenue, defaming the names of those he believed to have some remote Communist or Communist Front connections.

They were people like Hester McCullough of Greenwich, Connecticut, who was able to remove several talented people from the employable lists, simply by her letter writing campaigns.

They were organizations forced to use what was given them to destroy, at least temporarily, the lives of those people who were responsible for their own daily bread. I refer, of course, to the sponsors, their advertising people and the networks.

In the largest part, they were people like you and like me, who were willing to accept innuendo at face value because the lives of a few were inconsequential in the larger frame of things.

Who were the victims?

The victims were far too many to discuss in any one publication so, for my purposes I will treat only some of the cases of the 151 named in the *Counterattack* addition titled *Red Channels: the Report of Communist Influence in Radio and Television*. I will discuss the lives of many of those *Red Channels* blacklistees, who were still with us when this research began and were willing to talk about what it was that made them vulnerable to so heinous an attack. It is of the greatest importance to note that the list contained not one convicted party to subversion and in most cases the allegations were so remote that even the blacklistee was not totally aware of the circumstances being used against him or her. Furthermore, it would be difficult to find any of the remaining victims of *Red Channels,* who would not jump at the chance to clear the air about the gross injustice done to them.

This, then, is a chronicle of those horrible years using only the information obtained from those who knew the situation first hand. We will deal only with those listed in *Red Channels*, but the problem went far beyond that one single publication.

BOOK ONE
The Accusers

Chapter One
Overview

It was the worst of times! It was the worst of times! I know that is not the way Charles Dickens wrote it, but I believe that statement is very apropos to the conditions in the time that all of this was taking place to the detriment of our nation and all of us, as well. It was a time when we should have been able to feel good about ourselves, what with World War II recently concluded and most of our fighting men home to get on with their lives, those who survived, that is. Unfortunately it was also a time when many of those same men and women were re-conscripted to fight in an unsettling and mostly illegal police action in Korea, which accomplished very little with the exception of horrendous loss of life on both sides of the conflict. To make it even worse, those valiant veterans have been generally left without our thanks. They were forgotten during the events that followed after just a few years.

This book is not about the Korean Conflict, even though it became a large influence on what was occurring here at home. No, this is about a few would be do-gooders, who took it upon themselves to ruin the careers and the very lives of many mostly innocent people. It is about gross claims of guilt by innuendo, with little or no real evidence to back up the accusations that were made. It is about gross disregard for our Constitution and Bill of Rights. It is about the people mentioned in the prologue who radically misconstrued what infinitesimal data they dug out of questionable sources. While they had no direct connection to the junior senator from Wisconsin, Joseph McCarthy, they were a product of the time that is now known as the McCarthy Era or simply, McCarthyism. It is wholly about *Counterattack* and more specifically, *Red Channels: The Report of Communist Influence in*

Radio and Television that was published in June 1950 with devastating results. It made most of the parties listed un-employable for a period of several years. In some cases, the artists in question were never able to get back to productive lives, even though the charges made were spurious at best. We will get into the specifics of those charges, or citations as they were called, as we progress through the material, but the authors of *Red Channels* used a few guidelines that they never wanted to address publicly.

You stood a good chance of being listed for any number of ridiculous reasons, among them:

If you read the *New York Post*
If you admitted to living in Greenwich Village
If you had a history of helping with war relief
If you fought racism
If you were a liberal
If you opposed censorship
If you criticized the House Un-American Activities Committee
If you favored good relationship with the Soviet Union
If you had any connections with the University of California
And here's a good one...
If you helped Franklin Roosevelt get re-elected in 1944.

That may be over simplifying, but it should give a general notion of the criteria that were used. It was truly a broad brush approach. Communism was their target, but their efforts were extremely overzealous and in nearly in all cases, unsupported by reality.

Chapter Two
The Publication

While searching the world of printed matter, finding anything quite as disruptive and destructive as *Red Channels* would be almost impossible. In a true literary sense, it could not be called a book; it was simply a series of lists. It contained the names of 151 performing artists, 130 organizations, and 17 publications. Most of the blacklistees were arrived at by a "He said, she said" process and could not be backed up with solid facts. It was enough for the writers, most of whom remained anonymous, to hear on their grapevine any tidbit they thought to be suspect. The most devious thing about it was that they were using the same tactics as those they opposed to make their arguments stand up.

The worst of it all was the fact that so many people who had the power to stop the ill-founded crusade were more than willing to accept what they read on face value without doing their own investigation of the information that was presented to them. I am referring to the executives at the ad agencies and the networks along with the sponsors whose products were being hyped on the air.

In order to give some perspective to the whole situation, let me quote directly from the introduction to *Red Channels*, a part of the publication that very few ever read. You should notice how they said it all and, at the same time, said nothing of value, leaving the door wide open to scrutiny, but not to law suits, or so they thought. This segment was written by Vincent Hartnett, a man I will discuss at length in a later chapter. His proofs were never forthcoming.

"The information set forth in the following report is taken from records available to the public. The purpose of this compilation is three-fold, one, to show how Communists have been able to carry out their plan of infiltration of the radio and television industries, two, to indicate the extent to which many prominent actors and artists have been inveigled to lend their names, according to these public records, to organizations espousing Communist causes and three, to discourage actors and artists from naively lending their names to Communist organizations or causes in the future."[1]

There it is. In effect, he was saying in this statement, that neither he nor anyone else could actually verify the scandalous citations included in *Red Channels*. As I said, it was a "he said, she said" sort of third-hand data that was used to implicate their victims. If "A" said that "B" had told him in an offhand manner that he thought he had seen what looked like a copy of *The Daily Worker* on "C's" desk, then "C" must therefore be a member of the Communist Party USA. You must admit that is not what could be determined as conclusive proof of anything.

The publishers took this half-cooked bit of information and turned it into print in their shameful chronicle.

During that time, there was a major debate taking place about outlawing the Communist party USA, which had been established in 1919. Among those in favor of such a move were the American Legion and the Daughters of the American Revolution. Some of those opposed were J. Edgar Hoover and the American Civil Liberties Union among others. One of the most radical group leaders in favor of banning the party was Max H. Sorenson, the national commander of the Catholic War Veterans. He thought that all Communist Party USA members should be deported.[2]

One thing that was lost in the shuffle of the whole blacklisting scenario was that, like it or not, the Communist Party USA was, and still is, a legally recognized political party. In 1936, even Bill Paley, Chief Executive at Columbia Broadcasting System (CBS), gave equal air time to Earl Browder, who was Communist Party USA's candidate for president running in opposition to Franklin D. Roosevelt and Alf Landon. Did that automatically make Paley a

Communist? I think not. It was simply a part of the The Fairness Doctrine, a policy of the United States Federal Communications Commission (FCC), introduced in 1949, that required the holders of broadcast licenses to both present controversial issues of public importance and to do so in a manner that was, in the Commission's view, honest, equitable, and balanced. The Doctrine still holds true to this day. If equal time is requested, it must be granted.

It must be remembered that, when American Business Consultants published *Red Channels* in June 1950, it became the cornerstone of the blacklist for radio and television people. It took years to overcome the damage that had had been done.

Chapter Three
Kirkpatrick, Bierly & Keenan

How did *Red Channels* come into being? In the 1940s, there were many people behind it, but the three primaries were all extemporary employees of the FBI, who had worked mainly in their so-called Communist Squad, a group that pressed the envelope of legality in order to obtain information. They employed tactics that included wire-taps and even went so far as to examine the garbage of those they thought to be suspect.

Who was responsible for it? They were a pair of Midwesterners and a New Yorker, who, after leaving the FBI, decided they could do more damage, or in their minds, more good working outside normal parameters. The most convinced of these was Theodore C. Kirkpatrick, usually simply called Ted. He was born in Campbellstown, Ohio. He received his legal training at Earlham College in nearby Richmond, Indiana. The second was Kenneth M. Bierly from Peoria, Illinois, and then Chicago. He earned his law degree at Kent College of Law. The third was John G. Keenan, a native New Yorker, who was educated at Fordham University and St. John's law school.

Having worked together at the FBI, they commenced their anti-Communist battle by publishing the first of their series of anti-red newsletters titled *Plain Talk*. They did this with the aid of heavy financial backing from Alfred Kohlberg, a millionaire textile importer, whose primary markets were in the Orient. There were other notable backers of their movement including New York's Francis Cardinal Spellman and Chicago's Samuel Cardinal Stritch. Only a short time later in 1947, they began publishing the long-running missive they called *Counterattack- the newsletter of facts on Communism*. With very few exceptions, they were extremely careful to never directly refer to any of the people they chose to defame as Communists or Fellow-Travelers. They left it to the readers to draw their own conclusions.

Since none of them had any journalistic training, they hired Sam Horn, an editor with a proven track record to pull it together, who had contributed a twelve-part exposé to the Chicago Journal of Commerce under the pseudonym of Andrew Avery. *Counterattack* fell into a consistent format of 2,000 words on four pages every week, always being careful not to make any direct accusations against anyone in particular. Their aim was to purport guilt by innuendo while attempting to avoid any legal complications.

In the spring of 1947, the three aforementioned leaders of the pack formed a new organization that was intended to be for information gathering only. That entity was American Business Consultants and would later play a huge role in the clearing of those they had denigrated in *Counterattack* so that they could return to work. That part was mostly a money-making ruse that could only have been profitable in the tainted atmosphere of the 1940s and 1950s.

During the course of the run of *Counterattack*, they took on a wide variety of national and international targets. They accosted Trygve Lie, the Secretary General of the United Nations (UN), calling him 'Stalin's Choice,' and the UN itself for allowing subversives to work within their structure. On this, they were missing the most salient reason the UN had been created in the first place. The main purpose was to try to get every bent of political thinking out in the open rather that keeping it all underground. Admittedly, this did and still does not always work, but it was a step in the right direction.

Among other targets was a New York Supreme Court Justice for his use of the term 'Witch Hunt', a prominent Methodist bishop, Bishop G. Bromley Oxnam, for his attacks on the House Un-American Activities Committee, and a whole host of politicians, international statesmen, labor leaders, industrialists, ministers, artists, writers, and entertainers, with a heavy emphasis on performers.

Occasionally, they would put out a special edition to confront what they deemed to be a particular need. One of them was published on June 22, 1950 and was called *Red Channels: The Report of Communist Influence in Radio and Television*. *Red Channels* would become the Bible of blacklisting in the entertainment industry. It was a series of three lists, the first naming 151 performers, writers, and technicians involved in radio and television. The second section listed so-called Communist Front organizations, and the third part consisted of the names of publications thought to be anti-American. Some of the organizations named had closed their doors for business long before the release of *Red Channels*.

The results were devastating. It destroyed the businesses that had been established to entertain and educate us. The book was available on newsstands for $1, but was also distributed free of charge to the more than 4,000 subscribers to *Counterattack*. It was, by no means a financial success, however it proved to be the financial ruin of those parties it listed, for several years.

A few days after the release of *Red Channels*, *Counterattack* printed this declaration:

> "In an emergency, it would require only three persons—one engineer in master control at a radio network, one director in a radio studio, and one voice before a microphone—to reach 90 million people with a message."[1]

Here is what Kenneth Bierly had to say shortly thereafter:

> "We had been mentioning in *Counterattack* quite frequently, various phases of radio and television. We found that there was quite a good deal of interest in it and that was the principle reason we felt it might be good to publish a special report on radio and television. We felt it might be good to come out with something documented, and do it publicly to clear the air."[2]

The greatest fallacy in what he said was that the documentation he spoke of was sketchy at best and often totally without any real basis in facts.

At another time Bierly added:

"It was immaterial whether they were Communists; entirely immaterial to what we were trying to do. It had no bearing on whether they were Communists. In the second place, we couldn't find out if we asked who were pro-Communist and who were anti-Communist."[3]

What are my own feelings about that? Let's make an example. Suppose you were accused and convicted of perpetrating some heinous act without any evidence against you with the exception of one angry would be witness who had it in for you on a personal level. You could spend years in prison for something you did not do. Ridiculous, you say? Read the papers. Such things happen every day.

On the question of what constituted a Communist front, *Counterattack* said:

"Which organizations are really fronts and which are not, how can a jury be expected to distinguish? And if a jury does decide that a certain organization is a front, how can it tell whether the defendant helped it as a Communist or as an innocent? Some eminent persons, including Supreme Court Justices and conservative multi-millionaires have innocently sponsored Communist fronts."[4]

Once more, those words proclaim loudly, to anyone who is really listening to them, that *Counterattack* and *Red Channels* are mostly like fairy tales as from The Brothers Grimm—very grim. While all of this was going on, several governmental agencies were keeping a close watch on the activities of *Counterattack* and others working in the same vein. They made some strong denunciations, at best tongue in cheek, but they did little to stop them until much later when it was of no use to many of the victims. Here are the words of a spokesman for Lou Nichols, J. Edgar Hoover's assistant, in an interview for *Sponsor* magazine:

"We are aware of the activities of *Counterattack* and *Red Channels*, but since they are private citizens we have no legal control over their practices. Individuals who have severed their relations with the FBI, in no way, possess our endorsement or stamp of approval. Certainly, all of the FBI information is confidential, available only to those government officials so authorized to examine it."[5]

Mr. Hoover said, in comments made to *Newsweek* on June 9, 1950, shortly before *Red Channels* came on the scene:

> We can successfully defeat the Communist attempt to capture the United States by fighting it with truth and justice implemented by a few Don'ts.
> Don't label anyone a Communist unless you have the facts.
> Don't confuse liberals and conservatives with Communists.
> Don't take the law into your own hands. If Communists violate the law report such facts to your local law-enforcement agency.
> Don't be a party to the violation of the civil rights of anyone.[6]

At two separate speaking engagements in 1951, J. Howard McGrath, Harry Truman's Attorney General, made the following comments. The first is from an American Bar Association meeting.

> "We appear to be going through a period of public hysteria in which many varieties of self-appointed policemen and alleged guardians of Americanism would have us fight subversion by stigmatizing as disloyal all those who disagree with or oppose them. This hysteria appears in vigilante groups who decree beatings of purported Communist sympathizers, or who would in polite circles intimidate radio advertisers into silencing performers who they say have Communist leanings."[7]

In a Jackson Day address in Springfield, Missouri, he added:

> "We have an efficient Federal Bureau of Investigation to prevent sabotage and to keep track of Communist espionage, maneuvering and conspiracies, but Mr. Hoover and I are determined that there will be no Gestapo witch-hunts. The basic civil rights of the individual will be securely protected and defended as guaranteed by the fundamental laws of the land. Those who pose as saviors of our nation by seeking to abridge beyond reason our tradition of democratic freedom are as dangerous to American liberties as the Communists themselves."[8]

At a time when the dust was beginning to settle, John G. Keenan, one of three founding members and president of American Business Consultants, said in their publication *Counterattack*:

"After the hullabaloo of *Red Channels* and the Korean War, following after that and all of the hodge-podge and the mess we felt that we had laid an egg that was a bombshell."[9]

There is so much more I could add, but I believe Mr. Keenan hit the nail squarely on the head.

Chapter Four
Laurence A Johnson

In his middle sixties, Laurence A. Johnson, a self-proclaimed super-patriot, was old enough to know better and young enough to ignore the obvious flaws in his concepts. He was a respected grocer from Syracuse, New York, with a chain of four supermarkets in and around that city. While he was not one of the people responsible for *Red Channels,* he certainly made use of it in his crusade against alleged Communist Party USA supporters. He regarded it as his "Bible of Infamy."

Mr. Johnson made a constant practice of running up and down Madison Avenue in New York City with *Red Channels* in hand to harass the people at the radio and television networks, the ad agencies, and the sponsors responsible for hiring talent to do their shows. This included technicians, musicians, producers, directors, and writers, not just actors. Many of those contacted were willing to accept his data on face value without due diligence. This made some very astute artists and artisans virtually unemployable for long periods of time.

By speaking with the sponsors, he was hitting them where it really hurt, their financial bottom lines. He told them that, while he would not pull their products from his stores, he would be sure to post placards over them stating his feelings about the people they were allowing on their shows, people he thought to be subversive. By doing this, of course, he was stomping all over the Bill of Rights.

Some of those sponsors were coerced into going along with Mr. Johnson's allegations partially as a nod to a sign of the times because many of them were fearful due to the supposed "Red Scare." Just to document that statement, I want to cite some comments made by said sponsors.

For example, Stuart Peabody, an assistant vice-president of Borden Milk, wrote to him:

"I want to tell you again how grateful I am for the time and the help you gave me on Tuesday. It is no exaggeration to say that my eyes have been opened as a result of your cooperation."[1]

Also, from an unnamed Kraft Foods vice-president, who wrote to Johnson on September 8, 1952:

"It is indeed heartwarming to know that you are continuing your crusade. I sincerely hope you keep up the good work."[2]

Another unnamed president of General Ice Cream Corporation wrote:

"I think it is wonderful that you have taken this interest in ferreting Communists out of our entertainment industry. I wish there were more people like you."[3]

To show how terrified some of the sponsors became, here is what Paul M. Hahn, the president of American Tobacco Company wrote:

"The company which I represent is a publicly owned commercial corporation, engaged in the manufacture and marketing of trade-mark consumer goods, which are offered for sale to the general public. It is owned by some 85,000 shareholders. Its management is put into office by the shareholder for the purpose of safeguarding and increasing the value of their investments; of earning profits which can be paid to the 85,000 owners in the form of dividends. To perform the responsibility which has been entrusted to it, this management must strive to maintain and improve the company's business, which means maintaining and increasing the sales of its products to the purchasing public. When a company such as ours uses its corporate funds to sponsor a program on television or radio, it does so with but one purpose, to reach the largest possible number of the public as its audience and to present its products to that audience in the most favorale light.

> "Since it is the function of an artist employed on such a program to please rather than displease and since the successful promotion of consumer products depends in large measure on the impression left by sponsored entertainment, it follows that we would be wasting shareholders' funds were we to employ artists or other persons who, under company auspices, are likely to offend the public. We would disapprove of employing an artist who, in any respect, political or otherwise, has made him or is likely to make distasteful to the public."[4]

He stated clearly that the red scare was all about money, nothing else. Mr. Johnson used the economic playing card to perfection.

Talking about Laurence Johnson without including his daughter, Eleanor Johnson Buchanan, in the conversation is impossible. She was a huge factor in the whole muckraking campaign. She had her own personal axe to grind about Communism and Communists because her husband, Jack, a World War II veteran, who remained in the inactive reserves after his discharge, had been recalled and sent off to Korea. She had a meeting with her father and some of the members of the local American Legion Post in Syracuse to discuss her feelings. She was well-received, which led her to write back to the American Legion Post in June 1951. She had been collecting information from *Red Channels*.

> "Dad and I were pleased that you agree that manufacturers can be persuaded to remove Communist sympathizers from their advertising programs on radio and television. As you gentlemen pointed out in our meeting last Friday, the task is too great for me alone. I am grateful for your aid."[5]

She followed that up with many letters to local housewives containing material from *Red Channels* and quotes from *The Daily Worker*. This was really the start of her father's constant pressure along Madison Avenue. A month after that first letter, she gave a talk at the local Kiwanis Club:

> "My husband, a veteran of World War II, never received a penny for being a member of the inactive reserves. When he was recalled to service last October it meant leaving the small town on the Hudson where we had been so happy, the

company in which he'd been found to be a valuable asset, my small but interesting teaching position at Vassar College; all our plans for the future. And I know that Jack detested military life. He's very unmilitary about hanging up his clothes. But so many of our friends were reservists, I just took it for granted. Only now, faced with the prospect of being away from each other, I asked him one day why on earth he ever signed up for the reserves. He answered quietly and simply in one word—'Patriotism'."[6]

She then recited words from a letter she had received from Jack: "I have not been sick, which is a blessing in this land of loose bowels and bodies. The flies go from the dead Gook twenty feet away to the fish heads he left behind, to my C-rations, so I'm glad my stomach is strong."[7]

Eleanor continued:

"My stomach is not that strong. It sickens me to know of those banquets engineered by Communist sympathizers on radio and television to raise funds for their henchmen, and those do-nothing patriotic citizens who discuss the wrongs of the world over a dinner table while my quiet, unassuming Jack ate his lunch, surrounded by dead Chinese."[8]

Her campaign did not stop in Syracuse. She began to send her unproved information gleaned from *Red Channels* and *Counterattack* to all sorts of executives involved with the media in one way or another. It had profound, detrimental effects. It took many years and many destroyed careers before cooler minds took over and the dust settled over radio and television land. By then, it was too late for many of the victims of her project.

It is not too hard to understand her thoughts about her husband's predicament, but that was no excuse for her actions here at home.

Eleanor Johnson Buchanan also had a separate list of 188 names of people she also suspected of being on the wrong side of her conscience. She distributed it freely among the executives on Madison Avenue with her personal recommendation that they not be hired. The roster ran the gamut of the alphabet from Abbott & Costello to Robert Young.

Hugh Clegg, Assistant Director of the FBI, declared:

"Efforts by private individuals and groups to screen, process, and evaluate information pertaining to subversive activities, before reporting it to the FBI, are inconsistent with our best interests."[9]

The Johnson's devious work had far less effect in Syracuse than it did in New York City. Many Syracuse local folks tended to ignore them.

Chapter Five
Hartnett, McNamara & Aware, Inc.

Vincent Hartnett warrants much more attention. He was another self-proclaimed "walking file case" on Communist infiltration into the media. He went so far as to publish in *The Sign*, a leading Catholic news outlet, stories praising himself as "the protector of our freedom." He wrote those articles under an alias so as not to seem too arrogant or self-serving.

What made him the man he turned out to be? In order to understand him, we must go back to his earliest days. His father was an Irish immigrant, and his mother came from Irish-French roots. Vincent was born on July 4, 1916, which became a sort of slap in the face to the people he later persecuted. He attended Fordham University, where he achieved honor roll grades. He then transferred to Notre Dame, where he graduated *magma cum laude* with a degree in English. He continued on two years later with a master's degree, also at the top of his class. His major was in Apologetics, the defense and philosophy of religion. During this time, he began his study of Communism. Two of his courses were "Russia; government and philosophy" and "Communism and religion."

Three weeks after the Japanese attack on Pearl Harbor, Hartnett joined the US Navy, where he eventually became involved in naval intelligence, preparing reports on the Middle East and the Balkans. He learned enough to be able to see how the Soviets were taking control of Eastern Europe after the war was concluded.

Following his military service, Hartnett took a course on radio scripting at Columbia University, and not much later worked for Phillips H. Lord, the man most responsible for such shows as *Gangbusters* and *Counterspy*. In that position, Hartnett was to contact the actors who were to be on *Gangbusters*, a show directed by William Sweets. While doing his job, he decided that Sweets was leaning mostly to pro-left actors and technicians. When the show was removed from the schedule due to those allegations, Bill Sweets retired to Vermont, never worked in the industry again, and was later named as one of the 151 listed in *Red Channels*.

Hartnett resigned, saying that he could not work under those conditions. He spent the next couple of years writing articles and lecturing on his pet subject to any group that would listen. At the same time, he was authoring a *Counterattack*-like newsletter that he called *Confidential Notebook*. Prior to its publication, he heard about *Red Channels* and offered his services to do some of the writing. He often proclaimed himself as the author of *Red Channels*, but in reality all he did was write the extremely ambiguous Introduction. His rationale for such a proclamation was that he thought his knowledge of the subject was extensive, probably more extensive than any other potential blacklister. Whether the information locked in his head was true or not was totally irrelevant to him and, unfortunately, to many of the executives to whom he passed along his data.

At the time *Red Channels* was released to the public, Hartnett had his own publication in mind. He had previously written a book titled *File 13, Volume 1*. When *Red Channels* came out, Hartnett was working on *File 13, Volume 2*. He declared that *Red Channels* was a mere primer on the subject and contained less than one tenth of what Hartnett thought he knew. *File 13, Volume 2* would be directed at a select readership up and down Madison Avenue and would be sold for several hundred dollars per copy, a far cry from *Red Channels* cover price of $1 and its massive free distribution.

While some of his claims were indeed factual, the question remains whether many of those facts had any real ethical value. So much of his knowledge had no relevancy at all to the bigger picture, mainly amounting to a gross disregard for the civil rights of his victims.

When we think of Vincent Hartnett, we must ultimately speak of Aware, Inc., the organization he and others formed with the stated purpose of clearing blacklisted artists and actors so that they could return to work. Making money was Aware, Inc.'s game, although no one got rich.

Aware, Inc. was not alone in the clearance business; there were many others, including the networks themselves. What made Aware, Inc. somewhat unique was that before clearing anyone they had first made the accusations that started to whole process. This made Vincent Hartnett and his cohorts the most-feared and also the most-hated agents of the chaos on Madison Avenue. These vicious, two-faced tactics eventually caught up with Aware, Inc. after so much irretrievable water had flowed over the dam. For a long time, they were considered "the engine of blacklisting."

The fees Aware, Inc. charged for its clearance services could be very high, and when the process was completed, there was still no guarantee that it would have any real effect on the employability of those who had enlisted their services. Aware, Inc. set up "The Road Back," which were the twelve steps toward rehabilitation:

> Questions to ask one-self: Do I love my country? Do I believe my country is in danger? Can I do anything to relieve that danger? Will I tell the full, relevant and unfaltering truth?
>
> Recognition that, whatever the subject's intentions at the time, his name, efforts, money or other support gave aid and comfort to the Communist conspiracy.
>
> Full and frank disclosure, in written form, of all connections past and present with subversive elements, organizations, causes and individuals. Attach pertinent literature, correspondence, records of financial contributions, programs, newspaper clippings or other documentary material. Identify those who drew the subject in turn involved. (This disclosure may be used publicly or privately as the circumstances indicate)
>
> Voluntary and cooperative interview with Federal Bureau of Investigation on the basis of the forgoing full and frank disclosure. The content of such interviews remains inviolate with the FBI.
>
> A written offer to cooperate, as a witness or source of information with:

The Committee on Un-American Activities of the House of Representatives.

The Subcommittee on internal security of the Senate Judiciary Committee.

Subversive Activities Control Board.

Any other committee in Senate or House properly interested in some or all of the information the subject may have.

Any other security agency of the Federal Government, as may be appropriate.

Any State Legislature Committee or executive office investigating subversive activities.

Any local authorities interested in local subversive activities.

In the subjects union (s), he should make his new position on Communism clearly known by statements in meetings, letters or statements in union publications, etc. Whatever else he may do, he should not support the Communist or crypto-Communist element on any issue, no matter how attractive or insignificant it may then appear. Other union issues may then be freely debated without subversive interference.

Subject should make public his new position on Communism by all other means available; statements in trade publications, 'Letters to the Editor', personal correspondence to all who might be interested such as anti-Communist journalists and organizations, employees, friends and fellow professionals.

Outside the field of entertainment-communications many opportunities for establishing a new position are available: political, social and civic clubs, parent-teacher organizations, library and school committees, religious and cultural groups. They may be urged to increase the number of anti-Communist speakers, books, lectures, candidates, etc.

Support anti-Communist persons, groups and organizations.

The subject should keep himself informed by subscribing to recommended anti-Communist magazines, reading anti-Communist books, government reports and other literature.

The subject should support anti-Communist legislation having responsible endorsement.

If the subject's new convictions draw him to, or back to, religion, so much the better. He achieves the best of all reasons for opposing Communism. He can become actively anti-Communist in his church or other religious organizations. In church groups, as everywhere, he can combat neutralism and anti-anti-Communism."[1]

I believe the worst part of those twelve steps has to be #5. What they are asking for there is a great deal of time to be available to all of the many panels who were operating with anything but the best intentions toward the subject in question. Why, if you thought you were in danger, would you answer any of the questions posed by the various committees and agencies?

Many people in the business of radio and television production made uncomplimentary comments about the whole process. Among them was Dave Levy at Young & Rubicam, who said in an interview with David Susskind, "I deplore this practice as much as you do. We're caught in a trap. I have no alternative."[2]

That was not entirely true. It was the easy way out. As we will see later on, it only took a few determined people to stand up and bring an end to this deplorable era in American history.

In 1951, Vincent Hartnett was the first witness at the Senate Subcommittee investigation of subversive infiltration of radio, television. and the entertainment industry. What he had to say set many of the standards on what was to come. He spoke of alleged party members, collaborators, fellow-travelers, sympathizers, and dupes, without clarifying the differences. He said he considered *Red Channels*, a publication laden with supposition and innuendo, as definite proof of his indictments.

In 1955, the performers union, American Federation of Television and Radio Artists (AFTRA), took a vote on a proclamation to condemn Aware, Inc. The final vote was 982 for and 514 opposed, one of the first small victories for the good guys even though many members abstained from voting.

Here is what Jack Gould, radio and television columnist for the *New York Times*, wrote on July 11, 1955 after the vote was taken:

"The vote represented the first time that the union's administrative forces, which embrace a number of Aware members, went down to defeat in a mail referendum. The majority against Aware would not have been possible without the votes of many conservative federation members who, in the past, have opposed the union's so-called left-wing faction. Prior to the referendum, an official of both Aware and the federation had estimated that the vote against Aware would total only three or four hundred."[3]

In 1957, John Henry Faulk, a popular, folksy radio storyteller, was dropped by his long-time sponsor, Libby's Frozen Foods due to questionable reports received about his background. Though he was not among the 151 listed in *Red Channels*, he was among the many that were blacklisted and his case had dire implications for Aware, Inc.

Faulk filed a libel suit against Aware, Inc., and after a long dragged-out trial, he received the largest judgment for compensatory and punitive damages ever granted up to that time. That trial was one of the final straws that broke the back of the blacklisting era.

In an extremely-telling confession during the course of the Faulk suit, Paul Milton, one of the founders of Aware, Inc., said that he did not know if any of their allegations were true.

A report credited to the *New York Herald Tribune* yet first published in *The Daily Worker* said, "Aware sold a barrel of false information."

Whatever the source, that remark was the truth.

Chapter Six
The Fronts

To the folks at *Counterattack* and *Red Channels*, a Communist front was any organization that had even a remote connection to the Communist party USA. Undeniably, all of them worked under some Communist influence, and nearly all of them were formed with at least some humanitarian goals. From the time of the party's inception in 1919 until a much later date, their aims were mostly pure, fighting for the common man and his rights. Does that statement make me a Communist? I say no, of course not, but facts are facts and must not be ignored by even the most ardent anti-red advocate. They were deeply involved in the formation of many trade unions that were instigated to protect the there-to-fore downtrodden workers. They fought hard for racial and ethnic equality. They worked to prevent our entry into World War II, but after the attack on Pearl Harbor, they worked equally hard to assist in the war effort along with those who considered themselves super patriots.

Many of the 121 fronts listed as a separate entity in *Red Channels* overlapped each other and some that had ceased to exist long before *Red Channels* saw the light of day. Regarding the "Joint Anti-Fascist Refugee Committee," Part three of the *Red Channels'* citation reads:

"Formed in March of 1942 through the merger of the 'American Committee to Save Refugees,' the 'Exiled Writers' and the 'United American-Spanish Aid Committee.' The sponsors and officers, with a few exceptions, are admitted Communists and fellow travelers. The policy is in concert with the foreign policy of the Soviet Union. Much of the financing is undertaken by 'The International Workers Order'."[1]

In *Red Channels*, all five of the above-mentioned groups are also listed separately. Add to that the "Writers Congress," from which "The Exiled Writers" arose and the "League of American Writers," and you have no less than six duplications of the same information.

The "Joint Anti-Fascist Refugee Committee's" members were intimidated at the House Un-American Activities Committee hearings. One such un-friendly witness, Bishop G. Bromley Oxnam, was greeted by flash bulbs and klieg lights. He later commented, "There were, I think, seven microphones or recording devices in front of me, so placed that it was impossible to have my papers before me in any way that gave easy access. When I lifted my eyes to look toward the committee members I was almost blinded."[2]

In the 1946 questioning, the interrogator was Congressman John Rankin from Mississippi, who often proclaimed his affinity for the Ku Klux Klan.

Rankin said to Dr. Jacob Auslander, who had emigrated from Austria in 1924 and who had been a US citizen since 1929, "Do you realize that you are violating your oath of citizenship when you show contempt for this committee, and you are likely to have your citizenship canceled?" [3]

Rankin snapped when talking to another JAFRC member, Manuel Magana. "You are rubbing your nose right up against the gates of the penitentiary here."[4]

Tony Stackovich, a Seattle trade unionist and a man cut from much tougher cloth, when told by Rankin that he was nearing contempt, responded, "I do have contempt for this committee—a phony question from a phony Congressman. I think some of you guys ought to be investigated by psychiatrists."[5]

Another organization with multiple connections that were also all but one listed individually was "American Youth for Democracy," which began as "The Young Communist League" and was restructured as "The Labor Youth League."

Two other direct links were "The International Workers Order" (already mentioned in connection with JAFRC) and "The World Federation of Democratic Youth."

Part three of the *Red Channels* citation on "American Youth for Democracy" (AYD) stated:

> "Cited as a front formed in October 1943 to succeed 'The Youth Communist League' and for the purpose of exploiting to the advantage of a foreign power the idealism, inexperience and craving to join, which is characteristic of American college youth. Its high sounding slogans cover a determined effort to disaffect our youth and turn them against religion, the American home, against the college authorities and against the American government itself."[6]

This meant that colleges and universities across the land were hotbeds of activity in a time not favorable to liberals or free thinkers to be given free rein.

There were consequences. In October 1952, John Cherveny, who had once been chairman of the AYD chapter at Wayne University in Detroit, was tossed out of a good job at American Metal Products because he chose to plead his Fifth Amendment [7]* constitutional right at a House Un-American Activities Committee (HUAC) hearing to remain silent

During the same month, Paul Henley, a shop steward at the Chrysler-Dodge plant did likewise with the same result.

In 1947, Morris Judd, a philosophy instructor at the University of Colorado, had his contract nullified for refusing to ban the local branch of AYD.

Next up was "The Committee for the First Amendment." This one was a little different because, as *Red Channels* declared in their citation:

> "A recently created Communist front in the defense of Communists and Communist fellow travelers, its immediate purpose is to create favorable public opinion for the Communists who refused to testify before HUAC in Washington, DC."[8]

Did you catch the rhetoric there? What ever happened to innocent until proven guilty? And guilty of what?

This particular group was founded by John Huston, William Wyler, and several other Hollywood notables strictly for the purpose stated in the citation, but certainly not in those words. Their group had the support of at least four Senators.

In December 1952, a group of stars flew to Washington to plead their case. They carried with them a petition signed by the following at a rally held on October 15:

"Cornell Wilde, Gregory Peck, Bennett Cerf, Lucille Ball, Burt Lancaster, Robert Ryan, John Garfield, Myrna Loy, Frank Sinatra, Edward G. Robinson, Robert Young, Joseph Cotton, Clifton Fadiman, Van Heflin, Paulette Goddard, Henry Fonda, Irwin Shaw, Katherine Hepburn, Richard Brooks, Sidney Bookman, Joan Bennett, Pete Seeger, Leonard Bernstein, Ethyl Barrymore, Eddie Cantor, Louis Calhern, Jerome Chodorov, Kirk Douglas, Howard DaSilva, Agnes DeMille, Deanna Durbin, Melvin Douglas, Ava Gardner, Benny Goodman, Moss Hart, Uta Hagen, Harold Hecht, Ben Hecht, Walter Huston, William Holden, Canada Lee, Fritz Lang, Peter Lorre, Groucho Marx, Abe Polonsky, Ann Revere, Artie Shaw, Franchot Tone, Orson Welles and Billy Wilder."[9]

You must admit, that list is like a Who's Who of Hollywood in the 1950s. Not all of them could be wrong. Quite a few of them were listed in *Red Channels*.

A close tie-in to "The Committee for the First Amendment" was a group called "The Freedom from Fear Committee." *Red Channels* explained their aim in their own curious way:

"One of the Communist parties latest fronts which came into being in Hollywood and New York and was created to raise funds for the defense of the 19 unfriendly witnesses before the Congressional Committee on Un-American Activities investigation of Communist activity in Hollywood, Ten of which were cited for contempt of Congress."[10]

Once more, a presumption of guilt is there without so much as a trial. Some of those people were, at one time or another, party members, but that does not qualify them to have accusations of subversion hung on them.

The sponsors of "The Freedom from Fear Committee" were Richard Collins, Gordon Kahn, Howard Koch, Lewis Milestone, Irving Pichel, Robert Rossen, and Waldo Salt. Most of them were later blacklisted by one source or another while two of them became friendly witness in the 1950s, but on December 5, 1947, they distributed the following questionnaire:

> "Tired? Jittery? Sleeping Badly? Find out the reason. Test yourself. Here are ten questions. Score 5 for a yes answer. If you score 25 you're in the danger zone.
> Are you disturbed because you are a Jew?
> A Catholic?
> A union guild member?
> Are you haunted by your past?
> Remember your fourth vote for Roosevelt?
> The ambulance you helped send to Republican Spain?
> Your signature to protest lynching in the South?
> Are you thinking you'd better drop your subscriptions to a series of periodicals?
> Do you experience mixed feelings at the news that England has offered sanctuary to political refugees from the American motion picture industry?
> Do you think you're safe from the blacklists?"[11]

It was an open secret that nearly all of those in positions to hire talent denied the existence of a blacklist of any sort. It was very difficult to fight a supposed non-existent enemy even though they all knew it was a hard fact and was being used over and over every day.

Another front organization that grew from multiple roots (each of them listed separately in *Red Channels*) and was closely allied with ones I have already discussed was "The Civil Rights Congress." Item 2 in the *RC* citation said:

> "Cited as an organization formed in April 1946 as a member of two other Communist front organizations (International Labor Defense and The National Federation for Constitutional Liberties), dedicated, not to the broader issues of civil liberties, but specifically to the defense of industrial Communists

and the Communist Party USA and controlled by individuals who are either members of the Communist Party USA of loyal to it."[12]

One of their main functions was to set up a bail fund for those individuals who were being hounded by the HUAC and other government agencies. Between 1946 and 1951 they put together $1.5 million from loans and donations, which showed where the general feelings in the community could be found. Attorney General Tom Clark (Truman administration) said that "To defend the constitutional rights of a subversive is in itself a subversive action." He cancelled existing bails and confiscated $60,000 of CRC funds. In 1952, the Supreme Court upheld his decision by a 6 to 2 vote. Therefore, there would be no protection for the victims.

During this time frame, an ex-Communist unionist decided he would be wise to cooperate with the FBI. He named many names and then changed his mind. To escape further entanglements, he faked his own kidnapping and murder. Still later, he resurfaced to testify at the Subversive Activities Council Board in defense of CRC. He admitted at that time that many of the names he had given were those of people he did not know from Adam. By then, few could believe anything he said; the damage had been done.

Next came "The Progressive Citizens of America." The *Red Channels* listing stated:

"Cited as a new and broader Communist front for the entire United States, formed in September of 1946 at the direction of the Communist steering committee from the Communist dominated 'National Citizens Political Action Committee' and the 'Independent Citizens Committee of the Arts, Sciences and Professions'."[13]

The last one cited above was an offshoot of "The Independent Voters Committee of the Arts and Sciences," yet another crossover.

These organizations explain about the folks that wrote the *Red Channels* citations and how they were in an accusatory frame of mind when doing so and therefore chose words to fit their own feelings and convictions. In 1947, the Attorney General put out a list of alleged Communist front organizations. The people at *Counterattack* then took it upon themselves to add thirty-four more to that list simply because they had personal thoughts about them.

Ted Kirkpatrick and his cohorts always said to anyone who would listen that their information was reliable and public knowledge. They had two favorite sources for their data. One was the Communist newspaper, *The Daily Worker*, which they openly stated was mostly lies until using what they printed became convenient. Their other pet source was *Counterattack*. Enough said?

Chapter Seven
Clearance

"I can get you back to work, but it will cost you, not just money, but most of your self-respect, and that means more than cash."

That was the unspoken promise made by those vampire-like people that called themselves clearance experts or security men. They were more than willing to draw the very life blood from those mostly innocent victims of the blacklist in general and *Red Channels* in particular. You might, in some sense, compare them to the carpet-baggers that ran rampant after the conclusion of the Civil War, taking advantage of an already bad situation.

Two things that made these so-called clearers even more devious were, one, that the promises they made often amounted to zilch, and worst of all, the clearer was most times the very person who was responsible for getting his victim on the dreaded list in the first place.

In an earlier chapter I listed the criteria set down by Aware, Inc. that might or might not eventually get an individual back among the ranks of the employable, or at least partially employable; in other words, put on the graylist and off the blacklist.

The whole process was complicated and fraught with many possible pitfalls along the way.

Report on Blacklisting was written for the FBI, which explains the use of occasional anonymity. Here is how one well-informed yet unnamed public relations man described some of the traps that were inherent to the treacherous path to exoneration:

> First I examine his or her record to look for Communist party membership.

Once convinced he or she is not a Communist or had been, but changed opinions, I send him or her to the FBI to tell them everything he or she knows. (TRAP)

I find out where he is being blacklisted—radio, movies, television, the American Legion, etc.

I call the source, read his statement and plead his innocence.

If they will not accept his statement we are at a dead end. (TRAP)

If, on the other hand, I can get affidavits from some of the accusers exonerating the victim, I take the next step.

I present the data to one of the better known clearers like Jack Wren at Batten, Barton, Durstine & Osborn (BBDO).

If he does not think the party is clean it is over. (TRAP)

If he says okay, we'll give it a test. A job would be arranged in order to test the audience response. If the producers or sponsors get protest letters or calls—again, it's over. (TRAP)"[1]

Keeping a job when labeled a Communist was never easy and always involved at least several people to get through the process. There were those who successfully maneuvered their way through the complicated mine field and still found work hard to come by for several more years. Some never got back to the level of earning that they had enjoyed before the whole fiasco began.

One of the better known clearance people was the aforementioned Jack Wren. His background was akin to Ted Kirkpatrick, Ken Bierly, and John Keenan—the boys at *Counterattack*. He worked closely with them as an informer for the Communist Squad at the FBI. He was let go by them for what was determined to be a conflict of interest because, while he was still technically a federal employee, he was also an inside source of information leaked to *Plain Talk*, the precursor of *Counterattack*. Later, when he was established at BBDO, exclusively working on anti-red projects, he was also giving data to his previous co-workers at the FBI. Many thought he was still a member of the FBI. While firmly entrenched at BBDO, he tried to remain out of the limelight. Even though he was plainly listed on the company's directory in the lobby he had a very small office. He retained a certain degree of anonymity. Is that complicated enough, or was it just cunning?

The end results of most of Wren's clearances were dubious at best. After being cleared, the victim was often no better off in the job market than he was before the process. The irony was that some of the people who poured out names to the inquisitors—some of which were pure perjury—ended up with more work due to their deceit. They also made many life-long enemies among their one-time colleagues.

The other man I want to discuss was a West Coast lawyer, Martin Gang. He occasionally worked pro-bono, but usually his fees were whatever the traffic would bear. He tended to represent many of the so-called friendly people that spouted names to the various committees. Many of them were either present or past members of the party. His mainstay was arranging private hearings in his office with the House Un-American Activities Committee (HUAC) people and his clients, where he would bring up the reasons for their membership. Then he would bring out the stock question, "Are you now or have you ever been . . . .?" He demanded that format or else he would not allow his client to testify. Once again, this was a trap.

His theory was:

> The Fifth Amendment couldn't honestly be taken if a man was no longer a member of the Communist party, because if that person had been a member of the Communist party and had gotten out, he had no right to plead the Fifth Amendment because he was not guilty of any crime unless he had lied about not having gotten out.[2]

Howard Koch was a good example of someone who refused Gang's services. He said loudly and clearly.

> Mr. Gang himself is a good example of this schizoid process. I felt as if I was talking to two people, one identifiable with a progressive past, the other committed to an unprogressive present and future. For those of us who feel this way, the business of clearance is perhaps more complicated than if we were Communists, or at least repentant Communists.[3]

Gang's idea was to translate moral problems to tactical ones. This caused many clients to go from radical to informer. They could go back to work, but they suffered huge public relations difficulties.

Gang said he was not responsible for his client's pleas. He merely gave them options. They made their own choices. He worked closely with the HUAC and let them do the dirty work.

During this time, the large advertising agencies had nearly total control over the job market in the media. Among them, BBDO, J. Walter Thompson, Young & Rubicam, and McCann-Erickson all had their own surveillance people, and they all tended to cover for each other whenever it was convenient. One of those security men from one of the other agencies, who chose not to have his name used in print, thought it was all hogwash. He said, "They're as close to blackmail as any operation I know."

Still, the beat went on.

At Columbia Broadcasting System (CBS), if when interviewing someone in trouble, the information given did not match to their satisfaction, that interviewee was fired on the spot. There was no recourse.

The few cases I have stated could be cited all over the industry, as well as many other industries.

One anonymous clearance man was quoted as saying, "We cannot judge how valid the accusations against a performer are. That is immaterial. We're not here to promote justice."

Chapter Eight
Loyalty Oaths

Loyalty oaths were a very sensitive and disturbing subject, something that went far beyond the consideration of the individual civil rights of those affected by it. Loyalty oaths began for many well before the publication of *Red Channels*, but continued on long after that June 1950 date. Loyalty oaths first began to appear in front of government employees, but it was not long before they were used extensively in other professions including the entertainment industry.

As far back as December 2, 1947, E. B. White, a writer for the *New Yorker* magazine and author of such children's classics as *Stuart Little* and *Charlotte's Web*, had this to say in an article for the *New York Herald Tribune* about loyalty oaths:

> "The essence of our political theory in this country is that a man's conscience shall be a private, not a public affair, and that his deeds and words shall be open to survey, to censure and to punishment. The idea is a decent one, and it works. One needs only to watch totalitarians at work to see that once men gain power over other men's minds, that power is never used sparingly and wisely, but lavishly and brutally with unspeakable results. If I must declare today that I am not a Communist, tomorrow I shall have to testify that I am not a Unitarian; and the day after, that I have never belonged to a dahlia club. It is not a crime to believe anything at all in America."[1]

I believe he said what so many others were thinking during that terrible period in our history.

By 1950, a year when so much was occurring both overtly and covertly on the loyalty front, some tried to remain somewhat incognito while others boasted obscenely of their efforts.

Earl C. Anthony, President and General Manager of KFI, a National Broadcasting Corporation (NBC) station in Los Angeles, laid claim to the fact that he was the first in our nation to demand full loyalty oaths. On June 9, 1950, two weeks prior to the publication of *Red Channels*, he mandated that all 200 employees must sign a loyalty oath, including the cleaning staff. 199 went willingly to the slaughter, but Charlotte Aumack, the Network Traffic Manager for KFI, refused, saying it was an infringement of her rights as an American citizen. She was right, of course, but she was let go for her honesty and guts enough to say NO, even though she was well aware of the consequences of her actions.

Not to be outdone, James W. Gerrard, the head man at KNRO in San Bernardino, said that KFI's claim was untrue because he had had all of his people sworn by a State Superior Court judge two weeks earlier.

During July 1950, film director Cecil B. DeMille, one of the founders of the Screen Director's Guild (SDG) and the DeMille Foundation, and Joe Mankiewicz, President of the SDG, were two powerful alpha personalities that had dramatically opposite views on loyalty oaths. DeMille wanted to instigate them, but Mankiewicz would have no part in it. DeMille always thought Mankiewicz was a Communist fellow traveler, and he waited until Mankiewicz left for Europe for two months to shoot a picture, at which time he put his opinions to work. He did a thorough check of all the scripts Mankiewicz had turned into movies as far back as 1932, looking for what he thought were subversive references.

Mankiewicz returned and began to collect the signatures of other SDG members in an effort to stop what was going on. In the end, they signed a joint statement that they were not Communists, just what DeMille wanted all along.

Joe Losey, one of the 151 listed in *Red Channels* and also a member of the SDG, was not pleased. He said he would not be a party to it, but later, he, too, buckled under, saying it was one of the things that got the wrecking ball swinging. Not long after, he went to work in England and never returned to the USA.

In December 1950, CBS, which had been thought of as the most liberal network, instituted a compulsory, all-encompassing written document that all 2,500 employees nationwide were required to fill in and sign. The document was the brain warp of Executive Vice President and legal counsel Joseph H. Ream. He justified his move by saying, "We are faced with a new crisis in our national life."

Here is his CBS questionnaire:

> Are you now or have you ever been a member of the Communist Party USA or any Communist organization?
>
> Are you now or have you ever been a member of a Fascist party?
>
> Are you now or have you ever been a member of any organization, association, movement, group or combination of persons which advocated the overthrow of our constitutional form of government or any organization, association, movement, group or combination of persons which has adopted a policy of advocating or approving the commission of acts of force or violence to deny any other persons their rights under the constitution of the United States or of seeking to alter the form of government of the United States by unconstitutional means?[2]

By using the wording in item 3, they were doing exactly what they were asking about, that is, denying the civil rights of anyone who signed on.

On the reverse side of the form were long lists of organizations to be checked off individually with a yes or no. They included twenty-two Japanese-American, so-called totalitarian groups, twenty-two they dubbed Fascist, 137 alleged Communist fronts, and twelve that sought to alter our form of government. Some of them were listed under more than one category.

There was a great uproar over the whole affair, but ultimately, most complied. One of those who finally approved under protest was radio and television journalist Edward R. Murrow. Two of his close associates, Mike Bessie, an editor at Harper Brothers, and lawyer, Morris Ernst, sat up all night with Murrow trying to talk him out of signing. Bessie was later quoted as saying, "Morris and I tried to persuade Ed that if he signed the loyalty oath, the lesser people would also have to do likewise, and that if he didn't speak up, who would?"[3] Still later he said, "My recollection is that Ed was beaten down on the subject; that he was persuaded to go along."[4]

Murrow simply commented, "It was an absolute outrage."

One of Bill Paley's pre-war aides, William Fineschriber, said secretly, "It was a very stupid thing."

Shortly after the CBS debacle, Oscar Hammerstein III, President of the Author's League, made this comment: "It was more likely to condemn the loyal unjustly than to discover the disloyal."

The subject of loyalty oaths ran rampant throughout nearly every phase of industry during those trying times. In 1951, in his excellent book, *The Loyalty of Free Men*, Alan Barth discussed what was being done to teachers in this respect:

> "Why should teachers be singled out and asked to protect their innocence of an attitude which there is no good reason to suspect them of holding? Why stop at one profession? Let us require every legislator to swear that there are no illegal practices at his elevation and that he has never taken a bribe or purchased land knowing of a complicated improvement nearby. Let us require every lawyer to swear that he has never solicited clients by ambulance-chasing or otherwise; every doctor that he has never performed an abortion, and every business man that he has never violated the Robinson-Patman Act. (Legislature that basically leveled the playing field for all retail businesses, large and small) These offenders are far more frequent than disloyalty among teachers. Further, there is the very basic question of whether or not any private citizen has the right to investigate another, and equally important, to cut off his livelihood because of his failure to sign a loyalty oath."[5]

As E. B. White put it, "No one was watching the farm and there was no limit to the damage being done."

Chapter Nine
The Friendlies

What were "friendlies?" If you happened to be on the wrong end of the blacklist, it certainly was not your friend. No, they were the finger pointers who told all they knew, or thought they knew, or even made up just to get off the hook. They turned on their co-workers with a fury and by doing so, made themselves very unpopular. Many of these people were themselves on one list or another at one time or another, while others thought they were too pure to be bothered by the so called subversives.

Some of the worst of the finger pointers were actors Adolph Menjou, Ward Bond, Robert Montgomery, and John Wayne, but they were not really part of the group we call "friendlies," even though they and others did their share to make show business an uncomfortable place to be in the 1950s.

The group that I am referring to as "friendlies" were those who made it a point to testify before the various committees investigating what they called Communist activities in the industry. They were much worse than the mere finger pointers because much of the information they gave had no real basis in fact. They were burning other folk's bridges in an attempt to reestablish their own careers.

Martin Berkeley, for example. He was an ex-Communist Party USA member, who decided to turn on some of his old friends and a great many others he had no real knowledge of. You might say he was the #1 turncoat of them all because he named over 150 people, including some of his own close relatives. You can only imagine how that worked out at family reunions. Some were people he did not know at all. His own lawyers told him not to mention so many names because it would only get him in trouble later on, but he thought he would be making himself a hero in the eyes of the various committees and the American public. One of the committee investigators warned him that one mistake might get him killed.

The HUAC had just one purpose in mind during the hearings: not to legislate or even to discover subversives, but rather to stigmatize, humiliate, and denigrate their victims. This they did to perfection.

One of those friendlies was stage and film director Elia Kazan. He made some lifelong enemies with his testimony. Elia had been a Communist Party member for nineteen months between 1934 and 1936. He said he wanted to tell them all he knew about the Communist Party USA. He added that he had a taste of it and did not like it. In his testimony on January 14, 1952 and April 10, 1952, he expounded on what he felt the Communist Party's aims were:

> To educate ourselves in Marxist and party doctrine.
> To help the party to get a foothold in the Actor's Equity Association.
> To support the various front organizations.
> To try to capture the Group Theatre and make it a Communist mouthpiece.[1]

Kazan's appearances aroused a greater hostility and more bitter contempt than any other Hollywood informer. His extreme ego only made a bad situation worse.

Here are just a few of the comments made later by those who knew him well, for example, Warner Bros. Executive Producer, Jack Warner:

"This fellow is also one of the mob. I pass him by and won't talk to him."[2]

"I don't know why he gave names. He didn't have to. Perhaps he was fearful of losing his career in Hollywood, but he could have been distinguished in the theatre. I never discussed it with him since it's his personal problem." - a television director.[3]

"I believe, with great bitterness, that he sold off his most valuable possession." -a television writer.[4]

"After reading Kazan's testimony, I didn't think he truly believed anything he was saying," said screenwriter and Warner Bros. Producer Walter Bernstein.[5]

"What he did was diabolical. And what he did afterwards was diabolical—to try to reach out and offer work to blacklisted people, he tried to force them to accept him," said screen director Jules Dassin.[6]

"Kazan has a rotten character. In the end he was a stool pigeon," said screenwriter and director Abe Polansky.[7]

"His politics were very liberal at the time were supposed to be liberal, but he was a chauvinist and later, a fink," said screenwriter Marguerite Roberts.[8]

"I'd rather not talk about him. He was once my friend, my teacher. I've never been able to look him in the eye, nor he me, because he knows what I know," said director and actor, Martin Ritt.[9]

Another fink, or stool pigeon, was actor Lee J. Cobb, who was, in some ways, one of the most deceitful. As one of those listed in *Red Channels*, he had these citations to contend with:

American Peace Mobilization-Sponsor-American People's Meeting.
League of American Writers-Auctioneer-Benefit Books Auction Sale.
National Council of the Arts, Sciences and Professions-Signer for Wallace
Progressive Citizens of America-Member-Actor's division.
Daily Worker-Praised by the Daily Worker for refusing important role in The Iron Curtain
Scientific and Cultural Conference for World Peace-Sponsor
International Labor Defense-Affiliated

At first, Cobb denied any connections, but he reneged later and gave twenty names, his own wife.

In a statement he gave to the committee on June 2, 1953 he said:

"I would like to thank you for the privilege of setting the record straight, not only for whatever subjective relief it affords me, but if belatedly this information can be of any value in further strengthening of our government and its efforts at home as well as abroad, it will serve in some small way to mitigate whatever feelings of guilt I might have for having waited this long. I did hope that, in my delay to speak earlier, others of the people I have mentioned might have availed themselves of this opportunity for themselves to do likewise. I think by this time, I can reasonably assume that those who have desired to do so have taken the opportunity to make their position clear, and I can only say that I am sorry for those who haven't and that more haven't done so."[10]

At a later date, Cobb explained that he felt he was left with no options:

"In 1953, it was they (The Committee) who made the deal with me. I was pretty much worn down. I had no money. I couldn't borrow. I had the expenses of taking care of the children. You are reduced to the position where you either steal or gamble, and since I'm inclined more to gamble than steal, I gambled. If you gamble for stakes where you must win its suicidal—you lose. And that's what happened. When Elia Kazan testified I was shocked. I was offended. I wasn't in as deep. I thought, if I were in his boots, I'd die before they'd break me. If I had not been in need, I'd have never cooperated. My friends had the attitude that they'd rather eulogize me dead than to have me as an imperfect contemporary alive. They could say, "He didn't give in. He died pure.""[11]

Still later, Cobb added:

"When the facilities of the government of the US are drawn on an individual it can be terrifying. The blacklist is just the opening gambit—being deprived of work. Your passport is confiscated. That's minor. But not being able to move without being tailed is something else. Phone taps are expected, but the interception of a grocery bill? After a certain point it grows to implied as well as articulated threats, and people succumb."[12]

Cobb was far from the only one who felt this way, but he was one of the few who did turn tail and rat on his friends. As the old expression goes, "With friends like him, who needs enemies?" After his testimony, he found himself to be a pariah for many years. He constantly had to watch his back.

Chapter Ten
The House Un-American Activities Committee

Before moving on to the second part of this book I think it might be helpful to devote a chapter to a subject that will come up over and over again while talking about the cases of some of the individual victims of *Red Channels*.

That subject would be the House Un-American Activities Committee (HUAC) or as it is sometimes referred to the "House Committee on Un-American Activities." I think it is appropriate to discuss the historical roots of the HUAC. It had several ancestors.

The first was way back in 1918, the Overman Committee, which was presided over by Democratic Senator Lee Overman from North Carolina. The initial purpose of that panel was to investigate pro-German sentiments in this country during World War I. In 1919, they moved on to the area of propaganda resulting from the Bolshevik Revolution. The group passed from the scene before the end of 1919. The Overman Committee was, without a doubt, the seed that caused its followers to grow.

The next time a similar group came into the picture was in 1930. That one was called the Fish Committee. Their leader was Hamilton Fish III, a Republican Congressman from New York. Their favorite targets were the American Civil Liberties Union and the Communist Party USA.

The Fish Committee was short-lived, but it spawned the McCormack-Dickstein Committee jointly headed by Congressman John McCormack, a Democrat from Massachusetts, and Samuel Dickstein, who was a Democratic House member from New York. Their main function was to investigate how foreign subversive propaganda entered the United States and the organizations that were spreading it. Here is an intriguing note. During this time, Dickstein was reportedly being paid $1,250 a month by the Soviet NKVD to pass along congressional secrets about their information on the Communist Party USA. Whether he actually gave them any data is questionable, but that remains a moot point.

The Dies Committee, the actual HUAC panels, came into being in 1938 under Congressman Martin Dies, a Democrat from Texas. The Dies Committee's aims were basically the same as the previous committees with the additional purpose of looking into the Ku Klux Klan (KKK), until they were informed by John Rankin, a Democrat from Mississippi, that the KKK was an old, established American institution. Instead they went after the Federal Theatre and the Works Progress Administration (WPA) to search for purported Communists.

In 1945 and all the way up to 1975, the group became the Standing Committee on Un-American Activities to check into suspected threats of subversion or propaganda that attacked the form of government guaranteed by our constitution. In the process, they proceeded to trample all over several constitutional rights.

In 1959, ex-President Harry Truman was quoted as saying, "They are the most un-American thing in our country today."[1]

Throughout the years of the HUAC's existence, there were hundreds of people involved with the committee as the ever-changing House of Representatives went through its normal progressions, but I will list just six panels, because they were in place to question many of the people featured in this book.

Those six, along with some of their victims were:

> The 76th Congress (1939-1940), Interrogators on August 27, 1940 of Lionel Stander; Chairman Martin Dies, Texas; Members Arthur Haley (Massachusetts, later replaced by Joseph Carey, also Massachusetts), John Dempsey (New Mexico), Joe Starnes (Alabama), Jerry Voorhis (California), Noah Mason (Illinois), and J. Parnell Thomas (New Jersey). Their secretary was Robert Stripling.[2]

The 80th Congress (1947-1948), who questioned actor Edward G. Robinson on October 27, 1947; Chairman J. Parnell Thomas; Members: Karl Mundt (South Dakota), John McDowell (Pennsylvania), Richard Nixon (California), Richard Vail (Illinois), John Wood (Georgia), John Rankin (Mississippi), J. Harden Peterson (Florida), and Herbert Bonner (North Carolina, later replaced by F. Edward Hebert). Robert Stripling continued as secretary.[3]

The 81st Congress (1949-1950), which questioned Hazel Scott on September 27, 1950, and Edward G. Robinson again on December 21, 1950; Chairman John Wood; Members: Francis Walter (Pennsylvania), Burr Harrison (Virginia), John McSweeney (Ohio), Morgan Moulder (Missouri), J. Parnell Thomas, Richard Nixon, Francis Case (South Dakota), and Harold Velde (Illinois). The clerk was John Carrington.[4]

The 82nd Congress (1951-1952), which questioned actor John Garfield on April 13, 1951, writer Lillian Hellman on May 21, 1951, actor Jose Ferrer on May 22, 1951, and Mr. Stander once more on September 15, 1951; Chairman John Wood; Members: Francis Walter, Morgan Moulder, Clyde Doyle (California), James Frazier, Jr. (Tennessee), Harold Velde and Bernard (Pat) Kearney (New York), Donald Jackson (California), and Charles Potter (Michigan). The counsel was Frank Tavenner.[5]

The 83rd Congress (1953-1954, which questioned musician Artie Shaw and Philip Loeb on May 4, 1953; Chairman Harold Velde; Members: Bernard Kearney, Donald Jackson, and Kit Clardy (Michigan), Gordon Sherer (Ohio), Francis Walter, Morgan Moulder, Clyde Doyle, and James Frazier, Jr. Counsel was again Frank Tavenner.[6]

The 84th Congress (1955-1956), which questioned singer Pete Seeger on August 14, 1955, actor Zero Mostel on September 14, 1955, and writer Arthur Miller on June 21, 1956; Chairman Francis Walter; Members: Morgan Moulder, Clyde Doyle, James Frazier, Jr., and Edwin Willis (Louisiana), Harold

Velde, Bernard Kearney, Donald Jackson, and Gordon Sherer. Counsel was Frank Tavenner.[7]

Jack Tenney should also be brought into the discussion. He was not a member of the US House, but he did serve three four-year terms in the California legislature. He was responsible for much of the investigation going on out on the west coast in those days. He was quite outspoken on the subject of Communism. He once said, "You can no more co-exist with Communism than you can co-exist with a nest of rattlesnakes."[8] His main target was show business, which brought him firmly in line with *Red Channels*. He also worked to make loyalty oaths mandatory at the University of California. The Tenney Commission was yet another fine kettle of fish to be contended with.

While the whole red-baiting period is often called the "McCarthy Era", Senator Joseph McCarthy had absolutely nothing to do with the HUAC. His work was done in the Senate until his fellow legislators finally ostracized him with a thumping no-trust vote on December 2, 1954. The vote was 67 to 22 for censure.

BOOK TWO
The Accused

Chapter Eleven
Jean Muir

Citations:

Artists' Front to Win the War - Sponsor

International Workers Order - Available speaker - Concert & Lecture Bureau

Stage for Action - Member - Board of Directors

Congress of American Women - Vice-President - Cited by a former California Communist as having attended Communist study groups, loaned her car and home for Party purposes and met with Communist leaders

Southern Conference for Human Welfare - Supporter

Progressive Citizens of America - Supporter

Spanish Refugee Relief Campaign - Supporter

Moscow Arts Theatre - Sent individual cable of congratulations, 50th Anniversary Celebration

The Negro Quarterly - Sponsor

Actress Jean Muir was one of, if not the very first, person to feel the sting of *Red Channels*. She became the initial scapegoat for those aggressive witch-hunters, who would have made the prudes in Salem proud, but she never got a real chance to defend her honor.

She was the product of an upper-middle class family in Suffern, New York near the fringes of New York City, just over the line from Jersey. As a result, her early schooling took place in Richwood, New Jersey. Following high school, she attended the Sorbonne in Paris to study the French language. Acting was not even a remote part of her thinking while she had been in Europe.

On board the ship returning to America, she discovered that that the acting profession might be a good way to earn a living. That was in 1933, which turned out to be an eventful year for young Jean. During that fateful voyage, she came in contact with a traveling troupe of performers on their way to New Haven for a tryout of a play destined for Broadway. In route, Jean had many conversations with various members of the group and she became very interested in what they were doing. In response, they became interested in her and what they thought to be her possibilities. Some tests were conducted to see how she would react to reading and learning a script, and before the boat docked in Manhattan, she was hired to be the understudy for one of the parts in a play, *Bird in Hand*.

You might almost say Jean Muir became an accidental actress. As it turned out, acting was the only vocation she pursued for many years, with the exception of the time during which she suffered the humiliation of the infamous blacklist.

Not much later, she was discovered by a Hollywood talent scout. Jean was signed to a contract at Warner Bros. to appear in some movies. By 1937, she had appeared in over twenty films. By then, she became disenchanted with the acting profession; the roles she was cast in seemed to be less than challenging. Mostly, she played innocent ingénues in what could only be classed as "B" movies.

She felt she was destined for better things, so in 1937, she deserted the Hollywood lights to return to the stage. There were a few more films after that date, but they were the rare exceptions rather than the rule. Her return to the stage began in London in *People at Sea*.

By 1949, Miss Muir began to show up on television, which was still in its infancy at that time. Between that and her continuing work on the stage, she was kept busy until the fateful day that

Red Channels was published. Within a month of the issue date of *Red Channels*, the axe fell heavily on her employability.

She had been pegged to play Mother Aldrich in the TV version of the long-time radio success, *The Aldrich Family*. That never came to fruition because some people who thought of themselves as our would-be saviors came down hard on her. I should say they came down hard on General Foods, the show's sponsor. Both General Foods and the NBC network began to receive calls to complain that Jean was "a pinko" and should not be allowed to promote their products on the air.

Most of them came from the usual suspects. One was Hester McCullough, a lady who often did the same sort of thing to others she thought to be borderline subversives. Obviously, Hester did not have enough going in her life to keep her otherwise occupied.

Another of the verbal complainers was Alfred Kohlberg, the main financial backer of *Counterattack*.

Add to that list Rabbi Benjamin Schultz, leader of the Joint Commission against Communism, and Stephen Chess, Commander of the Catholic War Veterans post in Queens. Incidentally, Queens was also the home of Ted Kirkpatrick, who may have started the campaign. In all, NBC estimated there had been about twenty calls. General Foods put the number at over 200.

The sponsor turned chicken and ran scarred. All they were worried about was their bottom line. On a Saturday morning in August 1950, there was to have been a rehearsal for the first episode of *The Aldrich Family*, which would have reached listeners on the following Monday. That rehearsal never took place. The show was canceled and Jean was terminated. She was, however compensated for the full eighteen weeks her contract called for, because the powers-that-be were concerned about legal ramifications if they did otherwise.

General Foods issued a statement saying that Jean's appearance on the show would have provoked unfavorable criticism and even antagonism among sizable groups of consumers. They said they were not concerned with the accuracy of the allegations, only with audience perception. They claimed they were not conducting a political inquisition, but, of course, that was exactly what they were doing.

Michael Dann from the NBC public relations department said that there had been no discussion about the validity of whether or not she should be canceled, or whether or not there was any sort of injustice. He added that General Foods had made a decision and he would certainly support it.

Jack Gould, radio and television writer for the *New York Times*, wrote that the incident had dire implications for the future. The sponsor was setting a dangerous precedent by giving in to a small group of activists. He called them "Dictators of the Airwaves."

There were many more calls in Jean's favor than against her, but those made little or no difference to General Foods or NBC.

Jean felt she must respond to the whole flap. She said, "I am not a Communist; have never been one and I believe that the Communists represent a viscous and destructive force. I am opposed to them."[1] She desperately wanted to tell her side of the story to the folks at the HUAC, but they refused to call on her.

For a time, she fell into a deep depression and she turned to alcohol to mask her troubles. She did not return to show business until 1958, when she was hired by NBC, the same network that had fired her in 1950. After that, the pressure eased. She got back to work on television, and also her first love, the stage, but it was too late to recover all that she had lost.

During her down time, much was written about her from both sides of the spectrum. An article in *Counterattack* that was obviously aimed at her without using her name, said:

> "GIs in Korea are being murdered by those who have been helped by the people in this country who are members of, or who have given service to the Communist Party."[2]

The New Leader, a staunchly anti-Communist magazine took a different approach:

> "How does an actress in a TV comedy figure into the larger picture of the Cold War Conflict?"[3]

Ernie Pyle, noted war correspondent wrote:
"She was someone with a social conscience."[4]

When all is said and done, Jean was hardly a good target for *Counterattack* and *Red Channels*. Taking all the facts into consideration, it is very difficult to say that she warranted the behavior of those who opposed her. The only thing that was subverted was her life.

Chapter Twelve
Ireene Wicker

Citation:

Committee for the Re-election of Benjamin J. Davis-Sponsor

Ireene Wicker was perhaps the most glaring example of what *Red Channels* could do to a totally innocent person with its crusade by innuendo.

Ireene was a Midwesterner, born in Quincy, Illinois. All of her early years were spent in Illinois. She attended the University of Illinois at Champaign, where she majored in music and drama. In the late 1920s, she continued her education at one of the finest theatre groups in our nation, The Goodman Theatre. The Goodman Theatre got its start in 1925 thanks to a grant to the Chicago Art Institute, and was still going strong as of 2015. The Goodman Theatre was one of the most respected dramatic organizations in our land and one of the longest-running venues in the field.

Because Ireene was prominent on radio at the time, she drifted into that genre quite naturally. She worked on many of the early Chicago soap operas, but in 1931 she began a long run on her own show, *The Singing Lady*. It was a series directed at the children of that era and was, in fact, the first network show exclusively for a juvenile audience. She retold many of the old stories by such noteworthy authors as The Brothers Grimm, Hans Christian Andersen, Rudyard Kipling, and the like. She did all of the voices accompanied by a piano..

Through the years, Ireene was the recipient of award after award for her unique work. She practically owned the annual polls of *Parents* magazine, the *New York World Telegram*, the *Radio Guide*, and the *New York Journal*, among others.

Her trademark opening for those shows went something like this:

> "Children, you who wish to hear
> Songs and stories, come draw near
> Both young and old come hand-in-hand
> And we'll be off to story land
> For stories true from history
> And fairy tales and mystery
> So come along on wings of song
> Oh, come to story land with me."[1]

One group of stories she produced and performed was a series she called *When the Great were Small* on which she profiled the formative years of many of the historical masters of their chosen fields of endeavor. She profiled people such as Ludwig von Beethoven, Michelangelo, and Giuseppe Verdi.

In 1949, she successfully made the transition from radio to television on WJZ-TV in Baltimore. A few months later, her career came crashing down.

In June 1950, she received a call from John Crosby, radio and television writer for the *New York Herald Tribune*, informing her that she had been listed in *Red Channels*. Crosby then wrote a follow-up article titled, "Any of you children been subverted lately?" In it he wrote:

> "Somebody put her name down on the Committee for the Re-Election of Benjamin J. Davis and she has been smeared like so many people are smeared nowadays. In 1945—her most suspicious activity—Miss Wicker loaned her house for a benefit for Spanish refugee children. Miss Wicker was under the misapprehension that children were essentially non-political animals."[2]

Ireene decided to take the bull by the horns. She paid a visit to Ted Kirkpatrick at the offices of *Counterattack* to plead her case. The only item she had been cited for was her signature on that petition for the re-election of Davis to the New York City Council in 1945. She explained that she had never heard of the man and that she had not even been in New York at that time, making it impossible for her to have signed anything to that end. She told him of several patriotic programs she had done during that period and also that her only son, Walter Charles Wicker, Jr., had served in one of the Eagle Squadrons of the RAF and had been shot down and killed while flying over the English Channel in 1940. Kirkpatrick was unimpressed.

Ireene went a step further by securing a court order for her lawyer to examine the petition and its 30,000 signatures. Hers was not among them.

In October 1950 *Counterattack*, published her statement, adding that they had never said she was a signatory—a total lie on their part. They said that she was just a member of the committee.

Here is her statement as it was reported in *Counterattack*:

> "I emphatically declare that I am not, never have been, and never could be a Communist or Communist sympathizer in any case of these terms. The fundamental doctrine of Communism is abhorrent to me. It is in direct opposition to the American principals I have always upheld and advocated. The statement In Red Channels that the Daily Worker of September 15, 1945 reported me as a sponsor of the Artists, Writers and Professional Division of the Committee for the Re-election of Benjamin Davis is true. However, I was not aware of this fact until the publication of Red Channels. I absolutely deny the *Daily Worker* report. I categorically deny that I was ever a supporter of Benjamin Davis; that I gave my permission for their committee to use my name."[3]

She wrote a letter to the *Daily Worker* demanding a retraction. She received a reply from David Freedman of the law firm Unger, Freedman and Fleishcher stating that the *Daily Worker* story was based on a news release from the Davis Committee and did not contain the signatures of the sponsors listed. Freedman said that the *Daily Worker* regretted very much if that publication contained any error of fact.

Obviously, Kirkpatrick put too much credence in the *Daily Worker*, a source he condemned over and over. Once again, they did not fact-check the report because it served their purpose not to do so.

Another item that was brought up was her marriage to her second husband, Victor Hammer, the son of one of the founders of the Communist Party USA and the brother of Armand Hammer, an industrialist, who was later accused of money laundering for Soviet Russia. As Edward R. Murrow said, when he was fighting for the reversal of the charges against Milo Radulovich, who had been accused under similar circumstances, "We believe that the son shall not bear the iniquity of the father, even though that iniquity be proved. In this case it was not. Whatever happens in the whole area of the relationship between the individual and the state, we do it to ourselves. The line between investigating and persecution is a fine one. Cassius was right. The fault, dear brother, is not in the stars, but in ourselves."[4]

The end result of all of this was that Kellogg's, the sponsor of Ireene's television show, would not renew her contract, so she found herself virtually unemployable for a couple of years even though the folks at the HUAC had issued an apology, finding her faultless. She did return to the air in 1953, but she never regained her previous stature or reputation. However, she was rewarded in 1961 with a Peabody Award.

In case you are wondering about how the odd spelling of Ireene came about, let me explain. Early in her career when she was still using her birth name, Irene Seaton she came across a numerologist who told her that by adding an extra letter she would guarantee a successful future. Her surname came to her as a result of her first marriage to Walter Charles Wicker.

Chapter Thirteen
Philip Loeb

Citations:

American Committee for Democratic and Intellectual Freedom - signer - petition to discontinue Dies Committee

American League for Peace and Democracy - signer - statement on international situation

ARTEF - sponsor of fund drive

Artists Front to Win the War - sponsor

Council for Pan - American Democracy - signer - press release

End Jim Crow in Baseball Committee - sponsor - letterhead

Medical Bureau and North American Committee to Aid Spanish Democracy - member - executive board

National Federation of Constitutional Liberties - singer - message to House of Representatives

New Masses - signer - letter to President Roosevelt in defense of Communists

Negro Labor Victory Committee - entertainer - rally at Madison Square Garden

Non-partisan Committee for the Re-election of Congressman Vito Marcantonio - member

Progressive Citizens of America - sponsor

Stage for Action - member - board of directors

Statement by American Progressives on the Moscow trials - signer

Statement in Defense of the Bill of Rights against the Dies Committee - signer

Stop Censorship Committee - speaker by recording at Hotel Astor, New York City

Theatre Arts Committee - member - executive board

His was a truly tragic story, the life and death of a man who already had other monumental problems before his encounter with *Red Channels*.

Loeb was a stage, radio, and television American actor for more than forty years before his struggles began. On the Broadway stage, he had his premiere in 1919. He saw the final curtain fall in early 1955 while closing out an off-Broadway production that paid him the princely sum of $87.50 per week, a far cry from the wages he had been accustomed to earning earlier on in his career. Even as far back as 1955, that could not be considered much more than mere sustenance, if even that.

He had been a charter member of the Theatre Guild of New York, and did extensive work for Actor's Equity. During Loeb's years with Actors Equity, things began to turn sour for him. There were all sorts of rumblings that contributed to what befell him later on.

Beginning in 1940, when Congressman William Lambertson accused Loeb and six other members of Actors Equity of being Communists. Soon, the FBI confirmed that they could find no evidence to support that claim, but they did say they thought he might be a sympathizer or what they called a "Fellow Traveler," a title that carried bad connotations in those days, having nothing at all to do with tourism.

They said he was an instructive example of how the Communist movement could make a careless ally of a non-Communist leftist. By 1949, the FBI decided to cease their scrutiny, feeling that he was no threat.

Then, the 1950 publication of *Red Channels* happened, and Loeb's situation became untenable shortly after. He had a long list of seventeen citations in that book. He seemingly always had a soft spot for others who were in dire straits, no matter where they lived. He was more than happy to lend his name, his time, and his funds to many high-sounding organizations. He never denied this. Several of those organizations had long since been relegated to the annals of history before *Red Channels* came on the scene. At the same time, he swore under oath that he never was and never would be a member of the Communist Party USA.

He was by then working on both radio and television playing the role of Jake Goldberg opposite Gertrude Berg on the long running series, *The Goldbergs*. It was a character he had portrayed on stage in 1948 in a play, *Molly & Me*, based on the radio series that had been on the air since 1929 in a variety of different formats and on a number of different stations and networks.

The implications against Loeb in *Red Channels* were enough to make the show's sponsor, General Foods, nervous. They thought it would be better for all concerned if Phil found work elsewhere. Gertrude Berg was furious. She told her sponsor that if he was fired she would appear on every available platform coast to coast denouncing General Foods and advising people not to buy their products. The show's popularity was not enough to save Loeb. General Foods offered to buy out his contract for $85,000 if he would go quietly into the sunset. Loeb replied that he did not have a price. Unfortunately, that did not help his cause. He was let go. By the time he decided he needed to accept their money in 1951, the offer had dwindled to $40,000, which he had to accept due to his financial position. Then, General Foods dropped their sponsorship, and soon CBS cancelled the show, claiming that the ratings were poor, which was a lie. The television version came back on the air before long on NBC, but without Loeb as Jake. His career was over, with the exception of a few rare chances to perform on stage.

What did he have to say about all of this?

"After all I've done to correct the state of affairs, I am still blacklisted. I am deprived of work because of a cowardly, furtive smear campaign. I claim that, although innocent, I have been ousted from my work and hounded from my profession by a dirty undercover job."[1]

As time passed and his finances continued to dwindle, Loeb found he could no longer maintain his large apartment and way of life. He moved in with his dear friends, Zero and Kate Mostel, in order to share their limited funds. Zero had himself been a victim of *Red Channels* and was not doing a whole lot better, so the arrangement worked well for all concerned.

Loeb was only a shadow of the man he had once been. He would never smile no matter what crazy antics Zero would employ to try to cheer him up, as if he refused to be influenced by any other human being. Kate said she had noticed Phil on more than one occasion shouting out of the window at passing walkers.

Then one day in 1955, when Loeb did not come home as usual, Zero and Kate became very concerned because they both felt that he had been showing some disturbing signs. They and some of their friends called every New York hotel they could think of to see if they could locate him, but they did not find him until it was too late.

Loeb had checked into the Taft Hotel that afternoon using an assumed name. He then proceeded to take a massive dose of sleeping pills. He was finally discovered too late and he was dead, leaving no explanation note.

Kate Mostel summed it up in her own words. "Phil had had a rotten few years. The blacklist had not only kept him from working, it had humiliated him and beaten him down. He had a son who was seriously ill and cost Phil thousands of dollars to keep him in a good hospital. In addition, he had just had operations for cataracts and was terrified that he'd never be able to see well enough to work, even if the bad times would eventually be over."[2]

In the mid-1970s, Zero Mostel played a character called Hecky Brown in Walter Bernstein's movie, *The Front*. The role was based on both Zero's own life and Loeb's death. (In a later chapter, I will discuss that picture in some detail.)

Loeb had been a very high-energy, somewhat tightly wound individual throughout his adult life, always keeping busy with many different activities at any given time. When he was cited in *Red Channels* in June 1950, his world disintegrated piece by piece until he was a mere shadow of what he had been. He could no longer tolerate what life held for him. He decided to end his life at the age of sixty-four. Not long after, the FBI came out with a report clearing him of any Communist connections, but it came too late to do him any good.

To close this piece I think it is appropriate to quote the simple, but all-knowing statement made by his sister after his untimely demise.

> "He's been hurt so badly. Now see what they did to him. They took his living away. They took his life away. A person can only stand so much."[3]

Chapter Fourteen
Walter Bernstein

Citations:

Scientific and Cultural Conference for World Peace - Sponsor

Win the Peace Conference - Affiliated

Civil Rights Congress - Signer of statement in defense of Communist Party USA or Communist Party USA cases

Committee of 102 Writers and Artists to protest arrest of Pablo Neruda, Chilean Communist - Member

Masses and Mainstream - Signer - Open letter to Communist Writers

Mainstream - Affiliated

New Masses - Affiliated

May Day Parade 1947 - Sponsor

American Continental Congress for Peace - United States sponsor, Mexico City

Walter Bernstein deserves to have special notice in this book, so special that he will be featured in a much later chapter, as well as here. He is a great example of the people who were persecuted by the effects of *Red Channels*.

Walter was a native New Yorker, born in Brooklyn to Hannah and Louis Bernstein way back in 1919. His childhood was fairly uneventful, not at all like some of the others in this work. He got his higher education at Dartmouth College in Hanover, New Hampshire, which was also where he got his first job as a writer. He was the movie reviewer for the *Daily Dartmouth*, the campus newspaper. This was a very appropriate beginning when you consider his later extensive work as a screen and television writer. As was the case for so many others in those tumultuous days, he had to overcome some tremendous road blocks during his long career.

While he was at Dartmouth, he became a member of the Young Communist League, a small group of no more than four people at any given time, reduced to three by the graduation of one of them. They had no genuine contact with the Communist Party USA at that time. The Young Communist League was more of a social gathering than anything else. They would simply sit around and talk about the issues of the day that interested them, but they never took any active actions toward any of them.

When the Communist Party USA found out about their little group, they sent a local representative to try to get them to distribute the *Daily Worker* to their fellow students. As Walter said, this was out of the question because it was hard enough to get them to read the *Daily Dartmouth*, so nothing came of it. They just thought they should be in favor of anyone who opposed Hitler and his principals. The young party worker who called on them told of how he had been severely beaten when he was a union organizer. When he finished his unsuccessful pitch, the boys of The Young Communist League took him out for a few beers, where they discussed for hours everything and anything except politics. They found him to be a very likable chap. Ironically, that same young man met his death a few years later at Guadalcanal.

In 1941, Walter was drafted into the army. He reached the rank of sergeant. His main duty was to work as a correspondent for *Yank*, the army newspaper. His initial posting was to have been to Moscow, but due to all sorts of political red tape, that never came about. During the war years, he filed dispatches from the Middle East, North Africa, Sicily, and even Yugoslavia, where he got to interview Josep Broz (Marshall Tito). This was indeed a feather in his cap. Tito did not normally grant audiences to western reporters. Many of those reports were published in the *New Yorker* magazine. In 1945, a collection of them came to us in a book titled *Keep Your Head Down*. By that time, Bernstein had been a staff writer for *The New Yorker*, an association that would continue for several years thereafter.

When Walter was honorably discharged from the army after the conclusion of the war, he soon became a dues paying member of the Communist Party USA. He had many good reasons for doing so. Because of much of what he had seen, he thought it was a natural progression. He knew that our stilted friendship with the Soviet Union during the conflict had been only a convenient aberration that would soon become nothing but a blip in our history. He had read about and seen the Communist fight against fascism, racism, and colonialism. He thought that, while he knew they were far from perfect, they did have a vision for a better, more humane world. His emotions during that period were never directed towards anything that was in any way anti-American. He just wanted to be able to help those who desperately needed help.

In 1956, his affiliation with the party abruptly ended. The reason was the Hungarian revolt against their governmental system, for which they were rewarded with cruelty and Russian tanks patrolling their streets. 1956 was also the year that American memberships dropped precipitously because of that one event.

For a time after the war, Walter was also a member of the Duncan-Paris Post of the American Legion, a group that included many like-minded thinkers. They harbored the odd belief that the Bill of Rights should stand for something. It was a time when speech was anything but free. There was an ever growing attack on decency and reason. The post was drummed out of the Legion and its members were labeled Communist Party USA Agents.

In September 1949, Walter was present to witness a civil rights concert in Peekskill, New York that was put together by actor/singer Paul Robeson and included such performers as Pete Seeger and Woody Guthrie. That event that should go down in our history as a disgrace to all things American. It cemented his thoughts that he was on the right track. The concert went off nearly as planned despite the hecklers that had been brought in from all around. The real trouble arose when it was time to leave. The police had all the exits closed off except one. That meant that everyone leaving had to take the only exit left open, which led to a hilly, curvy, narrow path that offered no protection. As the performers attempted to exit, they were pelted with sizable rocks thrown by mostly American Legion members, and baseball bats with which they were assailed up close and personally. The only people the police shielded were the rioters.

One of those rocks was later embedded in the hearth around Pete Seeger's fireplace in his living room. It had been thrown through the windshield of his car during his departure. Pete resented it even more because he had his wife, Toshi, and his young kids in the vehicle.

Walter never forgot what happened that day. His car was also damaged by the bats. Maybe the worst of it was the curses that were screamed at them. They were called Nigger bastards, Red bastards, Jew bastards, and even Jewcommielikebastards, all slurred into one angry word. The ACLU, the NAACP, and *The Nation* magazine all demanded an investigation, but Tom Dewey, the New York Governor, refused to do anything about it because he said it was all Communist provoked.

In 1950, *Red Channels* was published and distributed. All hell broke loose. Walter Bernstein was one of the many souls who suddenly found it almost impossible to get work even though he was recognized as a great talent by all the folks who really counted in his industry. He tried to continue by writing under the pseudonym "Paul Bauman." He submitted television scripts through messengers, but that came to a screeching halt when a producer wanted him at the studio to do some rewrites. Of course, he could not show himself under the circumstances; too many people would recognize him. Then something very strange occurred that defied logical explanation. His agent told the producer that he had fired "Bauman" because he was so uncooperative, but that he had another client who would gladly make the necessary changes. That client turned out to be Walter Bernstein. Whether it was just a case of being up against tight production deadlines or some other reason, the rewrites were done and not another word was spoken. The show went on as scheduled. That proved to be an isolated incident. For the most part, Walter could still not find gainful employment, even from the producer whose bacon he had saved at the last moment.

He began using a long string of fronts. That did not prove to be very satisfactory. His contract with Paramount Pictures was not renewed. No one wanted to touch him. He did have some luck when Italian film director Carlo Ponti took him on to write a screenplay for him. Carlo said that the red scare was just a bad American joke. He would not listen to Walter's detractors.

During the 1950s, Walter was constantly shadowed by agents of the FBI. He said he could always spot them, even when they did not approach him because, as he put it, "They came in pairs and looked alike, but mismatched and from the same orphanage." Sometimes they came to his door and they always asked him very politely the same one question, "Are you ready to talk yet?" To this he would give them the same response before shutting the door; "NO!" The same brief dialogue would take place when they accosted him on the street occasionally. An FBI agent used to go through the same routine on the phone with regularity. He called himself special agent Graubard. Walter began to feel sorry for the man because he never got to first base. He was just doing his job.

All of this activity made him wonder why he had not been called on to tell his story under oath since several of his would-be friends had given his name to the House Un-American Activities Committee in order to try to clear themselves. Finally, near the end of the 1950s, Walter was served with a subpoena, but by then things were winding down and the Committee was rapidly disintegrating, so he never did get to testify.

Sam Moore, the president of the Radio Writers Guild and Walter Bernstein began distributing a newsletter called *Facts about the Blacklist*, sent mainly to ad agencies and network executives, the very people who constantly denied the existence of a blacklist. Some of them who had been afraid to speak publicly on the issue responded with documents contrary to what they had previously stated. They even received a letter from someone at CBS describing a meeting with the notorious Syracuse grocer, Lawrence Johnson, to go over lists of intended employees. Sam and Walter got many letters congratulating them for their courage, but all of these things were always done anonymously. No names were ever used.

Throughout the years, Walter wrote a plethora of movie and television scripts, many of which were never credited to him on screen. There is one that has become almost a cult favorite, Walter Bernstein's *The Front* (1976). In it, he took on the blacklist in retrospect, which will be the subject of a later chapter.

Chapter Fifteen
Zero Mostel

Citations:

Communist Party USA - Entertainer at social functions

American Youth for Democracy - Member

May Day Parade 1947 - Arts, Sciences and professions for May Day

Joint Anti - Fascist Refugee Committee - Benefit - Imperial Theatre - New York City

Civil Rights Congress - Reception for Hollywood writers - Park Central Hotel - New York City

Zero Mostel was a man who could be a different person at different times and was always unpredictable. He could be loving or arrogant, smiling or angry, easy going or impossible to get along with; all of these demeanors in a matter of seconds. Basically, he was a good man who could express strong feelings at any given moment, whenever he thought it to be appropriate.

A good example of this was expressed by Gene Wilder, his co-star in *The Producers*. When Gene was tapped to play his role opposite Zero, he was at first terrified. If you have seen that movie, you will remember one of the early scenes when the two first met and Gene's character, Leo Blum, was quavering with fear of Zero's character, Max Bialystock. That scene approximated their first meeting on the set. The outcome was surprising to Gene. Zero got up, went over to him, and planted a big kiss on him. From that moment on, the tension was gone. They became good friends.

Zero even made it a habit to pick up Gene every morning to go to the studio.

The relationship Zero had with Mel Brooks, *The Producers* producer, writer, and director, was quite a different story. When he first read the script, Zero wanted no part of it. Mel told him again and again to read it until, with the aid of Kathryn, Zero's wife, he convinced him it was good and he should do it. While shooting the picture, those two very strong personalities were often at odds as to how it should be done. Mel nearly always won those wars of words. In the end, that movie became one of Brooks' most successful efforts. Today, it is a cult classic.

The main problem with Zero and movies was that what he put into the characters he played was always too broad to come off well on the screen. His best work was on the stage. Also, Zero hated the screen scene, hated Hollywood and all it stood for. The only reason he did as many movies as he did was because the money was good and it gave him time to pursue his real true love. In his own mind, and in that of many others who had occasion to see his work, he thought of himself first as an artist, while entertaining was secondary to him. In his earlier days, he concentrated on building a future as a painter, and as a matter of fact, was quite good at it. He gave lectures at art museums, but due to his method of presentation, using humor to punctuate his discourses, he soon found that his audiences were spending more time laughing than taking notes. That turned him on to comedy.

Zero was obviously not his birth name. His parents, both of whom were from Eastern Europe, called him Samuel Mostel. What father or mother would hang the name Zero on their offspring? Zero was a stage name given to him by his publicity agent, Ivan Black, after he got him one of his first jobs at Café Society, a nightclub in downtown Manhattan, owned by Barney Josephson. Barney did not think Sam Mostel was an appropriate name for a comedian. Zero suggested "Fagel Bagel," but that did not ring true for anyone. Finally, Ivan settled on "Zero" because his client had started with nothing. The name stuck and was his ever after.

A funny sidebar to this was a biographical piece Zero wrote for the program notes while he was doing a play by Moliere called *The Imaginary Infidel*:

"Zero Mostel's real name is Talburnium Kohaaran von Eccelsex. He was born in Upper Slbeesing Holstein and is part Schnager. He traveled in a stock company with the immortal Keane Garret, Ben Johnson, and Birdie Tebbets to the far corners of the globe, until one day his brother smashed the globe to smithereens. He appeared in many films; *The Great Train Robbery, Greed, Grass,* and Pathé news reels. Mr. Mostel is doing a festival of plays in a diving bell for the submarine service. All he has to say is, "Heads off to Talburnium.""[1]

That all sounds like something reminiscent of the BBC's *Goon Show*.

Zero's name was listed in *Red Channels* along with the five previously stated citations. Eventually, he was called upon to testify before the House Un-American Activities Committee. Their main goal was not to prove guilt, but rather, to get their victims to name the names of others involved in what they spoke of as subversive activities. Most of the names they were seeking were already in their files. It was just a form of increased intimidation. Zero was careful not to give them any fodder to chew on. He invoked his Fifth Amendment rights whenever he felt his rights were being infringed upon, but he was very forthcoming on many issues. When asked by Donald L Jackson about The American Youth for Democracy, he strongly objected. "My point is that the organization for which I appeared was declared subversive by the Attorney General's list long after the inception of that particular organization."[2]

When asked directly if he was a member of the Communist Party USA, he said, "I refuse to answer that question on the grounds previously stated, sir, constitutional liberties, which I hear are granted to every individual in this land."

Jackson replied, "And which the committee does not question."

"I'm sure it doesn't," Zero said with sarcasm."[3]

He handled himself well under trying circumstances, giving no quarter. Here is another exchange with Clyde Doyle. "You are in a great field of entertainment of the American Public. From now on, why don't you get far removed from the groups that are known as Communist dominated or Communist controlled—that sort of thing? Why don't you remove yourself far away from that atmosphere, sir? You can be a much better inspiration and a joy to the American people if they just know that there is not a drop, not an ink point, not a pen point or a favorable attitude by you to the Communist conspiracy?"

Zero replied, "My dear friend, I believe in the antiquated idea that a man works in his profession according to his ability, rather than his political beliefs."

"I am not asking you about your political beliefs."

"My dear friend, I believe in the idea that a human being should go on stage and entertain to the best of his ability and say whatever he wants to say because we live, I hope, in an atmosphere of freedom in this country."

"That's right, and we will fight for your right to think as you please and be as you please provided you do it within the four corners of The Constitution."[4]

I do not think the panel was really operating under any constitutional premises. Zero went on to give an example of his thoughts. "I appreciate your thoughts. If I appeared there, what if I did an imitation of a butterfly at rest? There is no crime in making anybody laugh."

"If your interpretation of a butterfly at rest brought money into the coffers of the Communist party, you contributed directly to the propaganda effort of the Communist party."

"Suppose I had the urge to do a butterfly at rest somewhere?"

Doyle answered, "Yes, but please, when you have that urge, don't have such an urge to put the butterfly at rest by putting some money in the Communist party coffers as a result of that urge to put a butterfly at rest. Put the bug to rest somewhere else next time."[5]

At this point, the interrogators could see that they were getting zero from Zero.

"The witness is excused. Thank you, Mr. Mostel. Remember what I said to you."

"You remember what I said to you."[6]

Staying true to his convictions, Zero did not name any names, as was the case with many performers.

However, this was not the case for some of those called on to testify, such as Lee J. Cobb, himself listed in *Red Channels*, who ran off to the panel many names of those he suspected of being questionable, including Zero. As a result, he became a pariah in the industry, looked down on as a traitor to his own convictions. When they met by chance at a later date, Zero went into an instantaneous rage. No blows were struck because Cobb ran for cover.

Zero often asked himself and others why the committee was going after actors instead of spies. He said that to inquire into one's private or political life was against the intent of our constitution. Between 1951 and 1961, he was not asked to appear in any movies. His work on the stage was affected to a lesser degree, but even there he found many doors closed to him. He kept himself going during his down period by concentrating on his work as a painter. It did not bring in the kind of money he was accustomed to, but it did keep the wolf from the door.

In *The Front* (1976), a movie written by his good friend Walter Bernstein, he played a character loosely patterned on his own troubles with *Red Channels*. I will talk more of that picture later on. I will only add here that Walter was also a blacklistee.

Zero was very blasé about was the clearance process. He did not feel that he had done anything wrong. Ergo, he did not need to be cleared. He refused to play their game, sometimes to his own detriment.

On one occasion, when he had a good chance to get back on the air in a new television series, he was called to a meeting by the two writers of the proposed series. He was told to keep his mouth shut and let the others do the talking. He did better than that. He totally ignored the goings on and just sat there reading his newspaper. The only problem was that the paper he was reading was *The Daily Worker*. You can imagine how the meeting ended. It was just Zero's small way of exerting his rights, but of course, his ploy backfired.

When thinking of Zero, many will immediately think of his stage work as Tevye in *Fiddler on the Roof,* a role he played during two long runs. He did it first on the Broadway stage in 1964 and then repeated it during a road schedule in 1976.

There was so much more to the man, but I will leave that to his biographers, most notably Jared Brown in his excellent book, *Zero Mostel, a Biography.*

Chapter Sixteen
Pete Seeger

Citations:

   People's Songs - National Chairman

   Progressive Citizens of America - "Show Time for Wallace"

   Wallace for President Campaign - Led singing at rallies

   Communist Party USA - Entertainer

   American Committee for Yugoslav Relief - Sang at dinner - Hotel Pennsylvania

   Jefferson School of Social Science - Instructor

   Schools for Political Action - Instructor - Washington, DC

   People's Artists, Inc. - Participant

   Committee for a Democratic Far Eastern Policy - "Hail New China - Ally for Peace" - City Center Casino

   Voice of Freedom Committee - Participant - "The Case of the Loaded Mike"-Town Hall

   "Stop Rankin" meeting - Entertainer - Hotel Concourse Plaza

   American Youth for Democracy - Entertainer - Vet's Conference - Central Plaza Annex

   May Day, 1950 - Entertainer - "May Day Jamboree"

Singer/songwriter Pete Seeger was a caring man. He cared about the things that should be important to all of us. He was constantly working for causes that needed attention. At one time or another, he took on big business on behalf of the then non-union workers, civil rights where he joined with the downtrodden African-Americans throughout our land, the Vietnam War, and even the pollution in the Hudson River that flowed past his long-time log cabin in Beacon, New York that he and his wife of seventy years, Toshi, built with their own hands and where he was still living until he passed away. He survived Toshi by just a few months.

From his earliest days, he was exposed to music. Both of his parents were classical musicians, his father on piano and his mother on violin. Pete took a different route, but in 1955, he showed his versatility by releasing *The Goofing-Off Suite*, a recording blending traditional Appalachian banjo with classics from Beethoven's 7th and 9th Symphonies and also Bach's Cantata 147.

Of course, that sort of thing was not the main thrust of his music. He was in many ways the main reason for the overwhelming popularity of the Folk genre during the 1940s and 1950s. Many of his tunes reached high levels on the Top 10 lists in a time when the general trend of the industry was headed in an entirely different direction. The biggest winners were oft times recorded by others, but some included his own work, with one of the two major groups in which he was the driving force.

The first was *The Almanac Singers*, a group that featured Woody Guthrie, Lee Hayes, and Millard Lampell along with Pete. There were others in and out of the mix during their tenure, but those were the mainstays. During that time, Pete went from the four-string banjo to a long neck five-string banjo of his own design. He also sometimes played guitar.

The second combo, one you may have better memory of, was *The Weavers*. He was joined there by Ronnie Gilbert, Freddy Hellerman, and again Lee Hays. One of his earliest influences was Huddie Ledbetter, better known as "Lead Belly." Huddie's work left Pete in awe. His song, "Good Night Irene," recorded by *The Weavers*, topped the charts for thirteen weeks in the 1950s.

All of these people came at one time or another to the attention of the notorious red-baiters of various ilks.

Pete always wanted to share the lyrics of his songs with his audiences, wanting them to sing along so they could better understand what he was saying to them. The problem was that some of what he sang was considered subversive, not only for the words, but also from where they were performed.

Pete's hundreds of songs include those derived from worldwide folklore and others that were his originals, such as "Where Have All the Flowers Gone?" which was popularized by dozens of singers, including on *Peter, Paul and Mary,* the 1962 debut album featuring Peter Yarrow, Noel (Paul) Stookey, and Mary Travers, which spent five weeks as the #1 album in the country in 1962 and stayed on the chart for ten months.

Pete wrote the song during a very down time for him when he was enduring serious legal difficulties, and the melancholy tone clearly showed his mood at the time. Here is the final verse:

> "Where have all the young men gone?
> Long time passing
> Where have all the young men gone?
> Long time ago
> Where have all the young men gone?
> They're all in uniform
> Oh, when will we ever learn?
> Oh, when will we ever learn?"[1]

Another song Pete wrote was "If I had a Hammer," which he co-wrote with Lee Hays, and originally performed at a rally for some Communists that were on trial under the Smith Act (Alien Registration Act) in 1949. That immediately made the song highly controversial in the eyes of many beholders. In Pete's opinion, it was merely a statement to protest the current conditions when everyone became suspect. He felt very strongly on the subject. Here is the final verse:

> "Well, I've got a hammer
> I've got a bell
> And I've got a song

> All over this land
> It's the hammer of justice
> It's the bell of freedom
> It's the song about love between
> All of my brothers
> All over this land."[2]

After *The Weavers* recorded "If I had a Hammer" in 1949, they were taken to task by columnist Irwin Silber for the line, "All of my brothers," calling it male supremacist and demanding that it be changed to "My brothers and my sisters." Pete said that that wording did not flow, but in the end, when Peter, Paul and Mary and others later made a hit of it, they used those lyrics.

"We Will Overcome" was not a Seeger original but a song that he had first heard when Zilphia Horton taught to him to back the Black strikers on North Carolina tobacco farms. Pete, with his Harvard education, changed it to "We Shall Overcome," saying that it was not for grammatical reasons; it just came easier off the tongue. Toshi chided him about it for years, but "Shall" is how we all know it. While we associate it mostly with the civil rights movement here in our country, Pete sang the song with mixed success all over the world, wherever he thought it applied. In 1963, he did it in South Africa. In 1967, he sang the song in East Germany, much to the chagrin of the officials of the Deutsche Democratische Republik. In 1968, he joined Ralph Abernathy's Resurrection City protest in Washington, DC, where he sang the song over and over. He had been working for that movement as far back as 1959.

Pete never denied that he was a long-time member of the Communist Party USA; however his intentions were always pure. He always fought for the rights of the common man, even though, at times, that worked to his own detriment. Never did he do anything that could fall under the title of subversion except to those who chose to see it that way.

When he was called upon to testify before the HUAC, Pete made his intentions very clear. He had a huge decision to make. He could take protection from prosecution by invoking his Fifth Amendment rights and his troubles would be over, but by doing so he would forever be stigmatized as something he was not. His other option was to use the First Amendment and try to show that his right to privacy overruled any attempt to prove him guilty of what the committee accused him of. He knew this option would cost him dearly financially and personally, but he decided it was the best way to go if he ever wanted to clear his name once and for all.

On August 14, 1955, the HUAC attempted to drag him through the mud, but he gave them no quarter. He brought along his banjo to help make his points, but he was denied any use of it. His interrogators for this session were Frank Tavenner, Francis Walter, and Gordon Sherer.

First, he was asked about his residence and occupation.

"I make my living as a banjo plucker—sort of damning in some people's opinions."[3]

Tavenner asked him about an article from the *Daily Worker* that said that he sang for Communists.

"I refuse to answer that question, whether it was a quote from the *New York Times* or the *Vegetarian Journal*."

Sherer stated, "He hasn't answered the question and he merely said he wouldn't answer whether the article in the *New York Times* or some other magazine. I ask you to direct the witness to answer the question."

Walter said, "I direct you to answer."

"Sir," Pete replied, "the whole line of questioning . . . ."

"You have only been asked one question, so far."

"I am not going to answer any questions as to my associations, my philosophical or religious beliefs, or how I voted in any election, or any of my private affairs. I think those are very improper questions for any American to be asked, especially under such compulsion as this."[4]

Tavenner then asked him about the May Day rally in 1948.

Pete responded, "I feel that in my whole life I have never done anything of any conspiratorial nature and I resent very much and very deeply the implication of being called before this committee that in some way, because my opinions may be different from yours; that I am any less of an American than anybody else. I love my country deeply, sir."

Walter asked, "Why don't you make a little contribution toward preserving its institutions?"

"I feel that my whole life is a contribution. That is why I would like to tell you about it."

Walter replied, "I don't want to hear about it."

Sherer asked, "Let me understand; you are not relying on the Fifth Amendment, are you?"

"No sir, although I do not want to in any way discredit or deprecate the witnesses who have used the Fifth Amendment."[5]

When asked directly if he was paid by Communists for entertaining them, Pete said succinctly, "I am proud that I have sung for every American; Americans of every political persuasion, and I have never refused to sing for anybody because I disagreed with their political opinion, and I am proud of the fact that my songs seem to cut across and find perhaps a unifying thing; basic humanity."

Tavenner asked, "Did you hear Mr. George Hall testify yesterday in which he stated that as an actor the special contribution he was expected to make to the Communist Party was to use his talents by entertaining at Communist Party functions?"

"I didn't hear it, no."

Tavenner added, "It is a fact that he so testified. I want to know whether or not you were engaged in a similar tune of service to the Communist Party by entertaining at their functions."

Pete said, "I have sung for Americans of every political persuasion, and I am proud that I never refuse to sing for an audience no matter what religion or color of their skin or situation of life. I have sung in hobo jungles. I have sung for the Rockefellers, and I am proud that I have never refused to sing for anybody. This is the only answer I can give along that line."[6]

Tavenner said, "I hand you a photograph which was taken of the May Day parade in New York City in 1952, which shows the front rank of a group of individuals and one in uniform with military cap and insignia. Will you examine it please and state whether or not it is a photograph of you."

Pete answered, after a brief look, " It is like Jesus Christ when asked by Pontius Pilate, 'Are you the king of the Jews?'"

"Stop that!"

Pete added, "Let someone else identify that picture."

Sherer asked, "Again, I understand you are not invoking the Fifth Amendment?

"That is correct."

Sherer concluded, "We are not accepting the answers or the reason you give."

Pete concluded, "That is your prerogative, sir."[7]

The offshoot of all this was that he was cited for ten counts of Contempt of Congress. After many delays, on April 3, 1961, Pete was sentenced to one year in jail for each of the counts. When his lawyer requested bail pending an appeal, the very adversarial judge refused. When over a hundred demonstrators showed up on Pete's behalf, that decision was rescinded, and he remained free. Finally, on May 18, 1962, he won his appeal when the original indictment was ruled faulty by a higher court. His ordeal was over at last, but not without leaving some scars.

All during that period, Pete thought about a quote from Walt Whitman:

> "Have you heard that it was good to gain the day?
> I also say it is good to fail.
> Battles are lost in the same spirit they are won."[8]

Pete Seeger summed up his life with a song, "How Can I Keep From Singing."

"Some people sing because they're so happy they just can't stop.
Some people sing to keep their spirits from going five miles below hell.
And some sing just to keep their courage up.
How can I keep from singing?
My life flows on in endless song.
Above earth's lamentations
I hear the real, though far-off hymn.
That hails a new creation
Through all the tumult and the strife

I hear that music ringing.
It sounds an echo in my soul.
How can I keep from singing?"⁹

Chapter Seventeen
Millard Lampell

Citations:

Committee to Aid the Fighting South - Co-chairman

Congress on Civil Rights - Sponsor

Mainstream - Contributor

National Committee to Win the Peace - Vice-chairman

National Committee of the Arts, Sciences and Professions - Signer for Wallace - Speaker - Meeting to abolish House Un-American Activities Committee - Hotel Commodore - NYC

New Masses - Contributor

People's Radio Foundation - Member - Advisory Council - Leaflet

People's Songs - Member - National Board of Directors - Member - Advisory Committee

Veterans Against Discriminations of Civil Rights Congress - Sponsor - Chairman - Rally at Hunter College - NYC

The Worker - Contributor - Article - "Caste in the Army"

Writers for Wallace - Member

Scientific and Cultural Conference for World Peace - Sponsor

May Day Parade, 1947 - Sponsor

United Veterans for Equality - Member - Provisional Committee

Voice of Freedom Committee; National Council of the Arts, Sciences and

Professions - Chairman - Rally in defense of Bill Sweets - Hotel Abbey

American Continental Congress for Peace - United States sponsor - Congress held in Mexico City

Committee for Free Political Advocacy - Signer - Statement protesting prosecution of Communist Party USA leaders.

Stage for Action - Instructor

Voice of Freedom Committee - Chairman - Testimonial dinner to William S. Gailmor - Hotel Park Sheraton - NYC - Co-author of song, "We Got Gailmor"

Jewish Life - Contributor

Masses and Mainstream - Book reviewer

Millard Lampell was a prodigious activist throughout his adult life, but despite what was said of him by his detractors, he could never be called subversive in the true sense of the word.

Millard was born in Patterson, New Jersey, into a lower-middle class family, what we might call the working poor. His father was a Jewish immigrant from the old Austro-Hungarian Empire, a man who would take on any job that came his way in order to put bread on the family table. To say that his was a struggle at times would be putting it mildly.

Millard grew up with a deep appreciation of the trials and tribulations of the common man. His childhood gives us some insight into how and why he reacted in his later life when he saw things that disturbed him and his way of thinking. He spent most of his life fighting for those downtrodden people any way he could, often with detrimental effects on his own career.

After high school, Millard was rewarded with a full scholarship to West Virginia University based on his abilities on the gridiron. All was fine and good until he got injured playing and the school canceled his free ride. When finances became a stopping-block, he managed to cover himself by ghost writing Masters Theses for other students. In a very real way, that was the start of his writing career.

During those years at WVU, he became aware of the mountain folk music and musicians who were all around him in the hill country. In 1940, at the age of twenty, this led his to joining Pete Seeger, Woody Guthrie, and Lee Hayes in their group called *The Almanac Singers*. Millard is perhaps best-known for his award-winning work as a screen, radio, and television writer, but he also sang with and wrote lyrics for *The Almanacs*. Many of those lyrics and the people they were sung to would later become a major obstacle for all of them.

As Millard put it, "We found ourselves performing at union meetings and left-wing benefits for Spanish refugees, striking Kentucky coal miners and Alabama sharecroppers."[1]

Between 1939 and 1941, The Almanacs made it clear what their feelings were about entering the war, a feeling not too uncommon among the population in general. They did songs criticizing Franklin Roosevelt as a war monger and the British for their war against Nazi Germany. At the time, they even went after Eleanor Roosevelt in the song, "Ballad of October 16th" from their 1941 album, *Songs for John Doe*:

> "Oh, Franklin Roosevelt told the people how he felt
> We damn near believed what he said
> He said, "I hate war and so does Eleanor"
> But we won't be safe till everybody's dead."[2]

Those words, while they may be inflammatory, are still covered by the Bill of Rights under freedom of speech. Once the United States were actually involved in the war, *The Almanacs'* slant and tone turned 180 degrees on the subject.

In 1940, Millard and the others joined the Communist Party USA, not because of the party's leanings in international politics, but rather because of their position on the rights and privileges of the working man. That membership ended when Pete and Millard were drafted into the service. Millard often spoke of the Party meetings as a good way to catch up on much needed sleep.

The biggest target of *The Almanacs* was big business and their constant abuse of the very people who made them successful. At that time, labor unions were rare exceptions to the general rule. Workers had virtually no voice in how things were done.

One of the many pro-labor songs was "Talking Union," from the album *Talking Union*.

> "If you want higher wages let me tell you what to do
> You got to talk to the workers in the shop with you;
> You got to make a union, got to make it strong,
> But if you stick together, now, it won't be long
> You get shorter hours, better working conditions.
> Vacations with pay, take the kids to the seashore."[3]

Later Verse:

> "'Course, the boss may persuade some poor damn fool
> To go to your meeting and act like a stool;
> But you can always tell a stool, though - that's a fact;
> He's got a rotten streak a-runnin' down his back;
> He doesn't have to stool - he'll make a good living
> On what he takes out of blind men's cups."[3]

And if this was not enough, they also did one for the ladies in the factories titled, "Union Maid," from the same 1941 album, *Talking Unions*.

> "There once was a union maid; she never was afraid
> Of goons and ginks and company finks
> And the deputy sheriffs, who make the raids
> She went to the union hall when a meeting it was called
> And when Legion boys came 'round
> She always stood her ground."[4]

Not to be outdone by labor, the management had to have their say. The red-baiters came back with this little ditty called "Management Blues."

> "If you want higher profits let me tell you what to do
> You got to talk to the people who work for you
> Got to bust up the unions—they're much too strong
> Fire everybody who dares to belong!
> Get rid of the agitators
> Hire friendly people
> Willing to work for an honest wage."[5]

In the end, *The Almanacs* had a huge effect on the American labor movement. Even Henry Ford, an outspoken anti-laborist and racial bigot, was brought to the negotiating table. It seemed like every month another large work force signed on with the CIO.

In 1942, after *The Almanacs* disbanded, Millard was an important part of Norman Corwin's production of "Lonesome Train," a cantata based on the story of the train that carried Abraham Lincoln's body back to Springfield, Illinois for burial after his assassination. Earl Robinson wrote the music, and Millard wrote the words. "Lonesome Train" was later cited as subversive because it separated all too clearly the common man from the establishment types.

Here we have just one stanza:

> "A Kansas farmer, a Brooklyn sailor
> An Irish policeman, a Jewish tailor
> An old storekeeper shaking his head
> Handing over a loaf of bread."[6]

All three of the major contributors to "Lonesome Train," Corwin, Robinson, and Lampell, showed up on the pages of *Red Channels*, but when Jerome Lawrence and Robert E. Lee turned "Lonesome Train" into a stage play, they had no repercussions.

In 1945, Millard once again collaborated with Norman Corwin in his landmark production, *On a Note of Triumph*, which celebrated the end of the war in Europe. Millard wrote the words for "Round and Round Hitler's Grave," the theme that recurred throughout the show, each time with slight variations:

> "Hey! Round and round Hitler's grave
> Round and round we go
> We're gonna to lay that poor boy down
> He won't get up no more
> I wish I had a bushel
> I wish I had a peck
> I wish I had old Hitler
> With a rope around his neck."[7]

Considering the overwhelming feeling of utter joy at the end of the long conflict, no one could find much fault with that one.

By 1947, the boys at *Counterattack* were keeping a close watch on Millard. To them, he had been suspect for a long time. When *Red Channels* was published in 1950, Millard was one of the 151 names listed. He suffered the predictable results. In his own words, this is what he felt:

"There was no way of getting proof I was actually on a list, no easy way to learn the damning details. My income simply dropped from a comfortable five figures to $2,000/year. Finally I ran into a friend, a producer who had downed a few too many martinis, and he leveled with me. "Pal, you're dead; I submitted your name for a show and they told me I couldn't touch you with a barge pole." He shrugged unhappily, "It's a rotten thing. I hate it, but what can I do?" And with a pat on my cheek, "Don't quote me pal because I'll deny I said it."[8]

Millard sold his car and moved his family to a small apartment in a cheap neighborhood and began a long siege.

The Senate Committee on Internal Security, also known as the McCarran Committee, served Millard with a subpoena to testify in 1952. McCarran was the Senate equivalent of the HUAC. Millard did respond to the summons, but he refused to say anything that would aid them in their quest. Many who strongly opposed the blacklist thought this committee just an attempt to justify the witch-hunt, while smearing innocent people without any corroborating evidence to prove their accusations.

One of the items the panel found to be on the edge of Communist propaganda was a screenplay Millard had co-written with Sidney Buchman in 1951 called *Saturday's Hero*. It was based on Lampell's novel, *The Hero*, which, in turn, was more or less based on his own college experience on the football field, and the fact that, once he had been injured, he lost his free ride in the academic world. In the storyline, he and Buchman, who later was elected president of the Screen Writers Guild, told of every aspect of the so-called field of amateur athletics on the college level and how the players were exploited by their coaches, school executives, and alumni groups. They spoke of the overuse of pain killing drugs, the part-time jobs given to jocks that required absolutely no work, and the bonuses that could be earned for a good performance. Of course, none of this is allowed under the NCAA rule structure, but, as I am sure you know, it still goes on today. The committee found this kind of thinking not in keeping with the American way.

During the years he was forced to endure the blacklist, Millard used many ploys to try to earn a living at the work he did so well. He used several fronts and no less than four pseudonyms. Sometimes it worked; more often it did not. Once during that period, his friend, Hume Cronyn, wanted Millard to write a series that was being contemplated. When he submitted Millard's name, he was told, "No Way!"

Also during that time, he found some work writing industrial docudramas for clients, such as Air France in Paris, and International Business Machines (IBM) closer to home. There were always some avenues open, but never enough of them to compensate for what had been taken away.

After the situation had cooled down, Millard was again recognized for his immense talent. In 1965, he was awarded an Emmy for his teleplay, *Eagle in a Cage*, which was about Napoleon's exile on St. Helena. In the course of his brief acceptance speech, he said, "I think I ought to mention that I was blacklisted for ten years." When he finished, he received a standing ovation.

My, how times can change!!

Chapter Eighteen
Marc Blitzstein

Citations:

American Council on Soviet Relations - signer - open letter - official leaflet

American Friends of the Chinese People - entertainer

American Peace Mobilization - member - National Council - sponsor - participant - official program - signer of call

American - Soviet Music Society - affiliated

Citizens Committee to Free Earl Browder - sponsor of appeal - letterhead

Committee of Professional Groups for Browder and Ford - member - letterhead

Committee on Constitutional Liberties in America - sponsor - official program

Coordinating Committee to Lift the Embargo - representative individual - official booklet

First Conference on American - Soviet Cultural Cooperation - participant

Friday - endorser

International Labor Defense - sponsor - summer milk drive - contributor - Benefit Books auction sale

Jewish People's Committee for United Action against Fascism and Anti-Semitism - sponsor - letterhead

League of American Writers - supporter of Anti-War Movement - signer of call to 1941 Congress - attended 4thAmerican Writers Congress

Masses & Mainstream - signer - letter entitled "American Message—A reply to an Open Letter of Soviet Writers." A portion of this message reads as follows: "Your letter tells us that you are not deceived by the shots fired in the air by our press and radio, the furious wailing of paid mourners for the status quo—all of the caterwauling that passes for the voice of America"

New Masses - contributor - article—"A musician's war diary"

Musicians' Committee to Aid Spanish Democracy - sponsor - invitation

National Federation for Constitutional Liberties - signer - new release - signer - Sam Darcy appeal

National Wallace for President Committee - member - press release

New Masses - speaker - New Masses Theatre Night, NYC - signer - letter to the President protesting "Badgering of Communist leaders"

Open Letter for Closer Cooperation with Soviet Union - signer

Open Letter on Harry Bridges - signer

People's Songs - member - board of sponsors - sent birthday greetings

Progressive Citizens of America - sponsor - program

Schappes Defense Committee - sponsor - letterhead

Statement Defending the Communist Party - signer

Statement by American Progressives on the Moscow Trials - signer

Theatre Arts Committee - member - advisory council - letterhead

Veterans of the Abraham Lincoln Brigade - signer of protest

Washington Committee to Lift Spanish Embargo - signer - letter for the lifting of the embargo

May Day Parade, 1946, 1947 - affiliated

Progressive Citizens of America - Writer - "Showtime for Wallace" Cabaret

Moscow Library Gazette - signer - Open Letter offering to "share the public duty" assigned to Soviet intelligentsia

Scientific and Cultural Conference for World Peace - sponsor - official program

National Council of the Arts, Sciences and Professionals - composed song play, "I've got the Tune" - Carnegie Hall - official program—signer - advertisement, "We are for Wallace"—signer for Wallace

Committee for the Re-election of Benjamin J. Davis - sponsor

Wow! That was some list, twenty-five items in all, some of which overlap each other citing different occasions with the same groups, so it is not as long as it might seem.

This multi-talented composer and playwright was born into an affluent family in Philadelphia. He exhibited musical talent at a very early age. At seven, he was able to perform a Mozart piano concerto. He was the sort of prodigy that could and should be recognized and nurtured. He received the best of training along the way, including instruction from Alexander Siloti, who was himself a student of both Tchaikovsky and Liszt. Marc followed up at the Curtis Institute. He then went to both Berlin and Paris to polish his skills.

During his early years, Marc was a self-proclaimed intellectual snob, believing that true art should only be for the elite. This attitude did not make him many friends, but it was through his composition and performances that all of that changed, and his overall thought process, as well. He transformed from his narrow-mindedness to the opposite extreme over a period of not many years.

His compositions ran the gamut from concertos to incidental music and full scores for films and stage to symphonies.

The Cradle Will Rock, one of his better-known works due to its relationship with some long-time friends, was first performed against massive odds. It was arguably the most memorable debut in New York theatre history.

Actor and film producer John Houseman told me that *The Cradle Will Rock* was a production that was to be performed at the Maxine Elliott Theatre under the auspices of the Federal Theatre, a Works Progress Administration (WPA) organization created to give work and some cash to underemployed actors, writers, and technicians toward the end of the great depression. The producer and the director were Houseman and Orson Welles. The narrator, who was also the composer and musical director, was Marc Blitzstein.

They had completed rehearsals and were ready for opening night. At the last moment, the folks at the WPA decided that it would have to be cancelled or at least postponed because of the labor unrest that was happening at the time. The play was all about striking workers fighting for their rights, a subject too delicate to be handled under the existing conditions. In the eyes of Houseman and Welles, it was not a political statement, and they refused to allow it to be closed. They thought of it as simply a well-written piece that deserved to be seen and heard. The Maxine Elliott Theatre was made unavailable, and the talent union told the cast and musicians that they could not appear on stage in *The Cradle Will Rock*. They musicians would not even be allowed to enter the orchestra pit. The theatre was placed under lock and key, and all of the scenery and costumes were inaccessible.

With but a few short hours remaining before the intended opening, Houseman and Welles came up with what the temporary solution of sending their representatives to try to locate another theater that could adequately serve their purposes. At the very last moment, they received permission to use the Venice Theatre, which was a much larger house.

Prior to moving the production, they had sent Jean Rosenthal out to find and buy a truck and a piano because there could be none of the original planned music available. She was then told to just ride around with her purchases until the location could be solidified, which she did for several hours.

The other obvious problem was that the Venice Theatre was twenty-one blocks distant from the Maxine Elliott Theatre, where the audience had already gathered outside, restless because the theater was locked and they could not enter. When the word gradually got out as to what was happening, the already large contingent began their exodus. Some hailed taxis, some rode busses, but the large majority made the trip to the Venice Theatre on foot. The most amazing thing was that by the time they reached their final destination, their numbers had tripled. What they found upon entering the Venice Theatre was a bare stage with a rickety piano and nothing else. Marc came out, sat down at the piano with his sleeves rolled up, and the story began to unfold. Of course, the actors were still forbidden to appear on the stage, but they had a solution for that, as well. They were scattered throughout the house where they each delivered their lines from where they were as the evening progressed. The end result was an astonishing hit!

A few years later, Leonard Bernstein, a young undergraduate student from Harvard, took it upon himself to re-create the experience. He performed *The Cradle Will Rock* exactly the same way it had originally been done, with a cast that never set foot on the stage. When Marc heard about it, he attended an ensuing performance and was awe struck. That evening was the beginning of a long, close relationship between the two men.

Regarding Marc's connections with the Communist Party USA, he never denied his membership, which was severed in 1949. His reasoning was strictly humanitarian. We must remember that in the late 1930s, the USA was still clawing its way out of a deep economic depression. The situation was not limited to our own borders, as many people were desperately looking for a way to improve the existing state of affairs. The Communist Party USA was a possible option open to anyone who wanted to help the downtrodden people of the world. To many, it seemed to have possibilities, not for subversion, but simply to be able to help some of those in need. Granted, some of the party's aims were not good for our overall benefit, but on the other hand, some were. It was a matter of picking and choosing what part of their manifesto one wanted to adhere to.

Marc could have lived in the lap of luxury if he had wanted to use his talent to pursue pure entertainment, but he opted for a different route. Most of his work was about the human condition, something the general population was not always ready to accept.

In the late 1930s, he made a statement which I think of as his Credo, declaring quite clearly his opinion of the conditions at that time:

"I love this country. For that matter, I love all countries. What I love is people. I am ashamed of the meanness and stupidity which disorganizes people, and I am afraid of the insight and generosity which organizes them. If you were to limit me to my nation in the matter of love and loyalty and belief, then I might ask you to limit me also to the region, the state, the city, the house, the room, the corner I call my own, for my exclusive love and loyalty and belief. Really, you are asking me to recline, like the Greek Narcissus, gazing at myself in a pool with eyes of worship. I am against that. It seems to me that the complex that I am and the complex that I am not, which is to say the others, must have a traffic system, must join, must above all equate, before my conception of the way things ought to be will be satisfied. This is not nearly so unrealistic as it might sound to ears attuned only to 'Number One.' What I think I mean is culture, and I might reduce culture in definition to the smallest particles of join-up in this sense; wherever different people, plus time, plus experiences, simply living experiences, stack of a shapeless thing that gets shaped by more people, more time, more living experiences, a style is created. And when several of these styles are discovered to have joined, and shapelessly, slowly to have taken on a shape, we have lo, a culture."[1]

Shortly thereafter in 1940, J. Edgar Hoover sent this request to the FBI's New York office to try to clarify Marc's position:

"The above captioned individual has been reported to the bureau as being a Communist Party member who is also a playwright and entertainer. He has sponsored and participated in dramatic productions and balls for the benefit of such Communist front groups as the North American Committee to Aid Spanish Democracy and the Non-Sectarian Committee for Political Refugees. He attended the 10th National Convention of the Communist Party and has recently been associated with the various peace moves, having been elected to the National Council of the American Peace Mobilization at their Chicago rally in 1940. Please furnish the bureau with the present address of Blitzstein together with any recently available information reflected on the advisability of considering him for custodial detention in the event of a national emergency."[2]

In May 1958, Marc was subpoenaed to appear before the HUAC. When he responded, he was questioned in a closed executive session during which he refused to give names and thereby incriminate anyone else. He also questioned their right to interrogate him. He was told to make himself available the next morning to appear at an open hearing, but he was never called on that day.

He thought his troubles were behind him, but this proved not to be the case. After the hearing, the FBI was still trying its best to nail Marc with something—anything—even though he had long since ceased to be a party member and no longer had any ties to any of the front organizations. They still felt the need to conduct another interview in the hope that he would slip up and tell them something they did not already know. They thought this was possible because he had not been an entirely hostile witness at the HUAC. At the same time, they conceded that there was no evidence of any Communist Party USA activity since 1951.

In a memo from a New York special agent to the director:

"In view of the subject's history of psychoneurosis the bureau is of the opinion that he should be interviewed by two mature and experienced agents and that every caution should be exercised in order to preclude embarrassment to the bureau."[3]

The agents who did the interview identified Marc as though he was the subject of a wanted poster. Here is how they started off:

"Description—Build-small—Complexion-Dark olive—Hair-Black, bald on top—Eyes-Dark, deep set—Characteristics—Wears moustache, horn rim glasses, elongated, slightly hooked nose, soft spoken, theatrical mannerisms."[4]

After the interview they reported:

"The subject stated that he had nothing further to add to his testimony before the government committee and that he resented the attempts by the FBI to interview him as he considered it an invasion of his privacy. The subject was cold in his manner toward the agents and exhibited no inclination to cooperate. In view of the above no further efforts are warranted to interview him again. New York will remain alert for any information of subversive activity on the part of the subject and will reopen investigation if warranted in the future."[5]

Marc Blitzstein's life was never easy and not made any better when *Red Channels* published his name in 1950. Because of the nature of his work, he was able to get through it all because he was what could be called a private contractor, not always at the beck and call of others, as was the case with most of those on the blacklist.

In January 1964, he opted to take a working vacation on Martinique in the French West Indies because he wanted to get away from the cold weather in New York. It proved to be a terrible mistake. On January 22, he was beaten to death by three local sailors. Marc was an openly gay man, and the three sailors said that he had propositioned one of them. This can never be verified, but it is questionable. Marc was fifty-eight years old when he met his untimely end.

Back in New York, upon hearing of the tragic event, Leonard Bernstein stopped a concert to announce what had happened. He then dedicated the playing of Beethoven's *Eroica* to the memory of Marc Blitzstein. They had been dear friends for years and years, so it hit Leonard very hard.

This is what Eric Salzman of the *Herald Tribune* wrote about that performance:

> "The work was performed as if the conductor was rewriting Beethoven as he went along in order to express his personal grief. It was an incredible, agonized, unbearable reading, with its bursts of nervous energy, and wild relentless drive, left detail, clarity, accuracy and indeed everything but anguished, frenetic intensity far, far behind."[6]

Chapter Nineteen
Artie Shaw

Citations:

American Peace Mobilization - Sponsor of call

Committee for a Democratic Far Eastern Policy - Sponsor - Letterhead

New Masses & Mainstream - Sponsor - Rally to defend Howard Fast

New York Council of the Arts, Sciences and Professions - Vice chairman

Scientific and Cultural Conference for World Peace - Sponsor

National Negro Congress - Speaker

National Wallace for President Committee - Member

Statement Denouncing Hartley Committee - Signer

Voice of Freedom Committee - Member

Hollywood Independent Citizens Committee for the Arts, Sciences and

Professions - Member - Executive council

Civil Rights Congress - Sponsor

People's Songs - Affiliate

World Peace Congress, Paris, April 1949 - Member - American sponsoring committee

You probably would not have liked Artie Shaw as a person, but there was no one who would deny his genius as a musician. He was said to be the possessor of an IQ somewhere between 160 and 170, which is far above most of us. At the same time, he was thought to be arrogant and extremely self-centered. When performing, he tended to be stand-offish and disdainful of his audiences and often made derogatory public statements about their demeanor.

I do not in any way mean to distract you from his musical talent; quite the contrary. He was, with little dispute, the finest clarinet virtuoso we will ever hear. His experiments with various varieties of tuneful formats were always beyond the curve. He did some of the usual things that other Big Band leaders did, but far exceeded his competition. In his early years, his instrument was the alto saxophone, on which he excelled. It was not long before he graduated to the clarinet.

I remember a time back in the 1980s, when I was talking with Steve Allen, who had played Benny Goodman in The Benny Goodman Story (1956). Steve said he had to take some lessons on the clarinet in order to be able to show the proper fingering technique when mimicking Benny. Steve was a better than average sax player, but he told me that the clarinet was a much more difficult instrument. What you heard on the movie soundtrack was Benny playing, not Steve.

There was a long-running squabble between Artie and Benny over who was the best, to which Artie always replied, "Goodman plays the clarinet; I make music." Many believe that he was right.

Through the years, he fronted sixteen- and seventeen-piece bands with which he tried many combinations of sounds. For some time, he directed a thirty-two-piece orchestra with heavy emphasis on a large string section. The public was not always ready for what he did. When that happened he would move on to another style and usually catch the golden ring.

Many times during his long career he got frustrated and left the music scene for a time until he could come up with a new concept. He then returned with a new band and a new sound altogether. He did Jazz, Dixieland, and Be-bop. He had a small group of soloists from within the band that he called the "Gramercy 5." For a long time, he toured with the inimitable Billy Holiday as his vocalist, until she tired of the racial inequities, mostly in the South, but up North, as well. He even did solo classical work with the likes of Leonard Bernstein and the New York Philharmonic. All his life, Artie had a great love affair with the classics.

Shortly after the war, a New York *Journal American* columnist, Frank Conniff, and a writer for the *New York Mirror*, Lee Mortimer, dubbed him "The Communist Loving Clarinetist" because he played Shostakovich and other Russian composers. He said he would really be making a political statement if he did not play their music, since a good many of the modern composers were Russians.

While serving on the Executive Council of the Hollywood Independent Citizens Committee for the Arts, Sciences and Professions (HICCASP) in 1946, he was approached in his office by a man who would not identify himself, and asked to join the Communist Party USA. Artie wanted to find out all he could about them without committing himself. He wanted to find out how they operated within his organization. He was told he could not attend any of the Party meetings unless he joined their ranks, so he signed a paper after carefully reading it, not even dreaming it represented his intention to join up. He then attended several meetings strictly as a bystander to see what was going on. He heard a lecture about how the Executive Council of HICCASP should feel about the establishment of a Fair Employment Practices law and the extension of the Office of Price Administration. He did not pay much attention to it all, but he did go to a few more meetings before declaring himself out.

Unfortunately, when Kathleen Windsor, his sixth wife, filed her request for a divorce in the courts, she said he definitely had a Communist Party USA card. Her declaration was partially true. Artie did receive a card, but he claimed that he immediately tore it up.

In 1953, he was subpoenaed to testify at a HUAC session, something he had wanted to do for some time. His reason was so that he could clear his name. Of course, that was not the committee's intention. What they wanted was to hear him speak the names of others involved in what they termed subversive activities.

On May 4, 1953, Artie got his chance to speak out publicly. His inquisitors were Frank Tavenner, Kit Clardy, Gordon Sherer, Clyde Doyle, Donald Jackson, and the chairman, Harold Velde. Before Artie began his testimony, he made his intentions clear:

"May I say, first of all, that I am going to answer every question you ask of me as honestly and fully as I possibly can."[1]

He spoke of the cloak-and-dagger events in 1946 and how he had been hoodwinked—absolutely misled into attending meetings:

"I feel the use of my name on a lot of things should not have been granted, but at the same time I can only say that the intent on my part when I granted them was not to be anything disloyal. I never in my life have done anything disloyal to this country. Not since then will you find my name on anything outside of the American Federation of Musicians. I wouldn't sign anything today unless I had the advice of seven lawyers and the granting of permission of clearance by this committee."[2]

Sherer asked, "You realize, Mr. Shaw, you were thoroughly duped by the Communist group then, do you not?"

Artie replied, "Yes sir, I certainly was. I was a fool. I should not have signed."[3]

Doyle then said, "Maybe you should end your stage shows with a few uplifting words to the young people of the virtues and responsibilities of the American system.

Artie answered, "I think on occasion I have done that. Actually, you can pretty much upset an audience that way."[4]

Here is a portion of the actual testimony Artie gave on that day in response to questions from Frank Tavenner:

Tavenner asked, "So you attended four of these meetings?"

Artie replied, "Three meetings and one lecture."

"Over what period of time were these meetings held?"

"During the period I told you about—as I say, from a month to six weeks previous to July 1946. At this lecture meeting there was a lot of large—an awful lot of large statements made about international policy and so on and so forth and I wasn't very concerned with it-- didn't interest me very much and I sat there for about an hour, an hour and a quarter, and I listened to this man talk. At the end of that time I left. I informed someone I wasn't coming back to these things anymore and that was the end of any of these meetings."[5]

Artie continued, "I am at a point now where I am afraid to join any organization. I haven't joined any organization for three years because I don't know what any word stands for anymore. I am at a point today, if anyone says, 'Here's a committee for personal freedom,' I don't want any part of it. I don't know what these things mean anymore.

Jackson added, "They have been used by the Communist Party USA to the detriment of those words."

Artie responded, "I'm afraid that that is true. I used to think I knew what freedom and democracy meant."

Clardy interjected, "The meaning has been pretty well destroyed."

Artie said, "I'm afraid so. I had this discussion with a man not long ago. When he asked me how I could have been naïve enough to join the World Peace Congress—put my name on that, I said to him, "Do you know of any other peace congress I could join?" I want peace. He says, "That is a Communist inspired one." I said, "Get me a Republican Party inspired one and I'll join that. I don't care which one."

At that time, the audience broke into applause.

Verde stated, "We will countenance no further demonstrations, favorable or unfavorable."

Artie told him, "I wasn't bidding for applause, I assure you."

Verde agreed. "I am sure you weren't, Mr. Shaw."[6]

He ended his day in court in a very repentant mood, nearly in tears. The offshoot of it was not at all what Artie had expected. As a writer, he soon found that no publisher wanted to touch him. He did get the last laugh on that score by using a front. As a performer, he also could not get a spot on television, not even on panel shows.

One of the people who knew the most about him on a personal level was actress Evelyn Keyes, a lady I got to know quite well before she passed away back in 2008. She was the last of his eight wives, a marriage that endured through twenty-eight years even though they were not living together for many of those years. When she finally filed for a divorce in 1985, she cited his obsessive-compulsive behavior as her main reason. That was true. Throughout his life, Artie was never good to any of his women. He was a control freak, who always had to have everything done his way or the highway. Interestingly enough, Evelyn and Artie remained close friends as long as they both lived. She nursed him when he was sick and they even enjoyed vacations together several times. They loved each other, but they did not always like each other. When I called Artie for an interview back in 1987, Evelyn picked up the phone. That was after their official divorce in 1985.

Incidentally, I never did talk directly with Artie.

Chapter Twenty
Hazel Scott

Citations:

National Citizens Political Action Committee - member, women's division - vice-chairman, Campaign Committee

Citizens Non-Partisan Committee to Elect Benjamin J. Davis, Jr. - participant - "Harlem Event of the Year"

Progressive Citizens of America: Citizens Committee of the Upper West Side - affiliated, letterhead

Musicians Congress Committee - member, advisory board

American Committee for Protection of Foreign Born - guest of honor, "United Nations in America" dinner, NYC

American Peace Mobilization - sponsor, American People's meeting, NYC

Artists Front to Win the War - sponsor

Joint Anti-Fascist Refugee Committee - sponsor, letterhead

Civil Rights Congress - sponsor, dinner

Pianist and singer Hazel Scott was born in Port of Spain in the island nation of Trinidad and Tobago off the coast of Venezuela, where she lived with her mother until they came to New York City when she was only four. At the early age of eight, she was recognized as a musical prodigy by Professor Oscar Wagner at the Julliard School. She was far too young to be considered for a scholarship, but upon hearing her play Professor Wagner said,

"I am in the presence of genius." He took her on as a private student and worked with Hazel for several years.

By the time she was sixteen, she was performing with her mom in her "Alma Long Scott All-Girl Jazz Band." While Hazel is best remembered as an incomparable Jazz and Blues singer and pianist, she also was a capable trumpet blower. Her vast repertoire covered all the bases. Hazel was a trained classical performer and she worked from time to time as a guest soloist with many symphonic orchestras around the world. Her style at the clubs came to be known as "Jazzin' the Classics." She would start off with a classical piece and then gradually turn it into a Jazz form.

She was still in her late teens when she began working at *Café Society*, a very hip Jazz venue in New York run by Barry Josephson. *Café Society* was a unique club, and later two clubs, because they allowed no color line to exist on stage or in the audience. In the late 1930s, that was certainly not the norm. For Hazel, *Café Society* was her springboard to fame, as well as a millstone around her neck a few years later when the "Red Scare" was in full blossom.

Many of the regular performers and also their habitual customers eventually found themselves on one blacklist or another. The list of frequent attendees was long and included Leonard Bernstein, Eleanor Roosevelt, Lillian Hellman, Nelson Rockefeller, and Paul Robeson, a diverse group to say the least. On stage on any given night, you might find Zero Mostel or maybe Lena Horne.

Why was *Café Society* singled out to be victimized? Could it be due to their remarkable openness to all comers? Anybody who could think for himself or herself in those days was automatically suspect.

In 1945, at the age of twenty-five, Hazel earned the incredible sum of $73,000, the equivalent of more than $1 million in 2015.

1950 was a big year for her in both good and bad ways. She had her own television show, the first woman of color to do so, but then *Red Channels* published, and consequently her TV show was canceled.

In September 1950, she was engulfed with a combination of pride, fear, and rage. She had not received a subpoena from the

HUAC, but she wanted to clear the air. Against the advice of her husband, Adam Clayton Powell, Jr., she pled with the committee to hear her side of the story. They grudgingly agreed to listen only because of their respect for Adam, who was a leading member of the congress. He stated his overall opinion on the state of affairs that was so prevalent in those days. "I make no brief for Communism. However, I must defend the right of any individual to maintain whatever particular view he holds until such a view is declared illegal by an act of congress. Those of you who are afraid of red scares should have the guts to make Communism illegal. Until then it is legal."[1]

On September 22, 1950, Hazel appeared before the panel, which included John Wood, Burr Harrison, and Francis Walter, among others. During the course of her testimony, she refused to be brow-beaten by any of the interrogators. She gave fire for fire. She explained away each of the *Red Channels* citations one by one. She told the committee members that they might very well have important work to do, but she wondered if they had not become victims of "Headline-Seeking Super-patriots." She said, "I'm not going to relax my effort to get the rights for people of color merely because the Communist Party embraces that effort."[2]

When asked why she entertained Soviet troops in 1943, she said, "It's no small irony being accused of being unpatriotic for something, which five years earlier was considered the height of patriotism."[3]

As to her work for the political cause of Benjamin J. Davis, Jr., she said, "I don't recall exactly how that appearance came about, but I believe it was at the direction of Mr. Barney Josephson, my employer and manager, who often leant my name and time to affairs without consulting me."[4]

Barney never forgave Hazel for saying that.

She got into a rather heated war of semantics with Mr. Walter and Mr. Harrison over *Red Channels*. Walter asked, "Did the publishers of that pamphlet ever contact you in order to verify any of those statements?"

Hazel answered, "In no way. It was brought to my attention I was in that book. I never heard from them by wire, phone call or anything. *Counterattack's* failure to consult me before including my name in *Red Channels* establishes a presumption of their insincerity regarding the protection of innocents and genuine liberals. Until they have reasons for this, that fact alone damns them and calls for the cessation of their malicious activities."[5]

To Burr Harrison, she added, "May I ask you a question? If any committee, any official committee, lists me as having two heads, does that make me have two heads? And does that give *Red Channels* the right to publish that I have two heads?"

Harrison answered, "They make no bones of the fact that they do not evaluate the listings."

"They simply prepare a blacklist. Are we ready to say, in effect, that the Communists have taken over the whole country except for a few self-appointed patriotic virgins, such as the gentlemen at *Counterattack*?"[5]

At the end of the long, tedious day, Hazel summed up her thoughts to the committee, reiterating much of what she had said earlier in the session. "I for one, Mr. Chairman, am not ready to hand over America's entertainment industry to Moscow. A few cunningly contrived lies, some false statements, an impressively long list, such as *Red Channels*, and years of preparation, sacrifice, and devotion are killed. Instead of a loyal troupe of patriotic, energetic citizens, ready to give their all for America, you will demoralize them and end up with a dejected, wronged group whose creative value has been destroyed.

"Now that you gentlemen have heard me so patiently—may I end with one request? That is that your committee protect those Americans who have honestly, wholesomely and unselfishly tried to perfect this country and make the guarantees in our constitution live. The actors, musicians, artists, composers, and all of the men and women of the arts are eager and anxious to help, to serve. Our country needs us more today than ever before. We should not be written off by the vicious slanders of little and petty men. We are one of your most effective and irreplaceable instruments in the grim struggle ahead. We will be much more useful to America if we do not enter this battle covered with the mud of slander and the filth of scandal."[6]

When it was all over, Hazel departed for Paris, where she was able to put behind her all of the petty accusations, as well as the racial inequities that constantly plagued her. She became a hit in the cafes with her interpretations of many standards. They took on new meaning in the local language. She did not return to America until 1967.

Somewhere along the way, she commented on her past life and her thoughts on her own personality. "Stubbornness is one of my faults. If I believe that I am in the right, I will die before I allow myself to be dissuaded. No one has ever been able to make me swerve from a decision once I have made up my mind. It has never been my practice to choose the popular course. When others lie as naturally as they breathe, I become frustrated and angry."[7]

During Hazel's Parisian days, she continued to fight for the rights of her people back home. On August 23, 1963, she was at the forefront of a demonstration at the American Embassy to back Dr. Martin Luther King, Jr.'s March on Washington for Freedom and Jobs. She and her cohorts presented a petition to Ambassador Cecil Lyon for his support of the march.

In 1981, after landing her ideal gig at *Kippy's Pier 44*, she was performing to rave reviews. Then one night she was hit with unbearable stomach pains while doing her show. In spite of her agony, she managed to finish, but was then taken immediately to Mount Sinai Medical Center in New York where she was diagnosed with advanced pancreatic cancer. As she lay dying, Dizzy Gillespie was playing a muted version of one of her favorite songs, "Alone Together." She was only sixty-one, but she had lived a full life. She never left that hospital alive. Within a few weeks she was gone, a sad end to a feisty, sincere lady of the Arts. She never let anyone get the better of her no matter what.

Hazel was interred at Flushing Cemetery in Queens. She was to be in good company there. Gillespie was later buried there, as were other Jazz greats; among them were Louis Armstrong and Johnny Hodges.

Ezio Bedin, her second husband, said after their brief marriage and divorce, "Hazel was a Maserati, but I could only handle a Fiat.[8]

Chapter Twenty-One
Lena Horne

Citations:

American Committee for Protection of Foreign Born - Speaker, mass rally

Civil Rights Congress - Speaker, New York Conference, Manhattan Center

Citizens Non-Partisan Committee for the Re-Election of Benjamin J. Davis to the City Council - Supporter

New Masses - Received award from New Masses dinner Committee

People's Songs - Sponsor

Council on African Affairs - Sponsor, South African Famine Relief - Letterhead

United Electrical Radio and Machine Workers of America - Participant, Radio program, "Fighters for Liberty"

Southern Conference for Human Welfare - Fund Raiser

United Negro and Allied Veterans of America, Inc. - Affiliated - Member,

National Advisory Board - Letterhead

Outstanding woman who received praise of Elizabeth Gurley Flynn - Listed

Communist Party USA celebration in honor of Benjamin J. Davis - Announced as performer by Communist Party USA State Committee - Golden Gate Ballroom, NYC

There were some parallels between Lena Horne and Hazel Scott. In some ways, they were similar, but in many others they were quite different. Lena was born to an upper-middleclass family in the Bedford-Stuyvesant neighborhood in Brooklyn, which at that time was an integrated area of well-educated people. During her early, formative years she was not exposed to the level of racial prejudice she later endured. Her father, Teddy Horne, was a numbers kingpin who always did well financially. While she was being born in a small Jewish lay-in hospital, her dad was involved in a high-stakes poker game raising the cash to pay the hospital bill.

When Lena was three, he simply moved out, but he kept in touch by sending money and some rather lavish presents to both Lena and her mother. In later years, she and her dad became very close.

Lena was raised mostly by her maternal grandparents. Grandma was a stern but fair woman who devoted much of her time to the NAACP and the Urban League. As a result, Lena was enrolled in the NAACP at the tender age of two, making her their youngest member.

Her mom, Edna, was at loose ends for money resources after Teddy left, so, being a beautiful young lady, she tried her luck with an acting career. While on the road, she constantly warned Lena that her father was going to try to kidnap her, which had no basis in fact. As a result, she took her young daughter to a number of different locations in a wide variety of housing to keep her safe. Most of these were in the South, where Lena was suddenly exposed to the Jim Crow laws that were in effect there, as well as in many places in the North. Because she was not nearly as dark complexioned as most Black people, she really did not fit in well with any racial group. She experienced almost as much hatred from Blacks as Whites.

She was confused about her identity, a feeling she never entirely lost. During those early years, she was constantly protected from the so-called evil ways of the world. She grew up with very few friends her own age to play with. Nobody was good enough for her, according to mom and grandma.

By the time she was sixteen, she was put to work by Edna and her new husband. It was during the depression, a time when very few were doing well financially. This did not bother Lena because she was tired of school anyway.

Lena was hired as a dancer in the chorus line at the *Cotton Club,* the most segregated club in Harlem and in many ways a terrible place to work. Owney Madden, an Irish mobster, opened the club for sole purpose of having an outlet for the beer he was brewing in the heart of prohibition. Of course, Owney had enough politicians and cops in his pocket to avoid any serious problems.

The shows the *Cotton Club* presented were well-staged and well-performed by the best of the Black talent available, so the place earned an excellent name in the eyes of the elites in the surrounding area and beyond, but that included only the White elites. No Black person could ever gain entry. Conditions were so bad for the performers that they were even denied the use of the washrooms. The dressing rooms were a joke, just awful. Still, being a rather naive young lady, Lena mostly ignored the difficult conditions. The entire cast was often unfairly told they would have to do private parties without any extra compensation. On the good side, the *Cotton Club* was where Lena first met Cab Calloway and Duke Ellington, who became her lifelong friends.

Lena was called upon to sing in one of the shows, but she was ill-equipped. She felt that she was an awful dancer who just got by on her looks, and an even worse singer. She had never been instructed on how to project her voice without hurting herself, but she did as she was asked. Within three days, all she had left was a raspy sound. Her mom thought she had star quality. Lena definitely did not at that time. Once again, her beauty carried her through.

Eventually, Lena was hired by Noble Sissle to sing with his touring band, and after some training, she developed a signature sound. Her gigs at both the uptown and Greenwich Village *Café Society* clubs brought attention to her so-called Communist affiliations. Everyone who worked either of those venues earned immediate scrutiny from the red-baiters at *Counterattack* and *Red Channels*. That was because the original funding to open them came from *New Masses*, a known Communist publication.

Café Society is where Lena met Hazel Scott, and although they were never close friends, they had a great deal of respect for each other. Lena also came to know Paul Robeson. They became good friends during the ensuing years. He was eventually forced to permanently leave the country to avoid the constant persecution by the pseudo-patriots who made life so tedious for so many.

Lena was asked to testify against Robeson at a HUAC hearing, but she flatly refused. Her first contact with the committee was brought about when she was visited in her dressing room by a committee investigator named Alvin William Stokes, who happened to be Black. She asked him how a Negro could work for such an organization. When he requested that she go to Washington to tell what she knew about Paul Robeson, she said that, even though she didn't agree with his politics, he was a dear friend. She added that she would never speak to a panel headed by a southerner. As indignant as she was about it all, she thought it was too outlandish to take it seriously.

To a reporter, when asked about Robeson, she replied, "I don't know if Paul was a Communist; what's more, I don't give a damn. If he sought my company, I was happy to avail myself. He taught me the culture of my people."

The Tenney Committee in California listed her as Pro-Communist. Some of the others on their list were Paul Robeson, Frank Sinatra, Betty Garrett, Larry Parks, Fredric March, Edward G. Robinson, and John Garfield. Some of them never recovered from the implications. Suddenly, people were scrambling to avoid anyone who was not a close friend, and even some of those. Some would-be idealists turned tail and gave names to save themselves.

Let us take a closer look at some of Lena's citations in *Red Channels*. The Civil Rights Congress fought legal cases of racial injustice. The American Committee for Protection of Foreign Born defended the unjust deportation of non-American activists. The Southern Conference for Human Welfare was an inter-racial coalition that fostered democracy in the south. Incidentally, that one was a favorite of first lady Eleanor Roosevelt. The United Negro and Allied Veterans of America protected the rights of former Black servicemen. A name that comes up often in this book is Benjamin J. Davis. Yes, he was a Communist Party USA member, but he was also a fearless civil rights attorney.

I could go on, but as you can see, Lena was willing to sign onto any project that could help foster equality among the races. She never denied those affiliations, in fact, she was rather proud of them. Consequently, she was drummed out of Screen Actors Guild (SAG). When asked to write a letter to that organization to clear her name, she wrote, "I'm Black—I have these friends—I don't know anything about their politics." Nothing changed for her or her second husband, Lennie Hayton, a White man. She had cameo musical appearances in more than a dozen films made in the 1940s, but that source of income dried up. Lennie, who was a highly qualified musical arranger at MGM, did not have his contract renewed. Radio and television were even worse because they were controlled by wary sponsors. Lena and Lennie, like so many others, suffered greatly for several years.

The worst devil Lena had to combat was not *Red Channels* but an ongoing battle against racial bigotry. Here is a case in point: while working for the USO during the war, she was asked to entertain the troops at Fort Riley, Kansas. When she did her show in their large auditorium, she noticed that there were no Negroes in the large crowd. When she inquired about it, she was told that she would have to do another show the following day in the Negro mess hall. She rebelled at that idea because she was weary due to a tight schedule on a tour that was winding down, but she ultimately gave in. She would not abandon her own. Working in cramped quarters on a makeshift stage, she soon discovered yet another indignity. The front rows were filled with White men.

When she asked who they were, she was told that they were German POWs.

In another example, in 1947, when she and Lennie were looking for an apartment in Manhattan, they found that they had three strikes against them. First, she was Black; second, he was Jewish; and worst of all, they were married to each other.

Lena did have many highlights during her often troubled life. In 1957, she recorded a live album, *Lena Horne at the Waldorf-Astoria*, which peaked at #24 in the Billboard Hot 200 and became the best-selling record by a female artist in the history of the RCA Victor label up to that time.

At a much later time in the early 1980s, Lena appeared on the Broadway stage in a mostly one-woman show, *Lena Horne: the Lady and Her Music*. When the final curtain dropped, she had given 333 performances, but she was not done yet. Almost immediately, the show was taken on a 41-city tour throughout the United States and Canada. Then, after a month in London, the show concluded its long run in Stockholm.

Lena won many awards for her talent and her civil rights activism through the years. She passed away in 2010 at the age of ninety-two, leaving behind an unforgettable legacy of strength and endurance.

Chapter Twenty-Two
Leonard Bernstein

Citations:

Peoples Songs, Inc. - Sponsor - Letterhead

Scientific and Cultural Conference for World Peace - Sponsor - Official Program

American - Soviet Music Society - Affiliated

Hanns Eisler Concert - Sponsor

Protest against Deportation of Hanns Eisler - Signer

Committee for the Re-election of Benjamin J. Davis, 1945 - Affiliated

Progressive Citizens of America - Signer

World Federation of Democratic Youth - Affiliated

Voice of Freedom Committee - Affiliated

Southern Conference for Human Welfare - Affiliated

Progressive Citizens of America - Affiliated

National Negro Congress - Affiliated

Joint Anti-Fascist Refugee Committee - Affiliated

Civil Rights Congress - Affiliated

Committee for a Democratic Far Eastern Policy - Affiliated

American Council for a Democratic Greece - Affiliated

American Youth for Democracy - Affiliated

In the words of many of those in the know, Leonard Bernstein was "The finest musician America has ever produced." In the words of Joan Peyser, who wrote an excellent biography of the man and his work, "He was not only everything as it pertained to music, he was everything to everything." There was virtually nothing that failed to catch his interest. Leonard was like that for most of his life.

Born in Lawrence, Massachusetts, just a few short miles north of Boston, to Ukrainian-Jewish parents, his birth name was Louis due to the insistence of his grandmother, but oddly, even his parents always called him Leonard. That name later became official when he was in his middle teens. Leonard often claimed that he had been a sickly child, terrified by Anti-Semitic gangs that abounded in his neighborhood. He said that all changed when he was ten. That was when his aunt Clara, in the process of getting a divorce, had her old upright piano delivered to the Bernstein residence. It was an event that changed his life forever. He immediately took to the instrument. He regained his strength. He began to dream of being a renowned concert pianist and, in time, he became exactly that. His father was always opposed to Leonard's ambitions toward a musical career. He felt that his son would end up playing in fern-bars with an uninterested audience of drunks.

Because we usually think of him as a conductor and composer, we sometimes forget that he was also a world-class performer on the piano. It was not until his college days that he was convinced to pursue the worlds of composition and conducting.

After Leonard's early education at the Garrison School and the Boston Latin School, he attended Harvard, where he studied under Walter Piston. That was followed by his years at the Curtis Institute of Music in Philadelphia. There, he earned the only "A" grade ever issued by Fritz Reiner, who was on staff at that time. It was also where he switched his major to conducting.

During his Harvard years, in 1939, Leonard took it upon himself to produce Marc Blitzstein's *The Cradle Will Rock* in the same manner that it had been done by John Houseman and Orson Welles at the Venice Theatre in New York after a last minute change of venue. In a way, the circumstances were similar. Leonard had planned to do it in a theatre in Cambridge, but the city fathers would not permit that to happen. They said it was obscene and Un-American. Leonard moved the production to the Harvard campus, where he sat at the piano on stage while the rest of the cast were scattered throughout the house. The problems with the show, as some saw it, were that it took a dim view of labor/management relations, and that one of the leading characters was a prostitute. As it turned out, Leonard heard about it, so he was in attendance for the second performance. He was thunder-struck that this young college student could do such a fine job with his work. It was the beginning of a long, warm friendship between the two of them that lasted right up to when Marc was murdered on Martinique. It was also when the FBI opened a dossier on Leonard; yes, it was as early as 1939 that he came under their scrutiny, something that would never truly end during his life.

Many things had occurred during the years leading up to June 1950, the tragic date of the publication of *Red Channels,* After struggling mightily with his career for so long, things were finally beginning to come together for Leonard. With the backing of some close friends who could see his potential, he was gradually moving up the ladder to success. Those friends included Aaron Copeland, Dimitri Mitropoulos, Serge Koussevitzky, and the music director and principal conductor of the New York Philharmonic, Arthur Rodzinski. Rodzinski had been the music director of the New York City Philharmonic Orchestra since 1945.

Leonard had also made guest appearances at the New York Philharmonic, where he had been employed as an assistant conductor since 1943. One of his disappointments came in 1949, when he was rejected for the post of music director and principal conductor of the Boston Symphony to replace Koussevitzky, who would be retiring and who had recommended Leonard. Many reasons were given for that decision, not the least of which was his age. They also brought up his attitude, which could sometimes be trying. During that time, Leonard had guest-conducted with orchestras around the world.

Suddenly, when *Red Channels* published, the doors slammed shut. CBS, which had aired New York Philharmonic concerts for years, would no longer carry any of Leonard's work. There was a large connection between CBS and the orchestra. Several of the network's top brass served on the Columbia Artist's Management Board, including Bill Paley, the head-honcho at CBS.

The state department eliminated him from all of its functions, and in 1953, they denied him a passport, which effectively cut off his foreign appearances for several months. As was the case for so many others, their reasoning was based on gross innuendo.

The FBI then intensified their investigations. In one of their reports, an anonymous source, thought by many to be Hollywood producer Boris Morros, was quoted as saying, "How could a well-to-do Jewish left-winger be allowed to conduct the Israel Philharmonic?" In another statement, this one definitely from Morros, he said, "I could not hire a red." This is significant because Leonard had been working on movie scores and was looking forward to more. He had composed the film score for *On the Town*, the film version of his own show that had previously been produced on Broadway.

Leonard became enraged by what he called "A farce of informers in Washington." He considered it all ghastly and humiliating.

From the season of 1951-1952 until the season of 1955-1956, he was mostly unemployable.

In 1951, he was placed on an index based on the McCarran Act naming his as a person who should be incarcerated in the event of a national emergency. The list contained three possible categories; Communist, Social Worker, and Independent Socialist League. In Leonard's case, they chose Communist, once more with no facts to back up their accusations.

During the same year, having seen the writing on the wall and seeing that he was not on the list of associate conductors of the New York Philharmonic, he decided to take a sabbatical and relocate to Cuernavaca near Mexico City to work on his first opera, *Trouble in Tahiti*. Cuernavaca was also where several of the "Hollywood Ten" had taken refuge to try to continue their work using fronts and aliases. It was a trying time for all concerned.

After his passport had been revoked in 1953, Leonard took the bull by the horns. He wrote and signed an affidavit attempting to clarify his situation. He said, and I will paraphrase, that "He was not a Communist and had never followed the Communist line. If he had associated or supported certain organizations held suspect, he had done so casually, ignorant of their deeper purposes. He swore that he had never gone to any meetings of their organizations and did not know the names of their officials. He said that his association with Anti-Franco political forces had been, at best, nominal. His work for the Joint Anti-Fascist Refugee Committee had amounted to attending a dinner, and his association with Paul Robeson had amounted to a meeting when both were backstage during a concert. He swore that his participation at the Waldorf Conference in April of 1949, with among others, Aaron Copeland and Dmitri Shostakovich had nothing to do with the propaganda efforts promoted by the conference leadership. That he learned of his supposed failures from the April 4, 1949 *Life* magazine article and that he had purged and reformed himself. He declared allegiance to a politically orthodox religion, Judaism. Said he was active in Jewish philanthropy and the promotion of Israel as an independent state free from Soviet domination. As a Jew, he was necessarily opposed to Communism. He was chagrinned to learn that he might have been a source of embarrassment to the government of the United States. He strongly re-affirmed his loyalty."[1]

He was mortified to have had to do that, but it proved to be enough to get his travel privileges restored. However, it did not completely remove the stigma hanging over him.

By 1957, the tables turned upward for Leonard. He was named principal conductor of the New York Philharmonic, and, in 1958, he was made the music director for the orchestra, a post he would hold until his retirement in 1990.

As late as the 1970s, he was listed on Richard Nixon's "Enemies List" due to his stance on what was going on in Viet Nam. Had it not been for Hoover's death in 1972 and Nixon's sudden departure in 1974, he would have been subjected to constant harassment by the IRS, which would have made life very difficult for him.

One of the most memorable events in Leonard's long and illustrious career happened on Christmas Day 1989, just a few short months before he passed away. The place was the *Schauspielhaus* in what had previously been East Berlin until the wall finally fell. The event was the Berlin Celebration concert commemorating the re-unification of Germany after so many years of strife. The music he chose was one of the most beautiful works ever composed, *Beethoven's Ninth Symphony*. In the final choral movement, he took the liberty to change the words of Friedrich Schiller's poem, "Ode to Joy" to "Ode to Freedom." It was performed by a contingent of musicians and singers from both sides of the iron curtain, and in fact, from around the world. The concert was heard on that day by no less than 100 million listeners globally. As he always did, Leonard left all of himself behind on the podium when it was over. For him conducting was always an athletic and emotional, as well as artistic endeavor. He often lost ten to fifteen pounds during a concert.

He was not only active in the world of art music, he was also deeply involved with the Broadway stage and movies. Who can forget his marvelous score for *West Side Story*, along with other stage and film opuses? We should also not forget his *Children's Concerts* on CBS, wherein he taught kids how to listen to and enjoy the classics.

Leonard Bernstein was a man who never let music get in the way of his politics, or his politics get in the way of his music. Repeating what Joan Peyser wrote, "He was everything to everything."

Chapter Twenty-Three
William N. Robson

Citations:

Artists Front to Win the War - Sponsor

Hollywood Writers Mobilization - Speaker - Forum—Counter - Attack Against the Plot to Control America's Thinking - El Patio Theatre, Hollywood

National Council of the Arts, Sciences and Professions - Signer - Advertisement - "We are for Wallace"

Hollywood Quarterly - Associate

William N. Robson was a man who dared to take chances by writing and producing radio themes that few others would touch. A genius at getting his thoughts across is what he was, Bill made a very succinct statement to me when I spoke with him in the 1980s: "I was born in Pittsburgh, Pennsylvania in 1906. Radio was born in Pittsburgh, Pennsylvania in 1920. We were married in Los Angeles in 1933, and it was a happy relationship until radio died of terminal illness—television."[1]

Of course, Bill was making reference to the initial broadcast by KDKA reporting the presidential election results of the race between Warren G. Harding and James Cox. At that time, his father was an exploitation man or press agent for Paramount Pictures in the Pittsburgh area. He had heard that KDKA would be broadcasting the election returns so he took a receiver with him to the Olympic theatre. Every few minutes the movie was stopped so he could come out to tell what he had heard. It was very effective. It was estimated that more people heard the news by this indirect means than by any other method throughout the entire western Pennsylvania area, there being very few radio receivers at that time.

Not long after that, in 1922, young Bill was involved in his first actual broadcast on WCAE, also in Pittsburgh. This was also the work of Bill's father. As a member of his high school marching band, Bill was sent to Dayton, Ohio, to perform at a very important football game. As previously arranged, he sent telegrams to his dad as the game progressed to report what was happening, almost play-by-play. When the contest was over and his team had won, the band and the team rode the train back home in an elated mood. Upon de-training, they were escorted to the primitive studio of WCAE, where they performed a celebratory concert, Bill's radio premiere, so to speak.

In 1928, he graduated from Yale University and was hired by Paramount in California as a scriptwriter. In 1935, he was writing and producing a radio series called *Calling all Cars*, the first police-orientated show ever. It reached only California and some Arizona audiences, but when Bill Lewis got the job of Program Director at CBS in New York, he made a trip to the west coast looking for outlets there. When he met Bill, Mr. Lewis said, "If you're ever back east look me up."

That was all the incentive Bill needed. He had wanted to get back East for a long time, so he packed up his typewriter and made the trip with no real promise of a job there. Bill Lewis hired him on the spot and sent him to Chicago to clean up some problems with a show that was in the works there. Following the successful completion of that assignment, Bill returned to New York and became a fixture there for many years. That is not to say that he never worked again on the west coast, but the bulk of his endeavors took place in New York City.

He soon became one of the producers of *Columbia Workshop*. One of the many shows he was at least partially responsible for was the landmark production of Archibald MacLeish's *The Fall of the City*.

Bill was not immune to damage to his career by *Red Channels*. Although his list of citations was short, the end result was very much the same as it was for so many others.

Here is how Bill explained it to me:

"The problem started with the Hollywood Ten. The prescription was that if there were all these reds in Hollywood there had to be some in radio. A man up in Syracuse, New York, who owned a chain of supermarkets, Laurence Johnson, started the ball rolling by investigating these people and their shows. Cigarette companies, for instance—if they didn't get so-and-so off their show—he wouldn't carry their cigarettes as a boycott at the retail outlets. He started all of this. The advertising agencies went chicken, the networks went chicken, and heads rolled. If your name came up, you were not renewed. In my case, I was out to try Hollywood at the time, and the boss, Harry Ackerman called me one day. He wanted me to go to New York to do a new television show. So, I went, and Harry said to me, just in conversation, 'All right, you just be careful, you're such a dirty Communist.' I said, 'What the hell do you mean?' So, he unlocked his drawer and pulled out this booklet from his desk. It was *Red Channels,* and he showed me the citations. 'I never saw anything so ridiculous in my life,' I said. He said, 'I think so, too.' It had such things as I was a sponsor of Artists to Win the War, and I said, 'You know, among the sponsors on that particular list—at that particular rally—were Mrs. Roosevelt, Bing Crosby, and all kinds of celebrities.' But, of course, that citation in *Red Channels* came from the *Daily Worker.* That increased the Communist connection because they quoted it from the *Daily Worker.* Well, that was nonsense. I gave it no further thought. I set about putting together this one-hour, every-other-week mystery show. About three weeks in, I'm taken off it and no explanation was given. With the atmosphere at the time, I realized what was going on and that this had been what it was.

"I called Bill Paley's office and was told he was out of town. Then I called Frank Stanton. Stanton said, 'Can you get down here at one o'clock and have lunch with me?' I said, 'I'll be there before.' I went down to his office, told him what had happened and he said, 'The theory is you're a Communist.' I said, 'Of course

I'm not a Communist!' He replied, 'But you're in *Red Channels—* and you're not a Communist?' I said, 'No, I'm not. I'll give you any statement you require to that effect.' I added, 'You'll be losing a lot of money without me.' He told me not to worry about it, but that was the last I ever heard from him.

"I sat In New York for whatever it was in my contract. They paid me $600/week, but I was never reassigned to anything. Finally, when the contract ran out, I went back to the coast and found out that I was not acceptable. I said to myself, *All right, then I'll write under a pseudonym.* I used my two son's first names, Christopher and Anthony. That lasted three weeks until they figured it out.

"I was out of work for three years."[2]

He could hardly believe what had happened to him due to the biased opinions of a few red-baiters. Could it be true that the liberal management at CBS considered him a threat?

Bill had done some programming for them that could never be forgotten. One huge case in point was *Open Letter on Race Hatred* ,a docudrama about the race riots in Detroit. Helping him put it together was Walter White, then secretary of the NAACP and an old friend. Walter was the man who had presented the idea to CBS, but he said he would only want to do it if Bill Robson was the producer.

They ran into all sorts of difficulties before the program reached the airwaves. Care had to be taken to tell a bit of each side of the story so as not to seriously offend anyone. The rewrites were many, right up to the very last minute before the broadcast. It was a sustaining program, meaning no commercial sponsorship, so at least they did not have that to worry about.

The day before it was run, Bill Paley, the president of CBS, sent copies to many of his affiliates to test the waters. The result was predictable. One man, the manager of WBT in Charlotte, North Carolina, said, "You can count us out. We know how to handle our Blacks down here" ("Blacks" was not the word he used.) *Open Letter on Race Hatred* was never heard in most of the South, including the entire Texas network of five or six stations, which shows what kind of civil rights work the man was capable of doing.

No Help Wanted, another docudrama he did under the auspices of the BBC in London, was a program that was later called the finest dramatic program ever produced in the United States. The source for that statement was *The London Times*. Bill was later rewarded with one of his seven Peabody Awards for *No Help Wanted.* Done before the *Red Channels* scandal, *No Help Wanted* had originally been backed jointly by the BBC and the WPA. The cast, the technicians, and the musicians were all WPA employees. CBS would not directly take credit for it, even though it was to run on their stations. They did not want to handle anything that dealt with the New Deal. When push came to shove, the WPA wanted to cancel out, as well. The program was about the panic caused by the depression. They said they did not want Hitler to know about our financial dilemma. The WPA called Bill just a couple of hours before the planned performance, too late to get their wish. Bill told them he would have to contact Felix Greene, the local BBC representative, to have it aborted. He proceeded to tell Felix to get lost for a few hours until the broadcast was history. Bill would not allow the people at the WPA to reach him. Every time they called, he told them that he could not locate Felix. In the end, the program ran as originally scheduled. The reviews were terrific. It turned out to be just one more proof of Bill's intestinal fortitude.

Through the years, he was responsible for many cutting-edge programs and was never afraid to tackle any subject that came his way. Was that subversive? I would challenge anyone who dared to say so.

Chapter Twenty-Four
Norman Corwin

Citations:

Russian War Relief, Inc. - Signed statement - "These eminent Americans ask your help on behalf of the Russian People."

American friends of the Chinese People - "Stars for China Today" - Variety show - Town Hall - New York City

National Council of American - Soviet Friendship - Speaker - Madison Square Garden rally to honor three Soviet writers

American Russian Institute - Sponsor at dinner for American - Soviet post war relations - Commodore Hotel

American Youth for Democracy - Toastmaster - San Francisco

Committee for a Democratic Far Eastern Policy - On official letterhead

Civil Rights Congress - Initiating sponsor - Detroit

Committee for the First Amendment - (Religion - Speech - Assembly) - Signer protesting the House Un-American Activities Committee

Independent Citizens Committee of the Arts, Sciences and Professions - Executive council - Hollywood division

Progressive Citizens of America - Vice-Chairman

Scientific and Cultural Conference for World Peace - Sponsor - Speaker

Norman Corwin's upbringing was in a very tight-knit Boston family. They were anything but rich. Their home was a third floor tenement overlooking a railroad yard and round-house. From the very beginning, Norman, and his brothers Emil and Al, always looked after each other's interests. Emil was responsible early on for helping Norman to get hired by the *Springfield Republican*, a well-respected newspaper in Massachusetts, when Emil left that newspaper to go to Cleveland to become an editor for the Newspaper Enterprise Association. At that time, Norman had been working at the *Greenfield Register* near Boston, as a utility reporter covering all sorts of stories. When Emil talked the *Springfield Republican* into considering Norman as his replacement, Norman moved on to Springfield. Before he left the *Greenfield Register*, he told them that Al would fit in nicely in their operation.

A little later, Emil ran into some serious health problems and his doctors advised him to get away from the Ohio winters. He found a good position writing publicity for NBC in New York. Through some of the connections, he had made he found out about a similar job at 20th Century Fox, so he wangled an interview for Norman with Leonard Gaynor. It was the beginning of many years in New York for Norm. Before long, he joined CBS as a writer, producer, and director of quality programming. Norman knew how to help others and also how he had been helped himself.

Norman's father's father was Russian and his mother was Hungarian, which explains some of his feelings toward the situation some Middle-Europeans and other less fortunate fellow men and women found themselves in during and after World War II. As a life-long humanitarian, he could not ignore what was going on there and in the Far East.

As it turned out, he was one of the first people to be harassed by *Counterattack* and *Red Channels*, their second of the many victims to follow.

If you look over the names of the various organizations he was alleged to be in cahoots with, you will see that, while each may or may not have had connections with the Communist Party USA, they were mostly created in the interest of the downtrodden members of our worldwide society. Many of those relationships occurred during or shortly after the war, a time when most thinking people had grave concerns about what was going on. Norman was first, last, and always one of those deep thinkers who cared greatly for the plight of the common man, not only overseas, but here at home as well.

His monumental writings prove that to perfection. One of his landmark programs, *Document A/777*, which he wrote and produced under the auspices of the United Nations, showed exactly how he felt about the state of the world in 1948. It was based on a UN document titled, *Declaration of Human Rights*. His dialogue covered many of the dilemmas of that time. In truth, many of those same problems still exist to this day.

Is that Communist thinking? I think not!

While doing another opus called *One World Flight*, he had occasion to visit Russia, and he came away with one solid conclusion: they were neither the best nor the worst.

His main commitment, during and after the war, was to the fight against Pro-Fascists on our own shores. In a statement he made in a speech in 1942 at the Conference on Educational Radio, he gave them no quarter. He said, "They are equivalent to six battleships or a couple of Panzer divisions."

During the early part of the war, Norman wrote a program praising the Muscovites for their bravery and grit, and about a year later, he directed a show written by Norman Rosten called *Consider the Red Army*. Automatically, in some distorted minds, this made him a subversive despite the fact that we were all on the same side at the time.

In the late 1940s, the benevolent folks at *Counterattack* dubbed Corwin with the derogatory title, "Fellow Traveler."

Vincent Harnett of Aware, Inc. had other names for him. First he went after CBS by writing that they were thoroughly colonized by the Red Party. He followed that up by calling Norman "The Commissar of Radio" and "The Linchpin of the Communist Conspiracy." What a bad joke that was! No one was more loyal to the letter of the law written in the Constitution and the Bill of Rights.

At one point, Norman was called to testify before the HUAC, but after fifteen minutes the session was adjourned and he was never asked to come back.

He clearly stated to those congressmen that "Those accused are mainly decent Americans who have contributed much that is worthwhile to the culture, edification or just plain entertainment of their fellow Americans."

He became a strong worker against the blacklist and the HUAC and did all he could to defuse their efforts. He refused to clear himself because he was guilty of nothing. In a paper he wrote on the subject, he said, "I have been explicit as to what I mean by liberalism, and the United States Government has been lately most explicit as to what is meant by Communism. There can be no questions that, in official circles of the government, Communists and their fellow travelers were commonly understood to advocate and represent certain definite things."[1]

He added, "In my case, it is not a matter of being in a position to sneak a sentence into a speech. If I were a Communist or a fellow traveler, I had one of the best platforms in the world. I had the ear of millions of Americans—63 million in one night on one occasion. I had no interference in the form of censorship and none of the usual checks of supervision. I could say what I wanted and in a dozen or so years that I enjoyed that opportunity, years in which I did hundreds of programs. I would defy anyone to find anything advocating a foreign system of any kind superior to ours. I defy anyone to show that in whatever allusions I ever made to the forms and ideals of our government, as apart from the occasional abuses of those ideals, I had done anything but strengthen our respect and deepen our appreciation for the United States, its laws, its people, its Constitution."[2]

To sum up Norman's case, I must refer to several of the many conversations with him that I had the privilege to enjoy over a period of over twenty-five years. He talked freely about the situation he suddenly found himself in during the 1950s. He spoke of the fact that, while he was not affected as severely as many others, it certainly was not as easy to gain employment for a few years. He was never directly refused to use his talents, but sometimes the extended negotiations were unexplained and intolerable.

In a letter he wrote to one of his employers about why he was in *Red Channels*, he said, "My first reaction on learning that I was listed in the volume was one of anger. I resented both the action taken and the method of taking it—this not alone because I, personally, was affected. My resentment was against the whole idea of any private non-governmental and non-official organization appropriating into itself the dual role of prosecutor and judge to conduct a kind of trial-without-jury in which no evidence for the defense is asked for or allowed to be presented."[3]

There is the whole concept of accusation without representation, which is contrary to the laws of this land as set forth by our founding fathers. As stated earlier, *Red Channels* never, in any case, presented its readers with both sides of the story. They only wrote what they thought would prove their own very dubious claims. They did much more damage than good with their heavy-handed attempt at what they thought to be good citizenship.

Norman Corwin was a true patriot—never a subversive—and I am ready to argue that point with anyone who says otherwise. Better still, let's let his writing make that argument. Norman was always a strong advocate for world peace, but also a realist. In this excerpt from his wonderful, but not too well-known book, *Overkill and Megalove*, he wrote how he felt on the subject:

"How to endure on the earth?
Well, when the tilt of the globe awakens us each spring,
We extol living. We put out blossoms and scatter riches and
    are no poorer for it.
Out of the cloud comes our chemistry.
In the lash of the storm we grip harder.

"Here, beyond the squall of your freeways,
Unhurried roots pry in the clay and sunder rock.
Constellations of fruits are planned in secret chambers.
Leaf and needle negotiate with the near star for growth and
    green.
Time is easy.

"We're sorry for you, but wish you well.
It should only be that tribes of trees descend with your children,
To a day when the shade of the oak spreads wider than the shadow of war."[4]

To put this in context, I should explain that this was Norman's way of speaking in the voice of the trees, but it clearly shows his worry about a time when people were building bomb shelters in their back yards due to grave world unrest. It clearly shows a man who was concerned for the well-being of all of us and the planet we live on. He was talking survival, not subversion. If you do not understand this, I can only say, you should.

Chapter Twenty-Five
Arthur Miller

Citations:

- American Youth Congress - Signer of call
- Book Find Club - Writer
- Civil Rights Congress - Signer - Statement in defense of (Hans) Eisler—Signer -
- Statement in defense of Communist Party USA—Speaker - "Abolish America's Thought Police"
- Committee of Welcome for the Very Reverend Hewlett Johnson - Member
- International Workers Order - Defender of tax exemption
- *Jewish Life* - Contributor
- *Mainstream & New Masses* - Speaker - Rally to defend Howard Fast
- National Council of Arts, Sciences and Professions - Signer for Wallace—Member - Initiating Committee - Writers for Wallace—Co-Chairman -
- Performance—"The Journey of Simon McKeever" and "I've Got the Tune"
- New York Council of Arts, Sciences, and Professions—Speaker - Rally against "Foley Square" convictions.
- Progressive Citizens of America - Sponsor
- National Committee to Defeat the Mundt—(Ferguson) Bill - Sponsor—Pamphlet "Hey Brother"

Statement denouncing the Hartley Committee - Signer

Voice of Freedom Committee - Member - Dinner Committee

Scientific and Cultural Conference for World Peace - Sponsor - Waldorf Astoria

World Congress for Peace - American Sponsor

Amicus Curiae Brief - Signer - Petition to Supreme Court to review convictions of Dalton Trumbo and John Howard Lawson

American - Russian Institute - Attended dinner

National Council of American - Soviet Friendship - Speaker - Testimonial dinner for Reverend William Howard Melish

Playwright extraordinaire Arthur Miller was one of the most literate of all of those who crossed swords with the various HUAC panels. His responses were well-thought out and sometimes lengthy. Born in Harlem, New York City, he was one of the three children of Polish-Jewish immigrant parents. His higher education was received at the University of Michigan, where he majored in Journalism and then switched to English. He graduated with a degree in English.

Shortly after leaving school, he joined the staff of the *Federal Theatre*, a New Deal organization that provided some income to unemployed actors, writers, and technicians of all sorts. Arthur remained until it was disbanded in 1939, broken up because some members of the US Congress alleged that they had been operating under Communist influence.

While he was at the University of Michigan, Arthur worked as reporter and night editor for the student newspaper, *The Daily Michigan*. At that time, he also wrote his first play, *No Villain*, for which he earned the Avery Hopwood Award. The seed was planted in his psyche. He decided to go that route during his life, and what a great decision that proved to be.

Unfortunately, some of his later work created problems for him. One of those problems was a play called *The Crucible*, a story about the Salem witch-hunt back in seventeenth century Massachusetts, a subject he had been pondering ever since he took a course in American History during his college days. He did not write the play until a later date.

When Arthur was called on to testify in 1956, *The Crucible* got the Committee's immediate attention. He was asked if it was written to defy the panel, because of the parallels to the present that it presented. Arthur told them he could see where they were headed, but that their thoughts bore no relationship to reality. He explained how it all began at the U of M:

> "I never did anything about it because it was too absurd. Nobody could be made to believe that the people in a small village in seventeenth century Massachusetts would start killing each other over whether someone was a witch or not. But there were trials taking place in the United States in 1949-1950 where I heard the actual lines being spoken by American prosecutors which I vaguely remembered from reading about the witchcraft in 1692. At first, it was simply unbelievable, but I went back into history and there it was. It was mind-boggling that the same material could have arisen some 300 years later."[1]

He went on to say that what was occurring in 1950 was a similar moral inversion. Arthur said there was a deepening hysteria that was virtually defining the quality of culture. At that time, the accused was innocent, assumed guilty, and stripped of judicial power; the process perverted. To survive, you had to accept paranoid vision.

In the Beginning was the Word was another play brought up by the panel as being subversive. Arthur offered this description of the plot:

> "It is a story that might happen to an ordinary American should he wake up one morning to discover that the Bill of Rights has been abolished. An agent of the IRS tells the protagonist that citizens who mind their own business have nothing to fear. Those who argue are in trouble. Only one newspaper is allowed. Teachers cannot mention the Bill of Rights."[2]

Does this make you think of Orwell's *1984*?

A third play the committee objected to was *Death of a Salesman*, saying that it struck a blow against the values that have given our way of life and its passion and validity. There were other stage efforts that were met with the committee's disdain, but Arthur's plays were not the crux of their questioning, as you will see.

On June 21, 1956, a formal hearing was held in the caucus room of the Old House Office Building. Arthur was their victim that day. He showed up with his wife, Marilyn Monroe, which did not please the panel because she was thought to be above what was going on.

Arthur opened the proceedings with this statement, showing them he was not about to let himself be cornered and that there would be no compromising of his beliefs:

"I have never broken any law. No one accuses me of espionage, aiding a foreign power, or acting in any way inimical to the interests of the United States. No one accuses me of breaking any law or intending or conspiring to do so.

Why, then, am I subpoenaed by a committee of the congress to testify upon political matters? What legislation could conceivably be written as a result of a playwright's retailing his political and ethical views under order of a government body? Obviously, none!

The reason I have been called before this committee is, I believe, that my private opinions are anathema to those self-appointed vigilante groups such as the Catholic War Veterans, American Legion, and the publication, Counterattack. For myself, I not only admit that these people stand for things I abhor, but I declare this fact most proudly and emphatically."[3]

Throughout the day, he was asked about the citations in *Red Channels* one by one. To each, he gave a succinct and forthright reply, never denying any charge, but never finding guilt in them. Then they showed their true intentions. They wanted names. It had been agreed by all parties at a pre-hearing meeting that that sort of question would not be asked. As happened so often over the span of the hearings, the Committee reneged on their promise.

Chairman Richard Arens got this somewhat heated response from Arthur Miller:

"Mr. Chairman, I understand the philosophy behind this question and I want you to understand mine. When I say this I want you to understand that I am not protecting the Communists or the Communist Party. I am trying to, and I will, protect my sense of myself. I could not use the name of another person and bring trouble on him. These were poets, writers as far as I could see, and the life of a writer, despite what it sometimes seems, is pretty tough. I wouldn't make it any tougher for anybody. I ask you not to ask that question. I take responsibility for everything I have done, but I cannot take responsibility for any other human being. I will tell you anything about myself, which I have done, but I cannot take responsibility for another human being."[4]

Then, it was Bernard Kearney's turn. "Do you consider yourself more or less a dupe in joining these Communist organizations?"

Miller replied, "I wouldn't say so, because I am an adult. I was looking for a world that would be perfect. I think it was necessary that I do that if I were to develop as a writer. I am not ashamed of this. I accept my life. This is what I have done. I have learned a great deal."[5]

Referring once more to the fact that Arthur would not name any others, Donald Jackson said that that was not good enough, and that moral scruples did not constitute a legal reason for not answering the questions.

At the conclusion of a very long and tedious day, Arthur said, with unhidden bile, "I think it would be a disaster and a calamity if the Communist Party took over this country. That is my opinion that has come to me, not out of the blue sky, but out of long thought. We are living in a time of great uncertainty in this country. It is not a Communist idea. You just pick up a book-review section and you will see everybody selling books based on peace of mind, because there isn't any. I am trying to delve to the bottom of this and come up with a positive answer, and I have had to go to hell to meet the Devil. I believe in democracy. I believe it is the only way for myself and anybody I care about. It is the only way to live, but my criticism, such as it has been, is not to be confused with hatred. I love this country, I think as much as any man and it is because I see things that traduce certainly the values that have been in this country; that I speak. I would like more than anything else in the world to make positive my plays and I intend to do so before I finish. It has to be on the basis of reality."[6]

The hearing was over, but his troubles were not. Because he refused to name names, he was cited for Contempt of Congress on February 18, 1957, a conviction that was overturned by an appeals court in September of 1958. The HUAC had gone beyond their bounds when they so much as asked the question of other identities. To his credit, at no time during the ordeal did Arthur invoke his First or Fifth Amendment protections.

When the trials were over, he put out along and detailed press release:

"It should be easy for me to name the writers with whom I met some ten years ago. I am opposed to Communism and what ideology I profess is thoroughly democratic. Furthermore, I am and have been for some years now, on a blacklist that forbids the purchase of any of my works by motion picture or television companies in the United States. To get off this blacklist would mean a great increase in my income, and I can get off in the time it takes to say a half dozen names I remember or people I knew to be Communists. By uttering a certain number of syllables I would become what is called a 'Good American' and I should then be permitted to earn my living as an American writer ordinarily does.

"I am not going to say those syllables. It would be well, I think, for the American people to understand why.

I did nothing illegal in associating at one time with Communists. The government, in fact, does not even contend that it was illegal. It is merely using my refusal to lower myself in order to punish me and to destroy whatever influence my work exerts.

It is perfectly clear to me that the government knows the names it is demanding of me and this from its own informants.

The names of these people have no conceivable connection with national security, and I have had no connection with them for many years.

I do not believe that a person, under fierce pressure from government, who professes patriotism, is necessarily a patriot in his heart, and I refuse to join those who have degraded patriotism by mouthing its praises on pain of being relegated to the twilight zone of their profession.

I will not accede to the demands of the House Committee on Un-American Activities because in my case I believe those demands degrade the government of the United States.

The committee's chief counsel, Mr. Arens, recently held forth in New Haven, Connecticut. He took occasion severely to criticize a Rabbi for officiating at my wedding last summer, and at the same time called me a dangerous Communist.

The hope was expressed during my hearing in Washington that I would write more positively about America in the future. I am sorry to say that I did not respond at the moment as I would have after reflection, and as I do now. It is not the business of government or any of its officials what I write, how I write it, whether it is positive, negative or anything else.

A few days after my hearing in Washington, one of the members of the committee was quoted in the press as saying, in effect, that my indictment for contempt would be handed down just about the time I would divorce the woman I had just announced I would shortly marry. I do not detect in such a statement any sign of moral authority to which I might defer my own judgment of right or wrong, patriotism or treason, or even ordinary decency.

I do not deny the right of government to protect itself against a group dominated by a slavish subservience to Soviet Russia or any other foreign government. I affirm that right and that necessity. It happens that I am not a part of that or any other conspiracy, movement or ideology devoted to the advancement of Soviet ideas. But it does not follow that in the name of anti-Communism a writer can be rightfully hounded, or that the government has the right to defame him and bring him to his knees. If I cannot stand up outside I will stand up in jail, if need be.

I take this position not to defy the government, but to correct its errors. I do this because I love this country and will not be a part of what I conscientiously believe is a travesty upon its good name, and I ask of all reporters and editors who print these words or resumes of them, to print them with this statement; the prosecution of me and the campaign to destroy me does not represent the American spirit, but only a deformation of that spirit. I ask the people of the world not to conclude from my troubles that freedom is dying here."[7]

Here is an intriguing aside to all this. In 1955, J. Edgar Hoover stated that there were approximately 22,600 members of the Communist Party USA, whereas, in 1944, there had been about 80,000, and one third of those were FBI agents. As we now know, a good many of those 22,600 had absolutely nothing to do with any subversion or disloyalty.

Chapter Twenty-Six
Dorothy Parker

Citations:
- Joint Anti-Fascist Refugee Committee - Speaker - Rally for Spanish Refugee Appeal at Manhattan Center - Sponsor
- Scientific and Cultural Conference for World Peace - Sponsor - Official Program
- Amicus Curiae Brief - Signer - Petition to Supreme Court to review the conviction of Lawson and Trumbo
- American Continental Congress for Peace - United States Sponsor—Congress held in Mexico City
- Voice of Freedom Committee - Chairman
- American Relief Ships for Spain - Sponsor
- Artist's Front to Win the War - Sponsor
- Citizen's Committee for Harry Bridges - Sponsor
- Coordinating Committee to Lift the Embargo - Affiliated
- Equality - Member - Editorial Council of magazine
- Abraham Lincoln Brigade, Fund Drive for Disabled Vets - Sponsor
- Hollywood Anti-Nazi League - Sponsor
- New York Tom Mooney Committee - Sponsor

Medical Bureau and Committee to Aid Spanish Democracy - Sponsor

Civil Rights Congress - Affiliated

International Workers Order - Affiliated

Progressive Citizens of America - Affiliated

Stage for Action - Affiliated

Statement of American Progressives on the Moscow Trials - Signer

**"Men seldom make passes
At girls who wear glasses"**

Those few words may be the most quoted from the pen of Dorothy Parker, but they are not in any way an indication of her huge contribution to the world of poetry and her other writing skills. She was always thought to be a wit, sometimes caustic, but never mean. On the other hand, as humorous as she could be, her life was anything but.

Dorothy was born in 1893 to resentful parents. They considered her a late baby, a mistake and a burden. She was never allowed to forget that fact. Her mother died when Dorothy was not yet five years old, leaving almost no memories of her.

Not long after that, her father decided to remarry in 1900. Things went from bad to worse for young Dorothy. Her father was a man who gratuitously used physical abuse to keep her in line whenever the urge struck him. Never quite able to adjust to her new stepmother, Dorothy could never bring herself to call the woman "mom" or even "stepmom." Instead, she always referred to her as "The Housekeeper."

When it came time to attend school, the choice her elders made was a curious one. Her father was a Jew and "The Housekeeper" was a Protestant. Together, they selected for Dorothy a Roman Catholic grade school at the Convent of the Blessed Sacrament, an odd choice to say the least. Dorothy was a good student, but she found it difficult to accept some of what she was being taught. For example, she always questioned the concept of the Immaculate Conception. To her it was "Spontaneous Combustion." Of course, that wording did not bode well with the nuns, but it showed that, even at a tender age, she could construct her own way of thinking. Years later, she often said the nuns fired her.

Things got better in high school. She attended Miss Dana's Finishing School in Morristown, New Jersey—a girls boarding school with very progressive attitudes. She liked that much better and did very well academically.

After graduation, she refused to return to her father's home in New York City simply because she could not face that situation again. Soon, in 1913, her father died, leaving her destitute. Dorothy took up residence in a Manhattan boarding house and supported herself by playing piano for a dancing school. This was unheard of and most unacceptable for a young lady in that era. As was the case for all of Miss Dana's graduates, Dorothy was expected to go home and wait for "Mr. Right" to come along. To her, this was a ridiculous concept because she really did not have a home any more, and more importantly, she wanted to create her own destiny.

During this period, *Vanity Fair* began to purchase and publish her poetry. Not long thereafter, Frank Crowninshield, the editor of both *Vanity Fair* and *Vogue,* hired her as a staff writer.

Dorothy wrote for *Vanity Fair, Vogue, McCall's, The New Yorker, Life,* and *The New Republic* over the years. She wrote many well-received short stories and also some screenplays during a lucrative fifteen years in Hollywood. As a dyed-in-the-wool New Yorker, she hated Hollywood, but admitted that that was where the money was.

Before her stint on the west coast, she was a founding member of a very special intellectual forum in New York. She, along with Robert Benchley and Robert Sherwood, began meeting almost daily for lunch at the Algonquin Hotel to discuss everything and anything in depth. They called themselves "The Algonquin Round Table," and during its unique existence, their small group grew to include many of the deep thinkers of their day. You must keep in mind that this was the 1920s, a time of the "Flapper" and inane behavior prior to the stock market crash in 1929.

Dorothy's problems with the blacklist and her involvement with the Communist Front organizations began when she was cited in *Red Channels*. Those citations were published in 1950 from old information about her connections that pre-dated World War II, a time when the Communist Party USA was still a somewhat respected group. Dorothy never did actually become a member of the Party, but even if she had, it would have been no crime to do so.

In 1934, she declared, "I am a Communist." Those words were met with disbelief, even from actual Party members, because she never adhered to the Communist discipline. She was living in a Beverly Hills mansion, complete with a staff of servants, and to make matters worse, she absolutely adored both Franklin and Eleanor Roosevelt. She said she could never criticize the Communist Party USA because she felt they helped a suffering humanity. Dorothy identified with the depressed, in spite of the fact that she did not know any of them first-hand. One thing she deeply believed was that the rightists wanted to rule the working man, whereas those on the left wanted the working man to rule.

As a strong supporter of the Loyalist forces in the Spanish Civil War against the Falangists, Dorothy came into agreement with Ernest Hemingway, even though they had a virile dislike for each other on a more personal level. That war was a very divisive issue in our country because the Loyalists had the backing of Soviet Russia while the Falangists were supported and armed by Nazi Germany. It was hard to remain neutral under those conditions.

Speaking to the Congress of American Writers in 1939, Dorothy clearly displayed how she felt about those who preferred the status quo:

> "Out in Hollywood where the streets are paved with Goldwyn the word sophisticate means very simply, obscene. A sophisticated story is a dirty story. Some of that meaning was wafted eastward and got itself mixed up into the present definition. So that a sophisticate means one who dwells in a tower made of a DuPont substitute for ivory and who holds

a glass of flat champagne in one hand and an album of dirty postcards in the other."[1]

Dorothy continued to make speeches on behalf of the Anti-Nazi League in support of Spanish refugees to audiences that included many future blacklistees. Though her lifestyle may not have resembled her positions, it was eminently clear where she stood.

In 1940, one of her long-time friends, Donald Ogden Stewart, wrote a skit that was presented at the Philharmonic Hall in Hollywood. It was a protest to the words spoken by Martin Dies of the HUAC called "When Martin Comes." Dorothy was one of the performers. Here is her final oration from that work:

"The people want democracy—real democracy, Mr. Dies, and they look toward Hollywood to give it to them because they don't get it anymore in the newspapers. And that's why you're out here, Mr. Dies—that's why you want to destroy the Hollywood progressive organizations—because you've got to control this medium if you want to bring fascism to this country. We're grateful to Hollywood for our jobs and we're grateful for the opportunity it gives us to speak for American democracy."[2]

Always outspoken and often witty about every matter that came her way, Dorothy was a difficult person to really know. Even among her closest associates, she was given to tell many contrary versions of any story about herself.

Before she passed away, Dorothy put into her will a statement bequeathing her entire estate to the Martin Luther King, Jr. Foundation in order to aid yet another struggling civil rights organization. Her ashes became a source of controversy for seventeen years until they were finally enshrined in a memorial garden at NAACP headquarters in Baltimore where she is now honored with a plaque that reads:

"Here lie the ashes of Dorothy Parker (1893-1967) humorist, writer, critic, defender of human and civil rights. For her epitaph she suggested, 'Excuse my dust.' This memorial garden is dedicated to her noble spirit which celebrated the oneness of humankind and the bonds of everlasting friendship between Black and Jewish people. Dedicated by the National Association for the Advancement of Colored People, October 28, 1988."³

That lovely petite lady with her expressive limpid eyes did not live an uneventful life, but she always found a way to rise above her own problems and to help others much less fortunate.

Chapter Twenty-Seven
Lillian Hellman

Citations:

Independent Citizens Committee of the Arts, Sciences and Professions - Speaker - Theatre Panel

Progressive Citizens of America, National Arts, Sciences and Professions

Council - Participant, Cultural Freedom Conference

National Council of American - Soviet Friendship - Signer - Women's Committee. Greetings to women of the Soviet Union in celebration of International Women's Day

National Wallace for President Committee - Member

Harlem Women for Wallace - Speaker - Gave forceful tribute to Wallace

"New Party" (Wallace) - Member - Platform Committee

Writers for Wallace - Member - Initiating Committee

Moscow Art Theatre - Sent greetings to directors and members. Celebration of Moscow Arts Theatre's 50th anniversary

Progressive Party - Attended three-day conference

National Council of the Arts, Sciences and Professions - Signer - Statement calling for abolition of HUAC

Scientific and Cultural Conference for World Peace - Signer - Invitation to conference - Member - Program Committee

Amicus Curiae Brief - Signer - Petition to Supreme Court to review the conviction of Lawson and Trumbo

Moscow Theatres - Plays - "The Watch on the Rhine," "The Little Foxes," performed in Moscow theatres

American Committee for Democracy and International Freedom - Signer - Petition to discontinue Dies Committee

American Committee to Save Refugees; Exiled Writers Committee of the League of American Writers; United American Spanish Aid Committee - Chairman,

"Europe Today" dinner forum

American League for Peace and Democracy - Sponsor - Refugee Scholarship and Peace Campaign

Russian War Relief, Inc. - Signer - Advertisement asking for help on behalf of the Russian people

Artist's Front to Win the War - Participant

Citizens Committee for Harry Bridges - Member and sponsor

Equality - Member - Editorial Council

Friends of the Abraham Lincoln Brigade - Sponsor - Disabled Veterans Fund

Joint Anti-Fascist Refugee Committee - Sponsor - Dinner

The League of Women Shoppers, Inc. - Vice-president

National Emergency Conference for Democratic Rights - Signer - "Open Letter to the United States Senate"

Progressive Committee to Rebuild the American Labor Party - Member - Executive Committee

Statement by American Progressives on the Moscow Trials - Signer

Theatre Arts Committee - Member - Executive Board

Frontier Films - Member - Advisory Board

Lillian Hellman's life was complex. To learn more about her, one should read her three-volume autobiography, *An Unfinished Woman, Pentimento,* and *Scoundrel Time,* which are, for the most part, a sort of diary of her many experiences.

She was born in New Orleans, but she grew up spending equal time for several years in both Louisiana and New York City, six months at a time in each location. Because of that, she was exposed to two entirely different school systems and she could not adjust to either. In New York, she always seemed to be behind her classmates, while in New Orleans, she was usually ahead of the norm. Lillian did not much like school almost from the start, so she managed to stay away on at least one day of each week. In New Orleans, she had a favorite fig tree in which she could hide while spending her time reading and napping. Always an avid reader, she felt she could learn more in that tree than in a classroom. In spite of that, she did complete high school and later attended New York University for two years. Along with that, she also took some courses at Columbia University.

In 1929, she toured Europe. She took a liking to Bonn, Germany, so she decided to continue her education there. She became attracted to a student socialist group until she discovered their feelings towards Jews. She was a Jew, so she soon returned home.

During the 1930s, she became an ardent supporter of the International Brigades of non-Spaniards in their fight against the fascist regime of Francisco Franco. At one point, she did a radio broadcast from Madrid back to the USA to express her anxieties and overall feelings about the situation. Lillian did that report during constant bombing raids by the Italian air force.

On January 9, 1940, Lillian made a speech at an American Booksellers luncheon. She made her feelings quite clear:

"I am a writer and I am a Jew. I want to be sure that I can continue to be a writer, and if I want to say that greed is bad or persecution is worse, I can do it without being branded by the malice of people who make a living by that malice. I also want to be able to go on saying that I am a Jew without being afraid of being called names or end in a prison camp or be forbidden to walk the streets at night."[1]

In October 1941, she and Ernest Hemmingway co-hosted a dinner to raise money for the anti-fascists. The then Governor of New York, Herbert Lehman, had agreed to participate, but he soon withdrew because he said that many of the sponsors were associated with Communist activities.

Lillian replied, "I do not and did not ask the politics of any of the members of the committee and there is nobody who can honestly vouch for anybody, but themselves. Funds raised would be used as promised."[2] She provided an accurate accounting.

One month later she wrote to Lehman, "I am sure it will make you sad and ashamed, as it did me to know that, of the seven resignations out of 147 sponsors, five were Jews. Of all the peoples in the world, I think we should be the last to hold back help on any grounds from those who fought for us."[3]

In 1943 and in 1944, she was denied a passport because she was considered an active Communist. A year later, she was finally granted the right to have a passport.

Lillian then became a first-hand witness to the work of the Russian Army prior to their retaking of Warsaw during the waning days of World War II. She made that trip under the aegis of the State Department in order to compile information for a documentary on the valor of the Russian people. In order to get to Moscow, the jumping off point for her adventure, she had to endure an excruciating forty-day journey from Alaska and across Siberia, during which she contracted pneumonia. She traveled in the unheated cabin of an old C-46 transport aircraft that had to make many stops due to weather and fuel limitations. Some of those stops lasted for several days. Her accommodation was a sleeping bag on top of some shipping crates. Occasionally she was invited to sit in the cockpit to try to get warm. This only made it worse when she had to return to the frigid cabin.

The end result of that trip and her earlier life in Europe was predictable. She began to have serious problems with various anti-red factions.

In 1947, she was offered a long-term contract by Columbia Pictures. She refused to sign it because it contained a loyalty clause, which she said infringed on her rights of free speech and assembly.

Between 1938 and 1940, she had been a very casual member of the Communist Party USA because of their approach to the Civil War in Spain, although she never actually held a membership card. As time went on, she gradually drifted away from that connection. It seemed to her to be the wrong place to be. All she could recall of the experience was a bunch of people sitting around and discussing current affairs without ever coming to any conclusions.

In November 1947, the leaders of the film industry took it upon themselves to ban employment to anyone who refused to respond to questioning by the HUAC. Though she had not yet been subpoenaed at that time, Lillian found it necessary to respond. She wrote an article for *Screen Writer,* a publication of the Screen Writers Guild, titled "The Judas Goat." In part, she stated:

> "It was a week of turning the head in shame; of the horror of seeing politicians make the honorable institution of Congress into a honky-tonk show; of listening to craven men lie and tattle, pushing each other in their efforts to lick the boots of the vilifiers; publicly trying to wreck the lives, not of strangers, mind you, but of the men and women who have worked and eaten and played, and made millions.
>
> "But why this particular industry; these particular people? Has it anything to do with Communism? Of course not. There has never been a single line or word of Communism in any American picture at any time. There have never, or seldom, been ideas of any kind. Naturally, men scared to make pictures about the American Negro, men who only in the last year have allowed the word Jew to be spoken in a picture, men who took more than ten years to make an anti-Fascist

picture, those are frightened men, and you pick frightened men to frighten first. Judas Goats; they'll lead the others, maybe, to slaughter for you.

"They frightened mighty easy and they talk mighty bad. I suggest the rest of us don't frighten so easily. It's still not un-American to fight the enemies of our country. Let's fight!"[4]

In May 1952, the long expected subpoena from the Executive Committee of the HUAC was served on Lillian. She wrote a letter to the chairman, John S. Wood, stating the conditions for her testimony that she wanted to be read into the record prior to her appearance:

"Dear Mr. Wood:

"As you know I am under subpoena to appear before your committee on May 21, 1952.

"I am most willing to answer all questions about myself. I have nothing to hide from your committee and there is nothing in my life of which I am ashamed. I have been advised by counsel that under the 5th Amendment [sic] I have a constitutional privilege to decline to answer any questions about my political opinions, activities and associations, on the grounds of self-incrimination. I do not wish to claim this privilege. I am ready and willing to testify before the representatives of our government as to my opinions and my own actions, regardless of any risks or consequences to myself.

"But I am advised by counsel that if I answer the committee's questions about myself, I must also answer questions about other people and that if I refuse to do so, I can be cited for contempt. My counsel tells me that if I answer questions about myself, I have waived my rights under the 5th Amendment [sic] and could be forced legally to answer questions about others. This is very difficult for a layman to understand, but there is one principal that I do understand: I am not willing, now or in the future, to bring bad trouble to people who, in my past association with them, were completely innocent of any talk or any action that was disloyal or subversive. I do not like subversion or disloyalty in any form and if I had even seen any I would have considered it my duty to have reported it to the proper authorities. But to hurt innocent people in order to save myself is inhuman and indecent and dishonorable. I cannot and will not cut my conscience to fit this year's fashions, even though I long ago came to the conclusion that I was not a political person and could have no comfortable place in any political group.

"I was raised in an old fashioned American tradition and there were certain homely things that were taught to me: To try to tell the truth, not to bear false witness, not to harm my neighbor, to be loyal to my country, and so on. In general I respected these ideals of Christian honor and did as well with them as I knew how. It is my belief that you will agree with these simple rules of human decency and will not expect me to violate the good American tradition from which they spring. I would, therefore, come before you and speak of myself.

"I am prepared to waive the privilege against self-incrimination, and to tell you everything you wish to know about my views or actions if your committee will agree to refrain from asking me to name other people. If the committee is unwilling to give me this assurance, I will be forced to plead the privilege of the 5th Amendment [sic] at the hearing.

"A reply to this letter would be appreciated."[5]

Mr. Wood did reply:

"Dear Miss Hellman:

"Reference is made to your letter dated May 19, 1952, wherein you indicate that in the event the committee asks you questions regarding your association with other individuals you will be compelled to rely on the 5th Amendment [sic] in giving your answer to the committee questions.

"In this connection please be advised that the committee cannot permit witnesses to set forth the terms under which they will testify.

"We have in the past secured a great deal of information from persons in the entertainment profession who cooperated whole-heartedly with the committee. The committee appreciates any information furnished it by persons who have been members of the Communist Party. The committee, of course, realizes that a great number of persons who were members of the Communist Party at one time honestly felt that it was not a subversive organization. However, on the other hand, it should be pointed out that the contributions made to the Communist Party as a whole by persons who were not themselves subversive made it possible for those members of the Communist Party who were and still are subversives to carry on their work.

"The committee has endeavored to furnish a hearing to each person identified as a Communist engaged in work in the entertainment field in order that the record could be made clear as to whether they were still members of the Communist Party. Any persons identified by you during the course of committee hearings will be afforded the opportunity of appearing before the committee in accordance with the policy of the committee."[6]

His was not the response Lillian was looking for, so she was forced to do what she had said she would do. Her inquisitors at the executive session on the 21st were Wood, Frank S. Tavenner, and Francis E. Walter. Here is a segment from that hearing:

Tavenner asked, "Were you at any time a member at-large of the Communist Party?"

Lillian said, "I refuse to answer, Mr. Tavenner, on the grounds of the Fifth Amendment."

"Were you acquainted with V. J. Jerome?"

"I refuse to answer on the same grounds."

"John Howard Lawson?"

"I refuse to answer on the same grounds."

"Are you now a member of the Communist Party?"

"No sir."

"Were you ever a member of the Communist Party?"

"I refuse to answer, Mr. Tavenner, on the same grounds."

Wood then said, "See if we can be of mutual assistance to each other. You testified that you are not now a member of the Communist Party. On the grounds of self-incrimination, you have declined to answer if you were ever a member."

Lillian said, "Yes sir."

Wood asked, "What I would like to know is if you can fix a date, a period of time in the immediate past, during which you are willing to testify that you have not been a member of the Communist Party?"

Lillian replied, "I refuse to answer, Mr. Wood, on the same grounds."

"Were you yesterday?"

"No sir."

"Were you last year at this time?"

"No sir."

"Were you five years ago at this time?"

"I must refuse to answer."

"Were you two years ago at this time?"

"No sir."

"Three years ago at this time?"

"I must refuse to answer on the same grounds."

"You say you must refuse to answer. Do you refuse to answer whether you were?"

Lillian answered, "I am so sorry, I forget. I certainly don't mean to forget."

Walter continued. "Were you a member of the Communist Party in the middle of June 1937?"

"I refuse to answer, Mr. Walter, on the same grounds."

"As I remember your letter to the chairman, you didn't want to testify because you were afraid that you might bring bad trouble on people whose names might be mentioned in connection with your testimony. In view of that, Martin Berkeley has already admitted that he was a member of the Communist Party. What bad trouble do you think you would bring to him if you were to admit that you attended a meeting at his home?

Lillian replied, "I stand by my letter, Mr. Walter. I have worked very hard on it, and I tried very hard to explain exactly what I meant by it. I must refer back to it at this point."[7]

Lillian could not be shaken from her determination to keep the names of others out of the questioning. Because of her tactics, she could not be found in contempt. She was, as were many others, called a "Fifth Amendment Communist" for a long time thereafter. She should be admired for her tenacity in the face of adversity. What she really wanted to say to them, but did not, was, "You are a bunch of headline seekers, using other people's lives for your own benefits. You know damn well that the people you have been calling before you never did much of anything, but you've browbeaten and bullied many of them into telling lies about sins they never committed. So go to hell and do what you want with me."

Some of her problems arose because of her close friendship with Dorothy Parker and her thirty-one-year on-again off-again love affair with Dashiell Hammett. In those days, one could be marked a traitor with no evidence to support that claim.

In her later years, Lillian was given honorary degrees by many esteemed institutes of learning for her work as a playwright and screenwriter, which proves that some things are far more important than politics.

Chapter Twenty-Eight
Dashiell Hammett

Citations:
National Council of Arts, Sciences and Professions - Member - Initiating committee;

Writers for Wallace - Signer of statement - Handbill

Amicus Curiae Brief - Signer - Petition to Supreme Court to review the conviction of Lawson and Trumbo

Civil Rights Congress - Chairman, Trustees of Bail Fund - Advanced bail money for 11 U. S. Politbureau members convicted at Foley Square, New York, 1949 - President, New York Chapter - Letterhead

Scientific and Cultural Conference for World Peace - Sponsor - Official program

Motion Picture Artists' Committee - Chairman

League of American Writers - National Head, 1943

Statement by American Progressives in support of the Moscow Trials - Signer

Letter to President Roosevelt - Signer - Letter protesting persecution of Communist leaders

Robert Thompson and Benjamin J. Davis campaign - Supporter

Jefferson School of Social Science - Instructor - Catalog

Conference on Constitutional Liberties in America - Sponsor - Washington, D. C. - Official Call

How can one write about Dashiell Hammett, author of detective novels, short stories, and screenplays, without mixed emotions? We know a great deal about him and yet, at the same time, we know very little. Richard Layman put the proper spin on Dashiell's life when he titled his biography *Shadow Man*.

Dashiell's amazingly diverse accomplishments were done despite his poor health throughout most of his life. He was born Samuel Dashiell Hammett in Saint Mary's County, Maryland, and grew up in Philadelphia and then Baltimore. His formal education ended at the age of thirteen, when he felt he could learn more on his own than from any school. From the beginning, he was an avid reader, often studying material that far exceeded the norm for his age.

During those early years following his brief stay at school, he held many short-term jobs. In 1915, he joined the Pinkerton Detective Agency, a position he held until 1922, with some time off for World War I. In 1918, he enlisted in the army and was put to duty with the Motor Ambulance Corp. He contracted Spanish Influenza, which led to Tuberculosis (TB), a disease that had plagued his mother through most of her life. He was sent to Cushman Hospital (U. S. Public Health Service Hospital #59) in Tacoma, Washington to recover. There, he met a nurse, Jose (pronounced Josey) Dolan, whom he eventually married. Dashiell was transferred to U. S. Public Health Hospital #64 near San Diego because that facility could better serve his needs.

After his release and an honorable discharge from military service, he was able to return to the Pinkerton Agency. Because of his medical condition, he only worked sporadically for them as an operative until 1922. During that time, he was granted various levels of disability from the government at different times. TB is an odd infliction that comes and goes. There were times when he felt quite normal, but there were also times when he was so depleted that he could not work a full day.

By 1922, he was getting more and more uncomfortable with the Pinkerton Agency's strike-breaking tactics, so he resigned and began his writing career. He called upon some of his experiences as an operative to construct many of the short stories he later became famous for. Ultimately, he got to be known as "The Dean of the Hard-Boiled Detective Genre."

In 1929, Alfred Knopf published Red Harvest, the first of Dashiell's five novels. Also in 1929, his third novel-to-be, *The Maltese Falcon*, was serialized in *The Black Mask*, a detective pulp magazine, and in 1930, Alfred Knopf published *The Maltese Falcon* in its final complete form.

The Maltese Falcon featured a very cynical gumshoe named Sam Spade. The story was made into three movie versions, *The Maltese Falcon* (1931), *Satan Met a Lady* (1936) with Bette Davis, and *The Maltese Falcon* (1941) with Humphrey Bogart, Mary Astor, Peter Lorre, and Sidney Greenstreet.

Dashiell's last novel was *The Thin Man*, which was serialized in *Redbook* in 1933 and also published by Alfred Knopf as a book in 1934. *The Thin Man* (1934), MGM's movie version starring William Powell spawned a series, the first three of which were from screenplays written by Dashiell. After the third sequel, he lost interest in the project. All six were released through MGM and starred William Powell and Myrna Loy as Nick and Nora Charles.

Dashiell's problems with various government agencies before, during, and after the blacklisting days involves an unanswered question to this day about whether or not he was ever a member of the Communist Party USA, although more than likely, he may have been at one time or another. We know that he was a scholar on the subject and that he studied many philosophical works including the writings of Karl Marx. In 1948, Dashiell's brother, Richard, asked him directly if he was a Communist. Dashiell replied that he was "a Marxist," in other words, not giving a direct answer to his question. Lillian Hellman, with whom he lived off and on for over thirty years, said that he probably was a Communist, but that she would never ask.

On July 9, 1951, Dashiell was called upon to testify before the United States 2nd District Court in regard to his work for the

Civil Rights Congress (CRC), a group that had been established with the main purpose of raising funds to bail out convicted Communist leaders. At that time, the Communist Party USA was a legal entity. Dashiell had been the President and Lead Trustee for their New York Chapter of CRC. When he was questioned, he repeatedly used his Fifth Amendment rights. The judge was Sylvester Ryan, and the principal inquisitor was Irving H. Saypol:

Saypol asked, "Mr. Hammett, are you one of the five trustees of the bail fund of the Civil Rights Congress of New York?"

"Dashiell replied, "I decline to answer on the ground that the answer may incriminate me, and I am relying on my rights under the Fifth Amendment to the Constitution of the United States."

Ryan asked, "I direct you to answer the question."

Dashiell answered, "I decline to answer, your honor, for the same reasons."

Saypol said, "I show you exhibit six in evidence, the minute book of the bail fund of the CRC of New York, and I direct your attention particularly to the minute dated November 14, 1949, which reads as follows: 'The trustees agreed to post bail up to $1000 each for a thirty day period for the sixteen members of the Greek Maritime Unions now held at Ellis Island. It is reported that on November 3, 1949 bail in the aggregate amount of $260,000 had been posted in the case of the eleven Communist leaders convicted under the Smith Act. This action was taken in pursuance of the authorization given by the trustees at their meeting on July 22, 1948.' I ask you, have you seen this minute book?"

Dashiell said, "I decline to answer the question on the ground that the answer may tend to incriminate me."

Ryan repeated, "I direct you to answer the question on the same grounds."

Dashiell again stated, "I decline to answer on the same grounds."[1]

The hearing went on for some time, with Dashiell never willing to give his tormentors any quarter. Judge Ryan explained to him that, by his denials, he was in a sense producing the opposite effect of what he wanted to accomplish. The end result was predictable.

Ryan proclaimed, "Samuel Dashiell Hammett, I have found you guilty of Contempt of this court by reason of your refusal to answer questions and by your refusal to produce or give evidence of the location of certain books, records and documents in your possession, or under your control, relating to the bail fund for the Civil Rights Congress of New York, and more specifically as set forth in the certificate which I have made under rule 42(a) of the rules of criminal procedure. I have signed the certificate as was required by rule 42(a). Have you anything to say as to why judgment should not be pronounced upon you by this court?"

Dashiell answered, "Not a thing."

Ryan said, "I adjudge you and order that you, Samuel Dashiell Hammett, be committed to the custody of the Attorney General or his authorized representative for imprisonment for a period of six months or until such time as you may purge yourself of the contempt of court."[2]

In a highly irregular action, bail was granted and then denied. Dashiell never cracked during the period of his sentence, carried out first at the Federal House of Detention in New York City and then at the Federal Correctional Institute in Kentucky. His time was cut short by a few weeks due to his good behavior. He was a sick man when he went to prison and much sicker when he came out. During that time, Lillian Hellman never once visited him. They had agreed that it would be best not to aggravate her own situation by casting additional criticisms in her direction. She had enough of her own difficulties to contend with at that time.

A few short months after his release from jail, Dashiell again faced inquisitors from the Senate Internal Security Committee chaired by Joseph McCarthy. Chief Counsel to the committee, Roy Cohn, conducted most of the interrogation. By that time, Dashiell was in dire straits. He was only fifty-seven, but his health was continuing to deteriorate and he was nearly destitute. When he appeared before this latest panel, he was at first a bit more cooperative, but when the inquiry began to drift into familiar territory he once again relied on the protection of the Fifth Amendment.

Cohn began by asking, "You are the author of a number of rather well-known detective stories. Is that correct?"

Dashiell replied, "That is right."

"In addition to that, you have written, I think in your earlier period, on some social issues. Is that correct?"

"Well, I have written some short stories that may have. You know, it is impossible to write anything without taking some sort of stand on social issues."

Cohn asked, "You say it is impossible to write anything without taking some sort of stand on social issues. Now, are you the author of a short story known as 'Nightshade'?"

"I am."

"I might state, Mr. Chairman that some 300 of Mr. Hammett's books are in use in the Information Service today located in, I believe, some seventy-three Information Centers. I am sorry, 300 copies, eighteen books." Then, to Dashiell, he asked, "You haven't written 300 books. Is that right?"

"That is a lot of books."

"Now, Mr. Hammett, when did you write your first published book?"

"The first book was *Red Harvest*. It was published in 1929. I think I wrote it in 1927 or '28."

"At the time you wrote that book were you a member of the Communist Party?" "I decline to answer on the grounds that an answer might tend to incriminate me, relying on my rights under the Fifth Amendment to the Constitution of the United States."

"In the 1930s and 1940s, at the time you wrote your last book, were you a member of the Communist Party?"

"I decline...."[3]

The proceedings went downhill from there. The end result was not jail, but all of the Hammett books were temporarily withdrawn from the State Department Libraries around the country.

Regarding Dashiell's ill-fated marriage to Jose Dolan, they did have two daughters, but their union never stood a good chance for survival. The main reason was his Tuberculosis, which was contagious, and the Public Health people determined that he should not live with his three ladies. This made for a strange relationship. Later on, Jose obtained a divorce in Mexico that was never recognized by American authorities. Dashiell continued to support them as best he could throughout some difficult financially times, when he himself was living on the meager disability payments he received from the government.

Prior to his being released from prison, Dashiell was almost a millionaire from the royalties that continuously flowed in from his books, his movie work, and the radio spin-offs based on characters he had created. He had absolutely nothing to do with the radio productions, *The Adventures of Sam Spade*, *The Adventures of the Thin Man*, and *The Fat Man*, except to allow them to use his name. For that, he was paid handsomely. In 1942, after several rejections, he once again joined the U. S. Army. He was forty-seven at that time, highly unusual for a raw recruit. Most of his time in the service was spent on the little island of Adak in the Aleutians. His main task for the bulk of his time was the establishment and running of news sources to keep his cohorts informed of the state of the world.

When he was mustered out in 1945, Dashiell found the IRS waiting for him. He had been an excellent earner, but he was also a big spender. He had lived a flamboyant lifestyle whenever possible. During the war, that continued to be the case. He never gave much thought to his tax situation. The IRS stayed on his back for the rest of his life, taking nearly all of his income, which had been grossly reduced by 1945.

When he passed away in 1961, he was interred at Arlington National Cemetery, a privilege he was entitled to because of his service in both World Wars. Of course, that did not go down well with the many witch hunters who had hounded him for so long.

In a sort of odd way, he had the last laugh. His had been a constantly troubled but successful life, considering all he had had to contend with.

Chapter Twenty-Nine
Henry Morgan

Citations:
   Progressive Citizens of America - member - Actor's division

   Veterans against Discrimination of Civil Rights Congress - collection speech at Hunter College at City University of New York

   Stop Censorship Committee - speaker by recording - rally at Hotel Astor

Henry Morgan was many things to many people, but one thing he was not was subversive. He was witty. He was introverted to the point that it harmed his career at times. He was a master of the ad-lib. He was stubborn. He was lovable, but he could also be obnoxious. Most of all, he was a free thinking, caring person who would always take on any cause he thought needed his attention. He was also truthful to a fault. In my conversations with him, he held nothing back.

Henry's problems and his period of being unemployable all began when he was listed in *Red Channels*. As you can see, his list was very short.

Not much later, he received the following letter from Vincent Hartnett, the writer of the introduction to *Red Channels* and the head investigator for *Aware, Inc*. The comments in brackets are my own:

   "Dear Mr. Morgan,
   "As you know, I am the originator of *Red Channels* [Lie]. As you also know, only a small portion of your record in connection with Communist fronts was given in that book. [What kind

of game was he playing?] A new, much more complete book is now in preparation. It is not my intention to create undue hardship for anyone. [Since when?] Above and beyond telling the truth, I try to make it a work of supererogation [a big word that means "going beyond duty"] not to refer to the past the records of those who had conclusively broken with the Communist or Communist front movement."[1]

Hartnett goes on from there to explain how he, will take care of him if Henry will only come clean before a certain date. He told Henry that the entire matter must remain between the two of them, and if he should go to anyone else in an attempt to clear himself, all bets are off. One blatant falsehood that came up several times in the epistle was Hartnett's reference to being the author of *Red Channels*, which he was not. His own book was the aforementioned *File 13-Volume 2*.

The offshoot was that, while Henry did not ignore the missive, he also did not respond to it or heed the unveiled warning.

His response to the three citations was very firm and uncompromising. First, he said he never was a member of the Progressive Citizens of America, and had never actually even heard of them. As to the other two charges, his reply was equally adamant. He said that he did indeed make those speeches and would again speak out for any cause that opposed discrimination or censorship. He added, "How would I know that ten years later some smart ass would decide they were Communist fronts?"

Henry went on to state that he was briefly a member of something called the Duncan-Parris Post of the American Legion. As you should know by now, the American Legion was one of the most steadfast groups against anything with a red tint. After just two meetings, Henry discovered that this particular assemblage was Communist-dominated, so he immediately distanced himself from them. The last laugh was on the boys at the FBI and *Counterattack* because they totally missed that one.

Two years after he had been virtually put out of work by *Red Channels*, Henry received a call from Jack Wren, one of the most notorious "Clearance Experts."

"He asked me to come and see him about my problem," said Henry. "He told me he knew that I wasn't a Communist, but I would have to prove it. Why should I have to disprove, what was all a fallacy in the first place?"

When Henry asked Wren how he could say with certainty that he knew he was not a Communist, he was told that it was because Henry's cousin, Martin Berkeley, said he was not. If you recall from earlier in this dialogue, Berkeley turned out to be the #1 name-dropper. Henry was one of the few names Martin did not accuse. Since many of the names he gave were people he never knew at all, Berkeley was a very poor source of information. How could he be trusted either way?

Jack Wren then told him that he would have to meet with "certain" people to complete his clearance. He was sent to a lady whose name he said he could not remember. She assured him that they knew he was not a Communist. Their first conversation, as Henry remembered it, went like this:

The Lady asked, "Surely you must know some others—some you suspect."

Henry answered, "But lady, if I wasn't a member, how could I know? And if I just guess, wouldn't I be doing what has already been done to me?"

"You owe it to your country. Don't you love your country?"

"Yeah, yeah, I love my country, but I think naming names is un-American."[2]

They went through to same routine in two additional meetings. Each time, she got increasingly angrier because he wouldn't let her have her way.

Then, Wren sent him to the American Committee of the American Legion to meet with their head man. Once more, Henry could not remember his name, but he thought it was something like Oscar Barschlag. [The man was Karl H. W. Baarslag.] He was an ex-Communist Party member, who had been a big man with the Communists until he reversed his thinking after the Hitler-Stalin Accord. He and Martin, his cousin, were clearing his name from what they said they knew he was not; some sort of phony rehabilitation.

Finally, Wren asked Henry to attend a meeting of American Federation of Television and Radio Artists (AFTRA) to read a speech Wren had written denouncing Communism. Morgan would not do it, because, as he put it, "How the hell could I stand in front of my union and read something that started out, 'This rotten swine?'"

What was the real reason for his trouble? How did it all get started? It seems that it went back to the problems he was having with his first wife and her friends. Here is how he described the situation:

> "All her information came from friends whose conversation leaned sharply away from their relatively high incomes, which apparently, they found to be embarrassing in a world that harbored poor people. Their chosen method of being helpful was to attend meetings at one and other's homes and discuss the problems of the hungry hordes after dinner. I am not trying to be amusing. It is just what they did. A Party member was usually invited to lead the discussions. I was apolitical. To some that meant that I was either stupid or inner-directed, which meant, according to them, that I didn't care about my fellow man."[3]

So, it all came about over a gross misunderstanding, but Henry was never offered any sort of an apology from any of those who made his life so miserable for several years.

He may have been a man who could be hard to get along with at times, but he did not have a subversive bone in his body.

Chapter Thirty
Howard Duff

Citations:
Thanksgiving Program for Benefit of Hollywood Ten - Attended

Unfriendly witnesses before House Un-American Activities Committee - Endorser

Committee for the First Amendment - Member

Progressive Citizens of America - Member - Actors Division

Amicus Curiae Brief - Signer - Petition to Supreme Court to review conviction of Lawson and Trumbo

In the jargon of the titles of Howard Duff's favorite radio show, *The Adventures of Sam Spade*, we might call this chapter "The Misinterpreted Liberal Caper."

Howard Duff was born in the little town of Charleston, Washington, a stone's throw from Seattle across the waters of Puget Sound. His father was then Mayor of Charleston. You will not find that city in any current atlas because it was later incorporated into Bremerton.

During Howard's early days, his sole ambition was to pursue a career as a cartoonist, but that idea came to an abrupt end in high school. While there, he began acting in school plays. His dream of cartooning was quickly forgotten even though he displayed talent in that direction. He contracted the acting bug. Right out of high school, he auditioned for the Seattle Repertory Playhouse and, to his dismay, he was accepted to do plays by Chekov, Shakespeare, and Noel Coward, all classics. As he said to me in a conversation on September 23, 1986, "We didn't know what the hell we were doing, but somehow it came out all right." He said the Seattle Repertory Playhouse was like a university of acting. The director operated under a "Sink or Swim" philosophy because she felt that none of her protégés would be in her group if they could not act. Her theory usually worked out, but not always. However, Howard must have been doing something right because he stayed with the Playhouse for five years, building a solid foundation in his chosen field.

He was also doing a fair amount of radio announcing to get his feet wet in the audio world.

In 1946, Howard was hired for a new radio series called *The Adventures of Sam Spade*, which was based loosely on the private detective character created by writer Dashiell Hammett for *The Maltese Falcon*. Dashiell had absolutely nothing to do with the production except that he allowed his name to be used, for which he was handsomely rewarded financially.

The radio series ran for thirteen episodes on ABC in 1946 and for 157 episodes on CBS in 1946-1949. At initial rehearsals, the actors cast in minor roles sat waiting for the director, William Spier, but nothing was happening. As it turned out, they were being held up due to contract problems with an actor that had been hired to play Sam Spade.

Since they were working against time restraints, Spier had each of those present read a few lines as Spade. After Howard read, Kay Thompson, Spier's wife, urged him to hire Howard for the lead.

At first, William wanted him to do a sort of Bogart approach, ala, *The Maltese Falcon*. Howard told me, "I somehow or other worked out of that and tried to make it sound like somebody I could deal with on my own turf more than I could slavishly do a Bogart imitation. Bill allowed me to go my own way, and I did. Anyone who heard the show would know I wasn't doing a Bogart."

The show ran very successfully for five seasons and then trouble loomed. At a Christmas party given by film producer S. P. Eagle (Sam Spiegel), Howard ran into Lillian Hellman, Dashiell Hammett's long-time companion. He asked her, "Miss Hellman, can you tell me what Dashiell Hammett thinks of the show?"

She replied, "I don't believe he's ever heard it."

That was that, but at the end of the 1950 season, the remote connection with Dashiell plus Howard's *Red Channels* listing was enough to get the show canceled at the height of its popularity.

During our conversation in 1986, Howard put it this way when I asked, "When you were mentioned in *Red Channels*, nearly everybody in Hollywood who was a writer, a producer, a director, or who had any connection to the University of California, stood a good chance of being on that list."

Howard said, "I don't know about that. There were a few people who were not on it. I can remember joking with other people saying, 'Look at this, so and so has more credits than I have here.' It turned out to destroy me, as it did many others. I had a little trouble getting on the air after that for a couple of years, and Hammett went to jail. That was the unfortunate ending of a pretty popular show."

"It was automatic guilt by association. I had Bill Robson on my show a few weeks ago, and he told me what terrible effects undocumented information had on him. He actually tried writing under a combination name he made up from his two son's names, but even that didn't last very long."

Howard added, "I wasn't aware that Bill was on the list, but I guess he was. It was a sad time for a lot of people."

"And so uncalled for."

"I think so. Most of the people who were in *Red Channels*—including me—were by no means Communists, nor did *Red Channels* say they were. They implied that we were Communist sympathizers. Implication was all it took. Actually, what they were after was Liberals. I suppose I could have been classified as a Liberal and I still am; and proud of it."

I said, "I don't think many people looking at that list today would think very much of it, but at the time, it had disastrous effects for so many."

Howard replied, "You were around at that time. I'm sure you remember the McCarthyism going on. *Red Channels* had nothing to do with McCarthy, but it was part of the whole climate that most of us so-called Liberals didn't perceive."

"*Red Channels* was simply an offshoot of the misguided feelings of some at that time."

"Well, it was something that I was never ready for. I couldn't believe it until it happened. I just hope that sort of thing doesn't happen again."

"Unfortunately, history tends to repeat itself."

Howard added, "And of course, the climate these days is even more Conservative than it was then."[1]

Part of the problem was Jimmie Tarantino, a columnist for *Hollywood Life*. He did a lot of damage to a lot of people by taking half-cocked data and printing it as if it was the whole story. It was like throwing gasoline on a small fire. He wrote, "If anyone in this world, short of His Holiness, Pope Pius, had told me a few short years ago that this could happen in America, I would have shooed them away. It is almost unbelievable that so many so-called intelligent and prominent people would turn their affections and sympathies to butcher Joe Stalin and the Communist Party. Hammett is said to be responsible for selling the red banner to dozens of men and women, including actor Howard Duff, alias Sam Spade."[2]

Tarantino added more specifically, "Sam Spade Duff is a fellow traveler and red sympathizer. He has also given comfort and his well-advertised name to many Commie fronts. He was an unfriendly witness before the Washington House on Un-American Activities and a member of the Committee for the First Amendment, a Commie setup. Duff, on September 3, 1947 was a member of the Actors Division of the Progressive Citizens of America, a red front deal. He signed a petition to the U. S. Supreme Court to review the conviction of Lawson and Trumbo, two un-friendly Hollywood writers who were sent to jail."[3]

While there was some truth to his statements, Tarantino never took the time to back his data with the complete story behind each and every accusation. He left the basic issues up in the air. In those days, the average reader did not bother to investigate what he or she was told. Being marginally involved with any of the front organizations proved nothing about the political leanings of those unfortunates who had been named as subversives by people who had an axe to grind.

At the end of 1949, *The Adventures of Sam Spade* returned to the airwaves on NBC with Steve Dunne in the title role doing a rather poor imitation of Howard Duff. The new series lasted for one season of fifty-one episodes during 1949-1951. It could not hold a candle to the original.

Howard disappeared from radio altogether after 1950. He was also offered no substantive parts in films until a minor role in *Panic in the City* (1968), a major production. He also appeared in a few less than memorable movies during the 1950s.

If it had not been for his marriage to Ida Lupino in 1951—a union that lasted for thirty-three years—most of the time with rocky results—even those doors would have been closed in his face. As an actress and director, Ida held a bit more clout than Howard.

In 1957, Howard and Ida co-starred on a television series called Mr. Adams and Eve, which, in some ways, resembled *The Thin Man*. Howard said, "We got two hot seasons out of that one. I thought we ought to have done better than that, but that's the way it goes. We were perceived, I guess, as *I Love Lucy*, which we had no intention of trying to do."

Howard did a great deal of television work and continued to appear in some major films right up to the time of his death in 1990, but the scars of the blacklist were never totally forgotten. How could they be?

Chapter Thirty-One
Lionel Stander

Citations:

American Friends of the Chinese People - Entertainer

First Congress of the Mexican and Spanish - American Peoples of the United States - Signer

Open Letter for Closer Cooperation with the Soviet Union - Signer

United American Artists - Sponsor - Testimonial to Rockwell Kent

Actor Lionel Stander was born in the Bronx to Russian Jewish immigrant parents. Although the HUAC people denied that there was any anti-Semitism involved in what they did, a high percentage of the people they investigated came from Eastern European Jewish roots. There were members of that panel who were anti-Semitic, and that at least one of them had strong Ku Klux Klan (KKK) leanings. Is it just a coincidence?

Lionel was among the first batch of actors subpoenaed to testify as early as 1940. He also had the dubious distinction of having been blacklisted about the longest of anyone, from late 1940 all the way to 1965. As early as 1938, Harry Cohn, President and Production Director at Columbia Pictures where Stander was a contract player, is said to have stated that Lionel was "A Red son of a bitch!" Cohn went so far as to threaten the other studios with a $100,000 fine should they hire Lionel.

In order to keep food on his table during those down years, Lionel worked at all sorts of jobs that had little or no relationship to show business. He also was able to add a little to his income by performing at times on the stage, an arm of the industry that was somewhat less affected by the various lists. For fifteen years, he lived mostly in London since the going was much easier there for an actor.

When he returned to the USA, he was hired to play Max, the combination butler, chef, and chauffeur on *Hart to Hart*, an American mystery television series that premiered on August 25, 1979 on ABC with Robert Wagner and Stefanie Powers. He did that role for six years.

Lionel made his first appearance before the HUAC people at an executive session on August 27, 1940. As a result, he claimed he was put on the blacklist even though nothing substantive had been covered in that particular meeting—immediate guilt by innuendo, as was the case with most of the people on the blacklist and graylist. He said that he had even been forced to do some night club gigs after that because he became unemployable on stage and screen.

The actual heavy hitting began when Lionel was called back to testify at an open hearing on May 6, 1953. The first crossing of swords between very divergent personalities came almost immediately. When he was ushered into the room, it became obvious that the intention was to turn him into a performing monkey. Noticing the overwhelming lights and television cameras, he informed the chairman of the committee, Harold Velde, that the only times he would allow such conditions was if he was entertaining on television or at a benefit, and that that particular situation did not fit into either of those categories.

Chairman Verde told him that sometimes in the past the cameras and lights had been withdrawn if it seemed that the witness was too nervous.

Lionel simply replied, "I'm not exactly calm this morning."

He also objected vehemently to the fact that he was there mainly due to unproven information written about him in newspapers that stopped just short of actually accusing him of anything. He expressed his feelings to the committee on that. "Through newspaper headlines people get peculiar attitudes. Mere appearance here is tantamount—not just appearance; the mere fact, in my case, I was subpoenaed, is tantamount to being blacklisted."[1]

During his testimony, he invoked the Fifth Amendment protection at times, but in no way could it be said that he remained silent. For every thrust the committee made, he parried with careful, cagey, and often humorous replies. This caused the procedure to run longer than usual. Through it all, Lionel remained above the fray and never gave a direct answer to any question. He, like most of the other witnesses, did not feel that the panel had the right to make inquiries into his personal life. He twisted the knife into his interrogators while maintaining his decorum:

Lionel asked, "Does this committee charge me with being a Communist?"

Velde answered, "Mr. Stander, will you let me tell you whether you are charged with being a Communist? Will you be quiet just for a moment while I tell you what you are here for?"

"Yes, I would like to hear."

"You are here to give us information; facts and information which will enable us to do the work that was assigned to us by the House of Representatives, which has duly imposed upon us to investigate reports regarding subversive activities in the United States."

"Well, I am more than willing to cooperate—"

"Now, just a minute—"

"—because I have—I know of some subversive activities in the entertainment industry and elsewhere in this country."

"Mr. Stander, the committee is interested—"

"If you are interested, I can tell you some right now."

"—primarily in any subversive knowledge you have—"

Lionel added, "And I have knowledge of some subversive action."

"—in the overthrow of the government."

"I don't know about the overthrow of the government. The committee has been investigating for fifteen years and so far, hasn't even found one act of violence."

Velde replied, "Now, the record will speak for itself."

"Well, I have been reading the record."

"That is entirely—"

"I know some subversion, and I can help the committee if it is really interested."

"Mr. Stander!"

"I know of a group of fanatics who are desperately trying to undermine the Constitution of the United States by depriving artists and others of life, liberty, and the pursuit of happiness without due process of law. If you are interested in that, I would like to tell you about it. I can tell names, and I can cite instances, and I am one of the first victims of it, and if you are interested in that—and also a group of ex-Bundists, America-Firsters, and anti-Semites—people who hate everybody including Negroes, minority groups, and most likely, themselves."

"Now, Mr. Stander, let me—"

"And these people are engaged in the conspiracy, outside of all legal processes, to determine our very fundamental concepts upon which our entire system of jurist prudence."

"Now, Mr. Stander!"

"And who also—"

"Let me tell you this. You are a witness before this committee—"

"Well, if you are interested—"

"—a committee of the Congress of the United States—"

"—I am willing to tell you.

"—and you are in the same position as any other witness before this committee—"

"I am willing to tell you about these activities—"

"—regardless of your standing in the motion picture world—"

"—which I think, are subversive—"

"—or for any other reason. No witness can come before this committee and insult this committee—"

Lionel asked, "Is this an insult to the committee—"

"—and continue to—"

"—when I inform the committee I know of subversive activities which are contrary to the Constitution?"

"Now, Mr. Stander, unless you begin to answer these questions and act like a witness in a responsible, dignified manner, under the rules of the committee I will be forced to have you removed from this room."

"Well, I—"

"Mr. Stander, may I say—"

"I am deeply shocked, Mr. Chairman."

"Mr. Stander, let me—"

"Let me explain myself. I don't mean to be contemptuous to this committee at all."

"Will you—"

"I want to cooperate with it. You said something—you said you would like me to cooperate with you in your attempt to unearth subversive activities. I began to tell you about them and I am shocked by your cutting me off. You don't seem to be interested in the sort of subversive activities I know about."[2]

As you can plainly see, Lionel Stander was not about to be pushed around. For every ounce they threw his way, he returned a pound. A headline in the New York Times after his testimony read, "Stander Lectures House Red Inquiry."

During the course of his interrogation on that April day in 1953, Lionel often made it quite clear how he felt about the entire process. At one point, when he was asked if he thought he had been duped, he replied, "I am not a dupe, or a dope, or a moe, or a schmoe. I was absolutely conscious of what I was doing and I am not ashamed of anything I said in public or private. I don't want to be responsible for a whole stable of informers, stool pigeons and psychopaths and ex-political heretics who come in here beating their breast and say, 'I'm awfully sorry. I didn't know what I was doing. Please—I want absolution. Get me back into pictures'."[3]

His comment was an obvious reference to Artie Shaw, who had broken down in tears on the stand two days earlier. Here is an interesting side note: both Lionel and Artie had had their share of personal problems. Before all was said and done each of them had been married six times with limited success. That is where the parallel ends. In reality, they were as different as day and night.

At another time during his long testimony, Lionel made clear as a bell his opinion of the panel. "My estimation of this committee is that this committee arrogates judicial and punitive powers which it does not possess. Testifying is like the Spanish Inquisition. You may not be burned, but you can't help coming away a little singed."[4]

By the end of his life in 1994, Lionel had credited roles in just under seventy pictures. You can only wonder what that number would have come to if he had been allowed to practice his trade without interruption. He may have been outspoken, but he was never what could be termed as disloyal or subversive in any way, shape, or form.

Chapter Thirty-Two
Marsha Hunt

Citations:

Amicus Curiae Brief - Signer - Petition to Supreme Court to review the conviction of Lawson and Trumbo

Stop Censorship Committee - Speaker by recording - Rally - Hotel Astor

Hollywood Independent Citizens Committee of the Arts, Sciences and Professions - Signer - Statement protesting Tenney's attack on John Garfield and Lewis Milestone

Progressive Citizens of America - Speaker - Rally against House Un-American Activities Committee and in honor of the "Hollywood Ten" - Shrine Auditorium - Los Angeles

Committee for the First Amendment - Member

Statement Protesting House Un-American Activities Committee - Signer

Stop Censorship Committee - Participant - Rally against Cunningham Bill - New York City

 Marsha Hunt did everything correctly and above-board throughout her long life, but that did not prevent her from running amock of the dreadful rumor-mongers at *Red Channels*.
 Marsha was born into good circumstances in Chicago, but while she was still quite young, she and her family relocated to New York. He father was a successful attorney and her mother was a voice teacher/accompanist who gave early impetus to the di-

rection of Martha's life. At the age of three, Marsha was already drawn to thoughts of acting for a living.

She attended PS 9 in New York City, followed by the Horace Mann School for Girls and the Theodora Irving Dramatic School. During that period, she was a regular performer in school plays and at church functions. After high school, she did some work as a singer on radio and as a model for the John Powers Agency. Powers models were in big demand in those days. It would be no stretch of the imagination to say that she was then, and still is, an actress of note.

In 1934, at the still tender age of seventeen, Marsha and her older sister decided to give Hollywood a chance. At eighteen, she inked a contract with Paramount Pictures, where she made her film debut in *The Virginia Judge*. When that contract ran its course, she signed with Metro-Goldwyn-Mayer in 1937. She appeared on the silver screen in fifty-two movies between 1935 and 1949, an average of 3.5 per year, a lot of hard work by any standard.

By 1947, the outlook in Hollywood was becoming more grim day by day. The movie industry in general was being accused of perpetrating Communist ideals in the work they turned out. It was time to do something about this train of thought before it got out of control and completely destroyed some of the people involved in filmmaking.

On October 27, 1947, a group of about thirty movie people—there would have been more, but those currently in production could not go—got on a plane and flew to Washington, DC to hold press conferences and to attend some sessions of the HUAC hearings to see for themselves first-hand what was going on. They called themselves "The Committee for the First Amendment," and included many big names from show business, including Humphrey Bogart, Lauren Bacall, and Danny Kaye. Marsha was among them, as well as Evelyn Keyes. The whole affair had been organized by John Huston, William Wyler, and Philip Dunne, none of whom had any Communist connections.

After sitting in on a couple of days of hearings, the group was appalled at what they had witnessed, but they were not permitted to speak with anyone in control.

Upon returning to the west coast, all of the participants found that things had changed for them as far as opportunities to work were concerned. Some of them expressed regret for having gone. Marsha was not one of those. She could not believe that some had reneged, even though she understood their reasoning.

To further explain Marsha's tale of troubles and travails, let me refer to an interview she did with Glen Lovell a few years ago. He asked her about the effects of *Red Channels* on her career:

"Let's go back to June 1950, and the publication of the so-called Bible of the graylist, *Red Channels*."

Marsha said, "Oh gosh. Well, that ended my career. *Red Channels* came out in the summer, while—how's this for irony—I was in Paris being invited to dinner with Eleanor Roosevelt. *Red Channels* was concerned entirely with the broadcast field. The film industry had its own list of victims. *Red Channels* included me because I had been offered my own television talk show. I had beginner's luck on television, being, as you can see, very voluble. While my husband, Robert, and I were in Europe, I was branded a 'particularly suspect citizen' by *Red Channels*. When we returned, the offers vanished; just mysteriously vanished. I called my agent and said, 'I'm back you know. How are things?' He said, 'Haven't you heard?' Then he told me, and that was the first time I'd heard of *Red Channels*. They had listed several affiliations under my name—some I'd never heard about, complete lies. One, I think, had me attending a peace conference in Stockholm. I had never been to Stockholm, or to a peace conference. The rest were innocent activities that *Red Channels* viewed with suspicion. *Red Channels*, I think, is what sealed my fate."

"How bad was the news for you personally?"

"A few offers leaked through, although Stanley Kramer's *The Happy Time* was the only major film that was offered once the blacklist took hold. Before shooting began, I was in Seattle on tour in a play when my agent phoned me. He said the studio had received protests to my being cast in the film, and now they insisted that I sign a prepared statement or they would have to cancel my contract. In that statement, I must swear to my non-Communism, past and present, and vow my fervent anti-Communism from then on. It was full of mea culpa and what an innocent dupe I had been of Communists who had secretly masterminded the Washington flight, which I regretted with all my heart. I said, 'But that's not true! The flight was conceived by Willie Wyler, John Huston, and Philip Dunne, none of them a Communist. I can't sign and swear to what I know to be a lie.' My agent said, 'Well, then they'll break your contract, and you won't be in that or any other film.'

"I had just returned from a radio broadcast, selling US Savings Bonds as a public service for my country, only to hear by phone that I was suspected of being disloyal and perhaps even a traitor. After some pacing, I asked myself, *Well, what can I swear to? What can I say that would be the truth?* Then, I wrote out a statement expressing my pride and affection for my country's form of government, and saying that the flight to Washington had been a protest against the maligning of a good and patriotic film industry. I called my agent and said, 'Please get someone to take down what I've just written.' It was presented to Kramer's legal department, and they accepted it."[1]

Unfortunately, that was not the end of her troubles. Marsha continued to be called upon for meetings with an unnamed studio executive, who told her they were still getting protest letters from various American Legion posts around the country and also several other organizations threatening to picket the film if she was in it. She was asked again to sign all sorts of anti-Communist affidavits and to take out full page ads in *Variety* and *The Hollywood Reporter*. She responded, "I'll tell you what. If any of those shadowy groups want to step forward and accuse me of some wrong, I will answer, but I am not gratuitously going to take out a full page ad and beat my breast and shout, 'I'm not! I'm not! I never was!' Let somebody call me a Communist or charge me with subversive activities. Then I'll answer. I'm not going to fight shadows."[2]

Glen asked, "You were blacklisted—sorry, do you prefer graylisted?"

Marsha answered, "These shadings are beyond me. I was denied work, and I know I must have been on the list that the studios and networks consulted before they hired anyone. If that's black or gray or charcoal, it doesn't really matter. The result is the same."[3]

At another time, Glen asked her, "How long were you blacklisted? When did it end for you?"

Marsha replied, "Never really, never fully. I can't say that it never ended, but the momentum was never recaptured. I had a thriving, ongoing career. I made fifty-some movies before the dark ages. Since 1950, I've made about eight."[4]

Glen later asked, "After what you've been through, I can understand why it might take a lot to rattle you."

"The blacklist was an unhappy chapter in my life. When I did my book, *The Way We Wore*, which is principally about the styles of the 1930s and 1940s, I decided also to depict the era and the public mood. Now, having put it all down on paper, I suppose I have pulled the cork out of the bottle, and I seem to be approached again and again on the subject, which is curious because I was never subpoenaed. I was never a Communist. I was never a figure of public controversy. I just stopped working."[5]

To her everlasting credit, Marsha never changed or pretended to be anything she was not. Her leanings always were, and still are, very liberal. During the 1960s, when she was semi-retired from show business, she worked for many good causes, such as UNICEF, The March of Dimes, The Red Cross, and all sorts of civil rights issues. In 1983, she was made Honorary Mayor of Sherman Oaks, California, and later she served on the advisory board of the San Fernando Valley Community Mental Health Center.

She always was, and still is, a person to be admired, not discredited.

Chapter Thirty-Three
José Ferrer

Citations:

American Committee for Protection of Foreign Born - Sponsor

Artists Front to Win the War - Sponsor

Joint Anti-Fascist Refugee Committee - Program Chairman - Spanish Refugee Appeal benefit - Ziegfeld Theatre - New York City - Speaker - "Salute to Republican Spain" - Madison Square Garden

National Council of the Arts, Sciences and Professions - Sponsor - Committee to abolish HUAC - Sponsor of New York Council, "Theatre Pre-Conference"—vice chairman of New York State Council.

Scientific and Cultural Conference for World Peace - Sponsor

May Day Parade, 1946 - Affiliated

American Committee for Spanish Freedom - Sponsor - Letterhead

American Relief for Greek Democracy - Sponsor - Letterhead

Independent Citizens Committee of the Arts, Sciences and Professions -

Chairman, theatre division

National Wallace for President Committee - Member

Win the Peace Conference - Sponsor

Citizens Non-Partisan Committee for Re-Election of Benjamin J. Davis - Sponsor - Artists, Writers and Professions division.

Negro Labor Victory Committee - Entertainer - Madison Square Garden Rally

Veterans of the Abraham Lincoln Brigade - Sponsor

There were not many of those accused of Communist ties that were later honored by the very government and the same people that had previously made life so tedious for them. One of those few was José Ferrer. In 1985, he was invited to the White House, where he received the National Medal for the Arts. It was presented to him by President Ronald Reagan, a man who had seriously opposed him in the 1950s. More recently, in 2012, his image was featured on a United States postage stamp as a part of their Distinguished Americans series.

During his long career on the stage, in movies, and on radio and television, he received many accolades from his peers. He was awarded several Tony Award's, including one for his portrayal of Cyrano de Bergerac, a role he later repeated in the film version, for which he earned an Oscar. He was the first Puerto Rican and the first Hispanic to win that prize. He donated that golden statute to the University of Puerto Rico where it still resides today. If you know anything about the Academy Award system you know that being nominated is almost as prestigious as winning. He was so named for his work in *Moulin Rouge* (1952), a very testing part. He was enrolled in the American Theatre Hall of Fame for his directing skills for three successful Broadway plays, *The Shrike*, *My Three Angels*, and *The Andersonville Trial*.

Does that sound like someone we should fear? The answer is a definite no. He was born in San Juan, Puerto Rico, into a fairly well-to-do family. Today, his remains are interred in Old San Juan. It was a connection he never forgot. José was a well-educated man, beginning his higher education at the Institut le Rosey in Switzerland and finishing with a degree from Princeton.

In 1950, prior to the release of the movie *Cyrano de Bergerac*, he was beginning to see the writing on the wall. He took out full page ads in several publications to disassociate himself from his alleged past. He pleaded bad memory and naiveté. He said that he had very recently found out that May Day was a Communist celebration. He also admitted that he had backed Benjamin J. Davis, Jr. in his run for the New York City Council, not knowing at the time that he was a Communist. José said that he helped raise funds for Spanish refugees merely due to his roots.

When he was later asked why he signed on to anniversary greetings to the Moscow Arts Theatre in 1948, he said: "When I see something endorsed by the AF of L, of which I am a member, and the CIO; when I see Eleanor Roosevelt's or Fiorello LaGuardia's name, I drop my guard and say, 'Yes, I think it's safe to go along with these people.' I have been wrong time and again."[1]

On May 22 and 23, 1951, José got his chance to speak out about how he remembered some of the past events. You will notice that he often referred to his short memory of all sorts of things, a tactic he had been advised to use by his attorney, Abe Fortas, a man who, from 1965 until 1968, sat on the bench of the United States Supreme Court. His tactic worked to some degree, keeping the panel somewhat in the dark as to his intentions.

The committee for those hearings was chaired by John Wood, and consisted of Bernard Kearney, Donald Jackson, Francis Walter, and Morgan Moulder among others. Also present, serving as committee counsel, was Frank Tavenner. Tavenner asked him about his support of a statement asking for the abolishment of the HUAC and about a speech he made to over one hundred writers after the 1947-1948 Tenney hearings chaired by J. Parnell Thomas. The Tenney hearings were the west coast version of the HUAC.

José said, "I feel a certain amount of disproval of the way Mr. Thomas conducted the hearings."

Tavenner replied, "I did not ask you that question with the idea of indicating that you did not have the right to oppose this committee."

"I know you didn't, Mr. Tavenner. I know you didn't."[2]

You will notice that José really did not answer the question, which led to frustration for the committee. Tavenner then showed him an article from the *Daily Worker* that listed alleged members of the Communist Party:

José responded, "I am sorry to say, Mr. Tavenner, that this does not refresh my memory. I repeat that among these people are many people I know, whom I have worked with, and it is possible, even probable that I did allow the use of my name, but I cannot, in all honesty, say that I remember doing so."

Kearney said, "I would like to direct your attention, Mr. Ferrer, to the letter that the chairman spoke earlier about, under the date of May 21, 1951, directed to him, of which I believe all members of the committee received a copy."

José responded, "Mr. Tavenner just asked me about that, Mr. Kearney, and I told him that when I am now asked under oath, do I remember? I cannot honestly say I do remember. The reason I wrote this was—and I still say it was careless on my part—was that I come here to testify before you gentlemen assuming that most of the charges leveled at me are true."

Kearney asked, "Is this true?"

"I also permitted my name to be used in support of the candidacy of Benjamin J. Davis, Jr. as councilman of New York City. I don't remember, but I say it probably was, Mr. Kearney. Under oath, I don't want to say it was. For the purpose of brevity and simplicity, in this letter, I said it was true."

"We want to know if it was true."

"I can't honestly, completely say it was true."

"This letter was written two days ago."

"Yes."

"A lot of matters you testified about occurred in 1942, 1943, 1944, and 1945."

"Yes."

"Here, only two days ago, you stated definitely that you permitted your name to be used to further the candidacy of Benjamin Davis as councilman of New York City."

"Yes, sir."[3]

They went round and round without getting anywhere. A little later, Kearney asked him about his participation in a May Day parade.

"Mr. Ferrer, do you want this committee to believe that during all the years you lived in New York City, that you never knew that May Day was the Communist day in the city of New York and all over the nation?"

"I would like them to believe, but even if they don't, it is the truth."[4]

Toward the end of the second session on May 23, 1951, Donald Jackson took over the questioning:

He asked, "I don't believe you are a member, but I do believe you have given aid and comfort to the Communist Party."

"I wrote a letter to this committee offering all of my records and checks. I had an informal hearing before appearing formally, at my request. I have done my very best to help you. I believe in what you want to do. I am against the Communist Party. I don't want it. And however negligent I have been, my actions have never been other than Anti-Communist and Pro-American."

"I think that is a splendid statement."

"It is also true, Mr. Jackson."

"Splendid and probably true. I would have carried twice as much conviction a year ago as it carries today when your presence before this committee follows the service of a subpoena. I very frankly cannot place credence in some of the statements you have made."

"That I have just made?"

"No, in your testimony."

"In other words—I perjured myself?"

"That, I did not say. I say I can't place credence in some of the things you have said. This is as much my constitutional right as the constitutional privilege claimed by some of the witnesses refusing to testify."

"I am not questioning your constitutional rights."

Jackson said, "That is all."

Kearney then asked, "Mr. Ferrer, have you ever known an individual who was a member of the Communist Party?"

"I don't know him to be a member of the Communist Party, Mr. Kearney."

"Anyone?"

"At the time I did not know him to be."

"Have you ever known anyone to be?"

"I now know Mr. Davis is a member of the Communist Party."

"Any others?"

"I can't think of any at the moment. There may have been. If you tell me that Mr. (Howard) DaSilva is a member of the Communist Party, I know him. I know Mr. (Will) Geer, but I've never known them as members of the Communist Party."

Kearney said, "That is all."

Jackson said, "I think the record should show that I did not say that Mr. DaSilva and Mr. Geer were members of the Communist Party."

José replied, "I said, if you did say."

Moulder said, "This may be repetition. Are you now or have you ever been a member of the Communist Party?"

"No."

"Have you ever been sympathetic to Communist subversive activities?"

"No, sir."[5]

As you can see, it was a constant battle over semantics that was waged. To his credit, José never mentioned any names as members of the Communist Party with the exception of Ben Davis. In his case, his membership was common knowledge. José also never relied on the Fifth Amendment protection because he did not feel the need to do so. Overall, he acquitted himself quite well, maintaining his dignity at all times. That was not an easy feat under the circumstances.

Shortly after the hearings in 1952, his newest movie, *Moulin Rouge*, was released to rave reviews. That did not set well with the folks at the American Legion. They began picketing theatres where ever the picture played. José was the star and John Huston was the director.

What the Legion people did not realize was that Roy Brewer, a noted labor boss and clearance expert, had been working closely with both men to rid their names of suspicion. Two things happened to change their warped thinking process. First, they saw Mr. Brewer attending a screening of the movie in Los Angeles, and second, José made a speech criticizing Paul Robeson. At that point, the Communist Party USA attacked Ferrer. Consequently, the picketing ceased.

Chapter Thirty-Four
John Garfield

Citations:

American Committee for Yugoslav Relief - Sponsor

Civil Rights Congress - Sponsor

Hollywood Democratic Committee - Executive board member

Soviet Russia Today - Issued statement in support of USSR

Theatre Arts Committee - Member - Executive board

American Friends of the Chinese People - Chairman - Rally

American - Soviet Friendship Rally - Sent greetings - 1944

Progressive Citizens of America - Speaker - "Keep America Free Rally - NYC - 1947

Conference of American - Soviet Friendship - Speaker - 1943

China Aid Council - Sponsor - Hollywood branch - 1941

Motion Picture Artists Committee - Member - Executive board

Russian War Relief, Inc. - Endorser

Hollywood Community Radio Group - Stockholder

Medical Bureau of North American Committee to Aid Spanish Democracy - Endorser

Konstantin Simonov - Was among guests invited to a party on a Russian ship off Long Beach, California to honor Konstantin Simonov, the well-known Soviet writer - 1946

National Council of the Arts, Sciences and Professions - Sponsor - Committee to abolish HUAC

Stop Censorship Committee - Speaker by recording - Rally - Hotel Astor

Amicus Curiae Brief - Signer - Petition to review conviction of Trumbo and Lawson

American League for Peace and Democracy - Sponsor - Japan boycott

Statement of American Progressives on the Moscow Trials - Signer

Named in FBI Reports - FBI Reports, taken by Judith Coplon from Department of Justice files, were read into the record at her trial in Washington, DC. One of these reports identified John Garfield as having been praised by the Comintern

Marshall Plan - Stated, "The Marshall Plan is killing Communism in Europe—and that's good"

   This is the sad story of a man whose life ended much too soon. John Garfield was the son of Russian Jewish immigrant parents, and he was born into poverty in a lower-east side tenement in New York City. His birth name was Jacob Garfinkle, but while still an infant, Julius was added as his middle name. This is significant because, during most of his life, his friends and colleagues always called him Julie.

   When he was only seven, John's mother passed away and he was left to be handed on to any number of equally poor relatives in Brooklyn, The Bronx, and Queens, so he never had a real chance to call anywhere home during his developing years. When he got to school age, he decided that that was not for him, so he cut out every chance he got. Consequently, he was expelled no less than three times. This all led him to spending most of his time on the streets of some pretty seedy neighborhoods where he learned, in his own words, "All the meanness, all the toughness it's possible for a kid to acquire." The inevitable result of this pattern was John's membership in several different street gangs and eventual leadership.

Then something good happened. At thirteen, John's father enrolled him at PS 45 in the East Bronx in a sort of last ditch effort to get his life turned in a more positive direction. PS 45 was no ordinary school; it was the next step to detention without walls, but it was also a very progressive institution, where the kids were allowed to develop according to their own abilities and talents.

The director, Dr. Angelo Patri, took a particular interest in John because he saw something special about him. As time went on, he became more mentor than teacher. Dr. Patri spotted an ability to mimic performers in the youngster, both physically and vocally, so he helped him in those early steps into the dramatic arts. By 1930, he was a full-fledged working actor on the New York stage.

In 1934, he joined the Group Theatre, a collection of actors, writers, producers, and directors, who emulated the style of Constantin Stanislavsky at the Moscow Arts Theatre. Stanislavsky was the father of what was later to be called "Method Acting," a technique of using truly felt emotion rather than artifice to portray a character, thus bringing the stage to a more natural level, closer to reality. This was a near perfect fit for John's smoldering ability to project feelings. Later on, he was often referred to as "The Jewish Brando." He was the rebellious forerunner of people like Marlon Brando and James Dean.

There came a time when he was asked to do a screen test for Warner Bros. in Hollywood. He refused their overtures, preferring to remain on the stage. It all changed when Clifford Odets wrote *Golden Boy* specifically with John in mind. When he was passed over for the lead, he opted to go for the screen test he had earlier refused.

Over the next thirteen years, he appeared in thirty-one movies, most of them at Warner Bros. He had an unusual contract with them that allowed him to return to the stage every other year. It was a hard-fought battle to get that clause included in his contract because it was rarely done in those days. Warner Bros. was the ideal place for him because they, unlike other studios, handled real-life themes rather than pure entertainment.

On April 13, 1951, his testimony before the HUAC proved to be less than helpful to his cause, and ended his screen career. He was uncooperative and tended to be vague, indefinite, and inconclusive. He often employed memory lapse, the same tactic used by José Ferrer. He said that he did recall having had a drink on a ship off Long Beach with Konstantin Simonov, a Russian playwright, who had been invited to the United States by the State Department. He admitted to no memory of having introduced Paul Robeson at a dinner for the Joint Anti-Fascist Refugee Committee. He refused to name any names, saying that he did not know any Communists, past or present, in Hollywood.

Frank Tavenner began the questioning innocently enough by asking John his name and his occupation, but it was not long before he got into deeper water:

Tavenner began, "Mr. Garfield, after you were served with a subpoena to appear before this committee as a witness, the *New York Times* carried a statement attributed to you which is as follows: 'I have always hated Communism. It is a tyranny which threatens our country and the peace of the world. Of course then, I have never been a member of the Communist Party or a sympathizer with any of its doctrines. I will be pleased to cooperate with the committee.' Were you correctly quoted in the news article which I have just read?"

John replied, "Absolutely."

Tavenner asked, "Is it a fact that you have always hated Communism, as stated in the news release?"

"Absolutely, yes."

"Are you of the opinion and belief that Communism is a tyranny which threatens our country and the peace of the world?"

"I believe so. I think it is a subversive movement and is a tyranny and is a dictatorship and is against democracy."

"Have you ever been a member of the Communist Party?"

"I have never been a member of the Communist Party!"

"If you are willing to cooperate with this committee it will be necessary to ask you questions relating to your knowledge of Communist activities in the field, and especially about your own conduct in connection with organizations to which you have belonged and as to experiences which you have had. I understand you are willing to cooperate with the committee?"

John concluded, "I will answer any question you put to me."[1]

John did answer most of the questions, but not necessarily the way they wanted him to:

Tavenner said, "I have before me the December 10, 1936 edition of the *Daily Worker*, which has a column in it entitled 'A YCL Drama Against War' and a sub-heading entitled 'League Plans Gigantic Pageant for Lenin Memorial.' In the course of the article appears a statement that 'Jules Garfield of the Group Theatre is lending a hand in the promotion of the program.' The program, of course, was a Young Communist League program. Will you examine it and state whether or not you did participate in any way, lending your influence or help to the organization of that program by the Young Communist League of New York?"

"I have no knowledge of lending my name in this organization, particularly an organization called the Young Communist League, because; believe me, if I had heard such a name I would have run like hell. I have absolutely no knowledge of this; none whatever."[2]

Tavenner went on a little later to ask him about his connections with the Group Theatre. He was obviously leading up to something. "While you were a member of the Group Theatre, did anything occur to you to lead you to believe that there was Communist activity within the Group in the form of an effort to influence its action or the way in which it operated?"

John replied, "It was purely run on an artistic basis. Of course, the actors on Broadway used to call us peculiar because we didn't accept employment on the outside, and took much less money than we usually would get because we wanted to work in a certain way. They thought that was kind of strange."[3]

Tavenner was leading up to naming names. He questioned John about the summer camps the Group ran. "Do you recall any occasions when, at those camps, people were brought in who attacked the principals of our form of government?"

"I do not, sir. I do recall that one or two of the directors had just come from Moscow where they had seen the Moscow Art Theatre, and they talked about that. That is my best recollection. It is pretty long ago."

"What were the circumstances which led to your going to Hollywood?"

"Well, I had turned down Hollywood for five years. Then I was promised the lead in a play. It is a very personal story, but I don't mind telling you. I had a falling out with some of the directors in the Group on the basis of the part I was supposed to get and didn't get, so I was a little angry and signed a contract. Warner Brothers signed me at that time."

"Were you acquainted with Harold Clurman?"

"He was one of the directors of the Group Theatre."

"What part did he play in your going to Hollywood?"

"He was against my going to Hollywood. He wanted me to stay with the Group Theatre."[4]

John was then asked about several specific people, some of whom he knew only by name and others not at all. As hard as Tavenner tried to get John to incriminate these people, he got little or no satisfaction from him. "Were you associated at any time in a business way with Hugo Butler?"

John answered, "He was a writer."

"Were you associated with him at any time in the production of a picture?"

"Yes, yes, yes."

"What picture was that?"

"A picture called *He Ran All the Way*, just recently, six or eight months ago."

"Do you have any knowledge or information to cause you to believe that he was a member of the Communist Party?"

"None whatsoever. The only relationship I had with him was purely on a craft basis, the picture and the writing of the script."

"Are you acquainted with Herbert Biberman?"

"I know him casually. I didn't socialize with him."

"Did he at one time endeavor to get you to endorse an advertisement to Open the new Front Now—that program?"

"Can you tell me what year that was?"

Tavenner replied, "I should have said Second Front instead of New Front. It was the period along the latter part of 1942."

John said, "In other words, you mean the Russians! In other words, the period we were allies with the Russians?"

"Yes."

"I don't specifically remember it, but I certainly felt, as everyone felt, that the Russians were our allies, and therefore we tried to help them as much as possible.

Tavenner: I am not asking you about your views. I am asking about what Biberman did, if you recall."

"I don't know. I couldn't answer that."[5]

Toward the end of the two-day marathon of questions, Congressman Donald L. Jackson from California finally decided he had heard enough. He tried to pin John down. "You contend that during the seven and a half years or more that you were in Hollywood and in close contact with a situation in which a number of Communist cells were operating on a week-to-week basis, with electricians, actors and every class represented, that during the entire period of time you were in Hollywood you did not know of your own personal knowledge a member of the Communist Party?"

John said, "Absolutely correct."

"Have you been approached to assist at Communist Party functions or functions of Communist front organizations when you knew they were front organizations?"

"I would have run like hell!"

"One more question. I have before me a letter from the National Council of the Arts, Sciences and Professions which states, 'The Eighty-first Congress has a primary obligation to protect the civil rights of the American people. For years now the constitutional rights, the reputations, the jobs, and the private lives of many of our citizens have been recklessly attacked by the irresponsible Committee on Un-American Activities. This committee has been denounced by the President, by members of Congress, and by American leaders throughout the country. In its hearings it has failed to observe the most basic concept of Anglo-Saxon law. It has consistently used headline scare tactics to intimidate and to induce an atmosphere of fear and repression which is repugnant to our most precious American traditions. Its entire history has been one of flagrant violation of common decency and human liberty and has been an affront to one of the greatest institutions in our democracy—The American Congress. The Eighty-first Congress can and must abolish the Committee on Un-American Activities. We urge immediate action toward this end.' You are listed as one of a number of signers. Did you or did you not sign it?"

"I don't recall signing it."

"You do not recall signing it?"

"I do not recall signing it."

"Do you subscribe to the statements made in the letter?"

"No."

"You repudiate the statements made in the letter?"

"Yes."

"That is all, Mr. Chairman."[6]

In a final assessment of his political position, John made a brief statement, "When I was originally requested to appear before the committee, I said that I would answer all questions, fully and without reservations, and that is what I have done. I have nothing to be ashamed of and nothing to hide. My life is an open book. I was glad to appear before you and talk to you. I am no Red. I am no Pink. I am no fellow traveler. I am a Democrat by politics, a liberal by inclination, and a loyal citizen of this country by every act of my life."[7]

The committee persevered, turning the file over to the FBI, looking for grounds to charge John with perjury.

His good friend, Walter Bernstein, did not like what he saw. He said, "John's face was lined and drawn. He had the face of a Bar Mitzvah boy gone just wrong enough to enhance his appeal. He seemed old without growing into it. He still saw his friends, no matter their politics. He was loyal to what he still believed. He thwarted them all by dying."[8]

At an early age, John had contracted Scarlet Fever, which left him with permanent damage to his heart. At the young age of thirty-nine, not long after his HUAC appearance, he suffered a fatal heart attack.

All his life, he never did anything to subvert our constitution. His actions were always based on his care for his fellow man and should have been protected by the Bill of Rights.

In a final unpublished statement he titled, "I was a sucker for a left hook," he professed his belief that he had, at times, been duped by what he had considered a good cause.

Chapter Thirty-Five
Orson Welles

Citations:

American Committee for Protection of Foreign Born - Affiliated

Russian War Relief - Signer - Appeal - "These Eminent Americans Ask Your Help on Behalf of the Russian People"

American Student Union - Affiliated

Artist's Front to Win the War - Presided - meeting at Carnegie Hall

Citizens Committee for Harry Bridges - Sponsor

Coordinating Committee to Lift the Embargo - Affiliated

National Citizens Political Action Committee - Member

Daily Worker - Contributor

Exiled Writers Committee - Affiliated

Friends of the Abraham Lincoln Brigade - Affiliated

Hollywood Democratic Committee - Candidate for office on Executive Board

Motion Pictures Artists' Committee - Member

International Labor Defense - Affiliated

Joint Anti - Fascist Refugee Committee - Sponsor - "The Century of the Common Man"

League of American Writers - Signed call - Fourth American Writers Congress

National Council of American - Soviet Friendship - Speaker - Three Day Congress - Hotel New Yorker

Negro Cultural Committee - Member

New Masses - Affiliated

Theatre Arts Committee - Member - Executive Board

Sleepy Lagoon Defense Committee - Sponsor

Medical Bureau to Aid Spanish Democracy - Patron - Benefit performance and dance

Orson Welles was a native Midwesterner born in Kenosha, Wisconsin, where he lived his formative years, and also in Chicago. Although he spent most of his life in New York, Hollywood, and Europe, he always claimed middle America as his roots.

Ironically, in 1946, he seriously contemplated a run for the U.S. Senate representing Wisconsin, a seat that ended in the hands of none other than Joseph McCarthy.

Some of Orson's productions brought him into conflict with the folks at *Counterattack, Red Channels,* and other red-baiting people and organizations, beginning with *Panic* (1933), produced when Orson was still in his teens.

The producer, John Houseman, had been considering either Paul Muni or Edward G. Robinson, both actors with much more experience, for the lead role of McGafferty, a man in his late fifties. However, having seen Orson play an older character in *Romeo and Juliet,* his mellow voice and his ability to deliver poetic lines sold John on his decision to cast Orson. This began a long and often stormy relationship between the two men

Panic, written by Archibald MacLeish, followed a Wall Street power broker (McGafferty), who had been victimized by the stock market crash in 1929. The play lasted through just three performances at the Imperial Theatre in New York. It received mixed reviews including one that said it displayed Marxist thinking, expressing the political consciousness of the Communist Party. In all the reviews, Orson was praised for his work. Here is a small sample of the dialogue as spoken by McGafferty:

> "You think this creeping ruin is a shadow!
> You think its chance that the banks go one by one
> Closing the veins as cold does—killing secretly—
> The country dying of it—towns dead—land dead—
> Hunger limping every road—you think it's
> Chance that does it? You think? So did I!
> I do not think so now. I think they wish it.
> We cannot see them, but they're there: they loom."[1]

In 1936, both Orson and Houseman were working on an adaptation of an old French farce, *The Italian Straw Hat,* for the Federal Theatre Project (FTP) that was sponsored by our government as part of the WPA. The play had been partially translated and modified by Orson under the title *Horse Eats Hat.* At that time, the FTP and its leader, Halle Flanagan, were feeling a great deal of pressure from would-be patriots. For example, Harrison Grey Fiske wrote in *The Saturday Evening Post,* "The Federal Theatre's hair is full of Communists. They represent the Communist International program for this country. They find inspiration in the fact that Mrs. Flanagan cherishes the ambition to Russianize our theatre, to transform it into the true theatre which reflects the economic forces of modern life. She even invited the cast to tea to discuss Soviet Theatre".[2]

Flanagan shot back, not accepting that premise. "The Federal Theatre is committed to the belief that a people's theatre could be occupied in no better way than by the production of classics. It is no more Marxist than Franklin Delano Roosevelt. They share the belief in the mobilization of labor and to correct the flaws in the Capitalist system."[3]

Harry Hopkins, head of the WPA in the Roosevelt administration, said, "They are for labor, first, last and all the time. WPA is labor—don't forget that."[4]

A couple of years later on August 5, 1938, Halle Flanagan wrote in response to accusations by the Dies Committee, "I wrote to representative Dies asking him to hear me and our regional directors who constituted the National Policy Board. I told him that regional and state offices were waiting to give cooperation to the committee, but as yet no use had been made of available information, while in the meantime a half-dozen witnesses, not one of whom was in any position to know the broad sweep of the project's operation or administration, were making statements, which, as the committee could easily ascertain, were biased, prejudiced and often entirely false."[5]

She received no response, but in a matter of months the FTP was shut down. There is no doubt that there were Communist Party members within the group. Many people joined for their own good reasons that had nothing whatever to do with subversion. Of course, this reflected adversely on all of those involved with the project.

In 1937, Orson and Houseman produced Marc Blitzstein's *The Cradle Will Rock*, a hot potato for everyone involved. It was set in a fictional place, Steeltown, USA, and was about the problems of striking workers. The country was in a state of labor turmoil at that time. The Congress of Industrial Organizations (CIO) was attempting to unionize the steel industry and was met with violent repercussions. At a rally at Republic Steel in Chicago, ten demonstrators were shot to death including several who were shot in the back. In Johnstown, Ohio martial law was declared. The actors cast in *The Cradle Will Rock* were threatened with embargo should the play go on, but both Orson and John felt that the show must go on; the message was too important to be ignored, and they would not bow to governmental pressure.

In the final speech by Howard DaSilva (also blacklisted), playing a character named Larry, he said:

"When you can't climb down and you can't sit still
That's a storm that's going to last until
The final wind blows. And when that wind blows
The cradle will rock!"[6]

In 1938, more controversy arrived for Orson and John, who had by then created The Mercury Theatre and on radio, *The Mercury*

Theatre on the Air. On Halloween night in October 1938, they produced a radio adaptation by Howard Koch (also blacklisted) of H. G. Wells' *The War of the World,* a science fiction fantasy about an invasion from Mars. Those who tuned in late missed the disclaimer that the dramatization was fictional, and they mistakenly believed that the invasion was real. The chaos is well-documented, but as Houseman once told me, there were no long-term financial consequences due to the broadcast. Not one penny was ever paid to settle the many damage suits that were filed.

Elliott Lewis, who was very active in radio then, said that he always wondered why, if the Martians were devastating our planet, how come only CBS knew about it? *Counterattack* would later claim that *The War of the World* led right into the Communist's arms by seeding panic throughout the land.

In December 1938, the *Mercury Theatre on the Air* presented their version of *Danton's Death,* an old German classic that had always met with strong opposition from the time that it was written by Georg Buchner in 1835 until its debut on stage in 1902, long after Mr. Buchner's death. *Danton's Death* was a complicated story set in the time of the French Revolution. The basic theme is the constant battle between Georges Danton and Maximilien Robespierre over the wanton killing of thousands of French citizens.

The odd thing about this play and the reaction to it was that, while it trumpeted the rights of poor downtrodden peasants—the very lifeline of the Communist Party USA—most of the most vehement flack came from them. The Party hardliners felt that *Danton's Death* skated too close to demeaning Trotsky, Lenin, and Joseph Stalin.

Then in 1941, Radio-Keith-Orpheum Pictures (RKO) released Orson's famous *Citizen Kane.* The screenplay was jointly written by Joe Mankiewicz and Orson and was originally meant to be a composite of the lives of Robert R. McCormick (Owner of the *Chicago Tribune*), Howard Hughes, and Joseph Pulitzer. The final script turned out to be a thinly veiled biography of parts of the life of William Randolph Hearst, a man Orson often found himself in conflict with, a tenacious foe of everything liberal. Upon hearing about the movie, Hearst demanded that he be allowed to see it before it could be released. He then ran editorials in all of his newspapers blasting the film, Orson, and RKO. He said he would sue everyone involved if it was released to the public.

The American Legion also got into the act, saying they would lead a boycott against *Citizen Kane*. The pressure exerted against RKO was not enough to prevent limited distribution because there had been far too much money invested in it to set it aside. Hearst continued his crusade, saying that the picture was a Communist attempt to smear him inspired by Orson's close association with the Communist Party.

Citizen Kane was recognized as a masterpiece of innovative technique, (later ranking the lofty #1 position on the American Film Institute's list of fine film work). Hearst's futile attempts to stop distribution proved counterproductive, in effect fanning great interest among potential audiences. Many people may not have gone to see it if Hearst had kept his mouth shut. Nominated for Academy Awards in nine categories, *Citizen Kane* won an Academy Award for Best Writing (Original Screenplay) by Herman J. Mankiewicz and Orson.

During the ensuing years, claims about Orson's political beliefs constantly flew back and forth, led by the Hearst papers, yet Orson's radio audience share doubled after those attacks.[7]

New York Herald Express: "Welles broadcasts are spearheaded by red propaganda."[8]

New York Journal-American: "We must rid the country of every type of subversive propaganda."[7]

Chicago Sunday Times: "If it weren't so sad, it would be silly. William Randolph Hearst is piqued with Orson Welles. The rest is camouflage."[7]

Louella Parsons, the notorious Hollywood gossip columnist, took to openly calling Orson a Marxist. He sued her and easily won his case. He was never a man to let charges go unchallenged.

After the Parson's suit, Orson stated in a press release, "The Hearst papers have repeatedly described me as a Communist. I am not a Communist. I am grateful for our constitutional form of government, and I rejoice in our American tradition of democracy. Needless to say, it is not necessarily unpatriotic to disagree with Mr. Hearst. On the contrary, it is a privilege guaranteed me as an American citizen by the Bill of Rights. I want to say I am proud of my American citizenship. As a citizen I cherish my rights, and I am not fearful of uncertainty. I only ask that I be judged by what I am and what I do."[8]

The FBI opened a file on Orson that would not be closed until the very late 1950s.

John Houseman always maintained that he and Orson were apolitical and that they chose their material for artistic value only.

Much of what Orson accomplished was blown out of proportion by his high profile and huge ego, yet he was an artist in every sense of the word, and he was a survivor.

Chapter Thirty-Six
Edward G. Robinson

Citations:

American Committee for the Protection of Foreign Born - Sponsor

Civil Rights Congress - Initiator

National Citizens Political Action Committee - Member

National Democratic Committee - Member - Executive board

National Council of American Soviet Friendship - Affiliated

Soviet Russia Today - Red army anniversary dinner

Progressive Citizens of America - Candidate - Executive board

American Council for Yugoslav Relief - Sponsor

American Russian Institute - Participant - Conference on American Russian cultural exchange - University of California

Hollywood Independent Citizens Committee of the Arts, Sciences and Professions - Member - Executive Council

Edward G. Robinson was born in Bucharest, Romania, named Emanuel Goldenberg. He was the fifth of six sons. Rules and regulations in Romania at that time were strict in regard to the rights of anyone who happened to be Jewish. They were blocked from all but the lowest e trades. They were also not permitted to get any sort of decent education, and they had no real future in Bucharest. There was not enough money for the whole Goldenberg family to immigrate to America, but by scrimping and saving they were able to buy one ship card for Zach, the eldest son, was the best candidate to use it.

Zach sailed to New York, where he was able to find employment, not a great job, but one that allowed him to send back most of his earnings to purchase another ship card and bring his brother, Jack, to join him.

As time went by, their brother, Oscar, followed, and also their father, Morris. The remainder of the Goldenberg family, Mother Sarah, Grandma, Willie, Max, and Manny (Emanuel), boarded the *La Touraine* bound for New York. Since they were below decks in steerage, they spent most of the voyage seasick, so they were happy to get off the ship when they reached their final destination.

The land of milk and honey where the streets were paved with gold turned out to be anything but. In Romania, the Goldenbergs had been reasonably comfortable, in spite of the restrictions imposed on them, but in the Lower East Side of New York, they found residence only in a Jewish ghetto.

At the age of nine, Manny attended grade school. He could speak Romanian, German, and Yiddish, and could read Hebrew, but English was a total mystery to him. With the aid of understanding teachers, he not only learned English but managed to skip a couple of grades. He attended high school and then the City College of New York. He had become an excellent student.

Because of his interest in theatre, he eventually won a scholarship to the American Academy of Dramatic Arts. While there, his mentors decided that he should have an Anglo-Saxon name if he wanted to succeed in theater work. After some trial and error, they came up with Edward G. Robinson, the G standing for Goldenberg as a tribute to his roots.

In 1931, he got his first real break when he was cast as a ruthless gangster in *Little Caesar*, an image that stuck to him for many years thereafter. His true personality was diametrically opposed to low-life hood characters. He was a soft-spoken, genteel man who was by then fluent in seven languages, and he was a devoted patron of the Arts. His art collections through the years rivaled those of many fine museums. He scoured sources around the globe. Sometimes his lust for art and artists became a financial burden, but he was doing quite well in Hollywood.

He was always a humanitarian. He contributed to any organization that he felt was doing good work, never realizing that some of them were Communist fronts. He did know that they were active in the causes of the deprived put-upon victims of Nazi terror and our own economic unbalance. He lent his name to so many that he could not recall some of them. Many people in Hollywood thought Hitler was all right because he would prevent Communism from spreading. Manny was not one of them.

Edward never considered the fact that his humanitarianism would come crashing down one day, but that day came in the 1940s, when he was cited by the HUAC in Washington, DC and also in California with approximately the same list that later appeared in *Red Channels* in 1950.

In 1947, Edward received an invitation from the *Chicago Herald-American* to appear as one of the speakers at a forum at the Chicago Stadium, a big event that would include the swearing in of 500 new citizens. Then, he was asked not to attend by the same people due to the list put out by the HUAC. When all was said and done, after cooler heads prevailed, he was re-invited.

On May 19, 1947, he delivered his speech at the stadium. Here is a brief excerpt:

> "I love America with that special, special appreciation of millions. I was not born on this American earth, but emigrated here. This country and this people won't fail its destiny. We want every last American to enjoy the fruits of this land, at home, work and education of the children; to worship in a church of his own choosing. Tolerance—Democracy—Rights."[1]

He received the plaudits of the majority and thought the worst was behind him. In truth, his troubles were just beginning. On October 27, 1947, he was called to testify in the hearing room of the HUAC in Washington, DC. Francis Walter was the sitting Chairman at the time. Edward was questioned for hours about each and every organization he had any connection with. Finally, in desperation, he told them, "You are the only tribunal we have in the United States where an American citizen can come and ask for this kind of relief; and after you have looked over this rather exhausting testimony that I have presented to the committee, if you should like any further information, just the same as I have volunteered it to Mr. Hoover, I volunteer it to you. And if you find me innocent I would like to ask that you give these facts to the American people because my name is very dear to me, above everything else. I ask in all sincerity that you do this for me, because this is the most vital thing I have ever faced in my life. I am sorry if I have become a little bit emotional because I think that I have not only been a good citizen and I value this above everything else. I think that I may have taken money under false pretenses in my own business and that I may not have been as good a husband or father or friend as I should have been, but I know my Americanism is unblemished and fine and wonderful. I am proud of it and I don't feel it is conceit on my part to say this. I stand on my record or fall on it."[2]

He believed that only the HUAC could declare that he was not a Communist, but they denied that they could make that determination.

In 1949, the Senate Fact-Finding Committee on Un-American Activities released their fifth report. They said they were engaged in tracking down, taking testimony about, and attacking any person or persons as present or past Communists.

To this, Edward replied, "How can you prove you're not a Communist? Your word obviously means nothing because to belong to a political party that has at its very point the overthrow of the government by force means lying would be the least of your sins.

"I freely confess to all of these charges. What I do not confess to is the constant reiteration of 'A Communist Front,' 'A Communist Party Defense Fund,' or other similar characterizations. I also freely confess that from the start of this attack on me, I refused to believe that anybody would take it seriously.

"I shan't go into the whole history of what I call a witch hunt and others call an effort to rid America of subversive characters. I can only tell you of matters as they appeared to me; how they affected my emotions and my ability to make a living; how they affected my self-esteem."³

On December 21, 1950, Edward again testified before the HUAC. At that time, the main thrust of the questioning was to try to get him to admit he was hoodwinked. They wanted him to say he was a dupe, a sucker, a fool, an idiot, and an unsuspecting agent of the Communist Party USA. He refused to do so because he did not believe that he fit in any of those categories, all of which were insulting to say the least.

Finally, on April 30, 1952, during his third and last session with the HUAC committee, he was heartsick, worn out, and his defenses were down. He gave in, but he never named names. He said, in a very brow-beaten manner, "May I add that of the very many civic, cultural, philanthropic, and political organizations of which I have been a member and a contributor, but a small percentage, I later discovered, were tinged with the taint of Communism. It is a serious matter to have ones loyalty questioned. Life is less dear to me than my loyalty to democracy and the United States. I ask favors of no one. All I ask is that the record be kept straight and that I be permitted to live free of false charges.

"I readily concede that I have been used and that I have been mistaken regarding certain associations, which I regret, but I have never been disloyal or dishonest. I would like to find some way to put to rest the ever recurring innuendos concerning my loyalty. Surely there must be some way for a person falsely accused of disloyalty to clear his name once and for all. It is for this purpose that I come again before this committee to testify under oath. What more can I do? But, I repeat, I acted from good motives and I never knowingly aided Communists or any Communist cause."⁴

Congressman Francis Walter's response was demeaning. "Well, actually, the committee has never had any evidence presented to it to indicate that you were ever anything more than a very choice sucker. I think you are number one on the sucker list in the country."⁵ He then abruptly adjourned the session cutting off any response.

Life was not easy for the Robinsons for a long time. Aside from the loss of his ability to find work, their social life suffered. When they threw a small party due to their reduced income, many of those invited found some phony excuse not to attend for fear that the shadow of Communism would fall on them.

Of course, the worst part was the loss of a regular paycheck. He once explained how repeatedly calling his agent always brought a disquieting response.

Call 1: "Hell, Eddie, I've read a lot of scripts submitted for you and there isn't one right for you. Nothing but the best for you, Eddie, baby. You know that."

Call 2: "Business is in lots of trouble, Eddie, baby, post war adjustment and all that crap. I've got something really hot cooking, believe me, baby."

Call 3: "Eddie, it's not easy at your age; character parts, you know. After all, you're not exactly a baby, are you Eddie?"

Call 4: "There seems to be some opposition to you, Eddie. I'm looking into it. Whatever it is, we'll fight it with every penny we've got. You know that."

Call 5: (Taken by agent's secretary) "I'm sorry, Mr. Robinson, but Mr. B is out of town. I'll give him your message. He'll certainly call you at his earliest convenience."

Call 6: (No earliest convenience ever arrived).[6]

That was a story that could have been told by so many others in show business at the time.

In 1969, Edward was presented with a Life Achievement Award by the Screen Actors Guild, and in 1973, two months after his passing, an Honorary Oscar. At least he got some recognition from his peers for his massive body of work. He had appeared in 101 movies along with his radio and stage work.

Chapter Thirty-Seven
Langston Hughes

Citations:

Poem "Goodbye Christ" - Author - Is referred to as a typical example of vicious and blasphemous propaganda Communists use against religion.

Independent Citizens Committee for the Arts, Sciences and Professions - Affiliated

American League against War and Fascism - Affiliated

American League for Peace and Democracy - Affiliated

American Peace Mobilization - Affiliated

Communist Candidates in Election Campaigns - Supporter

Friends of the Abraham Lincoln Brigade - Affiliated

Veterans of the Abraham Lincoln Brigade - Affiliated

American Labor Party - Affiliated

American Youth for Democracy - Affiliated

Committee for a Democratic Far Eastern Policy - Affiliated

Coordinating Committee to Lift the Embargo - Affiliated

International Labor Defense - Affiliated

Joint Anti-Fascist Refugee Committee - Affiliated

League of American Writers - Signer, official call—Call stated that the League of American Writers would be affiliated with the International Union of Revolutionary Writers

Medical Bureau and North American Committee to Aid Spanish Democracy - Affiliated

National Citizens Political Action Committee - Affiliated

National Committee for the Defense of Political Prisoners - Affiliated

National Negro Congress - Affiliated

New Theatre League - Affiliated

People's Songs, Inc. - Affiliated

School for Democracy - Affiliated

Southern Conference for Human Welfare - Affiliated

Voice of Freedom Committee - Affiliated

Communist Book Shops - Supporter

Communist Party USA National Elections and its Candidates - Signer, Call for support - 1932

Committee of Professional Groups for Earl Browder and James Ford - Affiliated - 1936

League of Professional Groups for William Z. Foster and James Ford - Affiliated

Committee for the Re-election of Benjamin J. Davis - Affiliated - 1945

Reichstag Fire Trial Anniversary Committee - Signer - Declaration honoring Georgi

Dimitrov, General Secretary, Comintern - 1943

Statement by American Progressives on the Moscow Trials - Signer

Open Letter for Closer Cooperation with the Soviet Union - Signer - 1939

Soviet Union - Supporter

National Council of American - Soviet Friendship - Affiliated

Soviet Russia Today - Affiliated

May Day Parade, 1947 - Affiliated

Daily Worker - Affiliated

Mainstream - Affiliated

Midwest Daily Record - Affiliated

New Masses - Affiliated

Scientific and Cultural Conference for World Peace - Sponsor

Langston Hughes, an American poet, social activist, novelist, playwright, and columnist, was an intriguing Black man who, throughout most of his life, did not have to experience the poverty or many of the affronts that usually accompanied poverty. That is not to say that he was never a victim of racial prejudice, at times very deflating and humiliating, but he was more able to overcome most of what was thrown his way.

Langston was born in 1902 in Joplin, Missouri, into an upper middle-class family with a complicated family tree. Both of his great grandmothers were African-American women who had married White slave traders, mixing up his racial background. His maternal grandmother, Mary Patterson Langston, was a product of African-American, English, French, and Native American roots.

When he was still quite young, Langston's father, who was an educator, left the family to go to Cuba and later to Mexico to escape the prejudices that continuously dogged him. His mother then began to travel around looking for work, leaving her young son to be raised by Mary Langston in Lawrence, Kansas. Mary was a strong woman with strong convictions. She had been one of the first female students at Oberlin College in Ohio and had always fought for her civil rights. She instilled that attitude into Langston, a guiding light throughout his life, overwhelming his other emotions.

When his grandmother died, he went to Lincoln, Illinois to rejoin his mother. There, he graduated from grammar school and where he experienced a sort of reverse discrimination. Here, in his words, is what happened:

> "I was a victim of a stereotype. There were only two of us Negro kids in the whole class and our English teacher was always stressing the importance of rhythm in poetry. Well, everyone knows, except us, that all Negroes have rhythm, so they elected me class poet."[1]

Langston attended high school in Cleveland, Ohio, and he wrote for the school paper and was the editor of the school year book. He also began to write short stories, poetry, and some dramatic plays.

After graduating, he went for a while to live with his father in Mexico. It was not the best of times for him, but he wanted to go to Columbia University to study writing. His dad had the financial means to make it happen. The problem was that they had different ideas of what his major should be. His father said he would be glad to back him if he would study engineering, which was too good an opportunity to pass up. Langston knew that in any curriculum there would be room to squeeze in some of the courses he wanted to take. At Columbia, he maintained a B+ average, but he gave up after one year due to racial pressures.

For a couple of years, Langston worked a variety of jobs before he returned to academia to finish his education along the path he really wanted. He earned his degree at Lincoln University in Chester County, Pennsylvania, a well-known Black school.

In 1926, he wrote "The Negro Activist and the Racial Mountain," an article telling the world how he felt, and the article was published by *The Nation*. Here is an excerpt:

> "The younger Negro artists create and intend to express our individual dark-skinned selves without fear or shame. If White people are pleased, we are glad. If they are not, it doesn't matter.

We know we are beautiful and ugly too. The tom-tom cries and the tom-tom laughs. If Colored people pleased, we are glad. If they are not, their displeasure doesn't matter either. We build the temples for tomorrow, strong as we know how, and we stand on top of the mountain free within ourselves."[2]

His reputation as a published writer was growing by leaps and bounds. In 1932, he and some forty other Black Americans were invited to the Soviet Union to make a movie called *Negro Life*. The project was eventually scrapped because the Russians decided it was time to tone down the propagandist rhetoric. During this time, Hughes wrote "Goodbye, Christ," the poem that would later cause him so much anguish. Here are the first two stanzas:

> "Listen, Christ
> You did alright in your day, I reckon-
> But that day's gone now,
> They ghosted you up a swell story, too,
> Called it Bible-
> But it's dead now,
> The popes and the preachers've
> Made too much money from it.
> They've sold you to too many.
>
> "Kings, generals, robbers and killers-
> Even to the Tzar and the Cossacks,
> Even to Rockefeller's Church
> Even to The Saturday Evening Post.
> You ain't no good no more.
> They've pawned you
> Till you've done wore out."[3]

From a first quick reading, you may think the poem was irreverent, but if you take the time to think of the underlying meaning of it you will find it to be exactly the opposite. It is quite simply a statement about how the world had turned a blind eye to the prevailing situation.

A few years later in 1937, Langston traveled to Madrid as a correspondent for the *Baltimore Afro-American* and other Black news outlets. He was a strong supporter of the Republican faction of the Spanish population. While he was not a participant in their movement, he was sympathetic to their cause. This excerpt is from his poem called "Song of Spain":

> "Toros, Flamenco, paintings, books--
> Not Spain
> The people are Spain
> The people beneath that bombing plane
> With its wings of gold for which I pay
> I, a worker, letting my labor pile
> Up millions of bombs to kill a child--
> I bought those bombs for Spain!
> Workers made those bombs for a fascist Spain!
> Will I make them again, and yet again?
> Storm clouds move fast,
> Our sky is gray
> The white devils of the terror
> Await their day
> When bombs'll fall not only on Spain
> But on me and you!
> Workers, make no bombs again!
> Workers, mine no gold again!
> Workers, lift no hand again
> To build up profits for the rape of Spain!
> Workers, see yourselves as Spain!
> Workers, know the we too can cry
> Lift arms in vain, run, hide--die
> Too late!
> The bombing plane!
> Workers, make no bombs again
> Except that they be made for us
> To hold and guard
> Lest some Franco steal into our backyard."[4]

Because of his trips to Russia and Spain, and also because of his constant writing about civil rights here at home, he was ripe for the picking by the red-baiters. Since when can a man not express his thoughts? Is it subversive? I say, emphatically, NO! What ever happened to the Bill of Rights and to freedom of speech? Why should a man have to look over his shoulder after every comment he makes?

When *Red Channels* came out in 1950, Langston had more citations after his name than any other, over forty in all. In almost every case, he was simply listed as an affiliate, which indicates a personal grudge and some heavy-handed piling-on. Most of their claims had no basis in reality.

Secondly, almost all of the organizations on the list were long gone by 1950. During the 1930s, many of his poems and other writings displayed some favoritism to the Soviet way of life, but what was a Black man to think when things were far from good in his native land? He later expressed some regret for having written a few of them. Who among us can say that we have never done anything we lived to regret? If that is a fair criterion, we might all spend some time behind bars.

In 1941, Franklin Roosevelt made his now famous *Four Freedoms* speech. Here is an excerpt from which Hughes replied:

> "The president's Four Freedoms
> Appeal to me
> I would like to see those freedoms
> Come to be
>
> "If you believe
> In the Four Freedoms, too
> Then share 'em with me
> Don't keep 'em all for you.
>
> "Show me that you mean
> Democracy, please
> Cause from Bombay to Georgia
> I'm beat to my knees
>
> You can't lock up Gandhi
> Club Roland Hayes

Then make fine speeches
About freedom's ways

"Looks like by now
Folks ought to know
It's hard to beat Hitler
Protecting Jim Crow

"Freedom's not just
To be won over there
It means freedom at home, too
Now—right here!"[5]

Around the same time, he had more to say about the Jim Crow laws. This excerpt was from "Dixie Man to Uncle Sam":

"How can you
Shake a fist at tyranny
Everywhere else
But here?

"Do you not see?
I, too, in Dixie
Stand in need
Of being free

"Jim Crow's
Too Hitler-like
For you
Or me."[6]

In 1953, Langston was called to testify by the Senate Subcommittee run by Joe McCarthy and his henchman, Roy Cohn. When asked about his political leanings, Langston stated, "I never read the theoretical books on Socialism or Communism or the Democratic or Republican parties, for that matter. So my interest in whatever may be considered political has been non-theoretical, non-sectarian, and largely emotional and born out of my own need to find some way of thinking about the whole problem of myself."[7]

After the session was over, he spoke with Lloyd Garrison, a liberal lawyer, and then sent the following statement to his own attorney. "If you think it wise (and I do) you might send the FBI a copy of the transcript of my testimony for their files, with a brief covering note, since Cohn told us that Hoover once used 'Goodbye, Christ' in a speech, and perhaps should therefore be advised that this no longer represents my views in any way. Lloyd Garrison feels that we might also draw up a brief statement using portions of the transcript of the open hearing to send to the American Legion, who might pass the word down to the red-baiters in their Indianapolis office who've been sending out mimeographed material ala *Red Channels* on a number of writers and artists, to correct the material on me, at least to the extent that it conforms with my sworn testimony. All of my publishers are pleased with the outcome of the hearings, have backed me up beautifully and are going ahead with their publishing plans in relation to my work. But it would do no harm to have a brief resume and interpretation of my testimony on tap, if needed."[8]

Langston was never at any time a member of the Communist Party USA. His main concern was always to seek the promised rights for his own race. When someone asked him directly why he never joined, he declared, "It was based on strict discipline and the acceptance of directives that I, as a writer, did not wish to accept."[9]

In conclusion, allow me to add one more excerpt from one of his 1955 poems, *"Brotherly Love,"* which was written at the height of the red-baiting fiasco and clearly shows how he felt throughout most of his years:

> "In line of what my folks say in Montgomery,
> In line of what they're teaching about love,
> When I reach out my hand, will you take it?
> Or cut it off and leave a nub above?
>
> "If I found it in my heart to love you,
> And if I thought I really could,

If I said, "Brother, I forgive you"
I wonder, would it do you any good.

"So long, so long a time you've been calling
Me all kinds of names, pushing me down--
I been swimming with my head deep under water,
And you wished I would stay under till I drown.

"But I didn't! I'm still swimming! Now you're mad
Because I won't ride in the back of your bus.
When I answer, Anyhow, I'm gonna love you,
Still and yet you want to make a fuss.

"Now listen, white folks!
In line with Reverend King down in Montgomery--
Also because the Bible says I must--
I'm gonna love you—yes I will! OR BUST!"[110]

Chapter Thirty-Eight
The Others

I cannot deal with each and every one of the 151 people listed in *Red Channels* individually in one book so I will just list the others here along with the number of citations each received in brackets following their names. There may be many names that you do not recognize after so many years, but also some that you will know. Each of them made an impact with their particular skills, and each of them suffered, to varying degrees, from the implications that were made.

As you read through the names, I am quite sure you will find some surprises, as you probably have in some of the preceding chapters. Also, as you read through this lengthy catalog of unfair persecution, be aware that the charges against nearly all of them were not—and could not—be substantiated with facts.

Remember too, that *Red Channels* was just one of the many sources used by the blacklisters.

Quotes are word for word directly from *Red Channels*.

Larry Adler - Harmonica player-[13]

Luther Adler - Actor - Stage, screen, radio-[5]

Stella Adler - Actress, director-[12]

Edith Atwater - Actress-[8]

Howard Bay - Scenic designer - President, United Scenic Artists, Local 829 - Brotherhood of Painters, Decorators and Paper Hangers of America-[15]

Ralph Bell - Radio actor-[1]

Michael Blankfort - Writer-[12]

True Boardman - Writer-[2]

Millen Brand - Writer - Screen Writers Guild Award, 1948, as scenarist in the motion picture, *Snake Pit*-[29]

Oscar Brand - Folk singer - Master of ceremonies on folk song program-[6]

J. Edward Blomberg - Actor-[20]

Himan Brown, AKA Hi Brown, Hy Brown - Radio director and producer-[3]

John Brown - Radio actor - Portrayed Mr. Foster on *Date with Judy* - Al on *My Friend Irma*-[2]

Abe Burrows - Humorist - Master of ceremonies on *This is Show Business, We Take Your Word*-[4]

Morris Carnovsky - Actor-[23]

Vera Caspary - Writer, novelist-[8]

Edward Chodorov - Writer - Stage, screen, radio-[21]

Mady Christmas - Actress-[9]

Marc Connelly - Playwright-[11]

Aaron Copeland - Composer, writer-[21]

Howard DaSilva - Actor - Stage, screen-[12]

Roger DeKoven - Actor - Radio-[1]

Dean Dixon - Musician, conductor-[7]

Olin Downes - Music critic of *New York Times*-[26]

Alfred Drake - Actor, singer - *Kiss Me Kate*-[8]

Paul Draper - Dancer-[19]

Clifford J. Durr - Former commissioner, Federal Communications Commission-[9]

Richard Dyer - Bennett - Folk singer-[12]

Louise Fitch - Actress - Radio-[1]

Martin Gabel - Actor, director, producer - Radio, screen, stage-[3]

Arthur Gaeth - News commentator-[6]

William S. Gailmor - Radio news commentator-[7]

Will Geer - Actor - Screen, stage, radio-[11]

Jack Gilford (Guilford) - Actor, comedian - Stage, nightclub-[11]

Tom Glazer - Folk singer and song writer-[3]

Ruth Gordon - Actress, writer-[6]

Lloyd Gough - Actor - Screen, stage, radio-[2]

Morton Gould - Composer of popular music-[12]

Shirley Graham - Poet, writer-[17]

Ben Grauer - Radio announcer - Council member, American Federation of Radio Artists-[5]

Mitchell Grayson - Radio director - instructor, Sarah Lawrence College - Author of radio play, *Labor on the March*-[3]

Horace Grenell - Musician - Children's Record Guild - Formerly president of *Young People's Records*-[8]

Uta Hagen - Actress-[19]

E. Y. (Yip) Harburg - Composer - Stage, screen-[22]

Robert Heller - Radio program director-[6]

Nat Hiken - Comedy writer - Radio and television-[3]

Rose Hobart - Actress - Screen, stage, radio-[6]

Judy Holiday - Actress - Screen, stage, radio and TV-[10]

Roderick B. Holmgren - Radio news commentator-[2]

Leo Hurwitz - Director - TV and radio, films-[12]

Charles Irving - Announcer, producer, actor - Radio and TV-[6]

Burl Ives - Folk singer, entertainer-[11]

Sam Jaffe - Actor-[14]

Leon Janney - Actor - Radio, television-[3]

Joe Julian - Actor - Radio-[2]

Garson Kanin - Writer, director, producer - Screen, stage-[6]

George Keane - Actor - Stage, studio, TV-[4]

Donna Keath - Actress - Radio-[2]

Pert Kelton - Actress - Radio, TV-[2]

Alexander Kendrick - European news correspondent, author-[4]

Adelaide Klein - Actress - Radio, TV, screen, stage-[7]

Felix Knight - Singer - Radio, opera-[2]

Howard Koch - Writer - Radio, screen, stage-[5]

Tony Kraber - Guitar player-[9]

John LaTouche - Writer, lyricist - Radio, stage - Co-author, *Ballad for Americans*-[7]

Arthur Laurents - Writer - Stage, screen - Wrote *Home of the Brave*-[6]

Gypsy Rose Lee - Strip-Teaser-[4]

Madeline Lee - Actress - Radio-[2]

Ray Lev - Concert pianist-[15]

Ella Logan - Singer - Radio, stage-[2]

Alan (Allan) Lomax - Folk singer, composer - Author of book *Mr. Jelly Roll*-[8]

Avon Long - Dancer-[6]

Joseph Losey - Director - Radio, theatre-[3]

Peter Lyon - Writer - Radio-[8]

Aline MacMahon - Actress - Member of Equity Council-[6]

Paul Mann - Actor, director - Stage, radio-[5]

Margo - Actress, dancer-[11]

Myron McCormick - Actor - Stage, screen, radio, television-[2]

Paul McGrath - Actor - Stage, radio-[2]

Burgess Meredith - Actor, director, producer - Stage, screen, radio, TV-[7]

Ben Myers - Chicago attorney - Legal counsel for radio and TV Director's Guild, AFL-[7]

Meg Mundy - Actress - Lead in *Respectful Prostitute*-[2]

Lynn Murray - Choral director, radio composer-[2]

Arnold Perl - Radio writer-[5]

Minerva Pious - Actress - Radio-[7]

Sam Raphaelson - Playwright-[2]

Bernard Reis - Accountant - American Federation of Radio Artists-[7]

Anne Revere - Actress - Screen, stage-[6]

Kenneth Roberts - Radio announcer-[2]

Earl Robinson - Singer, composer - Wrote score for *Ballad for Americans* - Also for motion pictures *The Roosevelt Story* and *A Walk in the Sun*-[17]

Harold Rome - Composer-[11]

Norman Rosten - Writer and poet-[12]

Selena Royale - Actress - Screen, stage - Appeared in *Hollywood Screen Test*-[8]

Coby Ruskin - Actor, director - Stage-[4]

Robert St. John - Author, lecturer, news commentator-[9]

Lisa Sergio - Radio commentator, author, lecturer-[9]

Irwin Shaw - Dramatist, critic - Author of *Bury your Dead*-[10]

Robert Lewis Shayon - Former president of Radio and Television Director's Guild-[3]

Ann Shepherd - Actress - Radio-[1]

William L. Shirer - Radio commentator, news correspondent, author-[3]

Allan Sloane - Writer - Radio-[2]

Howard K. Smith - Radio news commentator-[3]

Gale Sondergaard - Actress-[11]

Hester Sondergaard - Actress-[8]

Johannes Steel - Radio commentator-[31]

Paul Stewart - Actor - Stage, screen, radio and TV-[3]

Elliot Sullivan - Actor - Stage, radio and TV - *The Big Story*-[4]

William Sweets - Former director of *Gangbusters* and *Counter-Spy* - Former national president of Radio and Television Director's Guild-[8]

Helen Tamiris - Choreographer-[14]

Betty Todd - Director - Radio - Secretary, Radio and Television Director's Guild-[1]

Louis Untermeyer - Poet, writer - Frequent guest on radio shows-[23]

Hilda Vaughn - Actress - *On Whitman Avenue*-[4]

J. Raymond Walsh - Radio commentator-[17]

Sam Wanamaker - Actor, director - Radio, TV, stage, screen-[9]

Theodore Ward - Author of *Our Land*-[13]

Fredi Washington - Actress-[9]

Margaret Webster - Author, director, producer-[16]

Josh White - Singer of folk songs-[11]

Betty Winkler - Radio actress-[2]

Martin Wolfson - Actor - Radio, TV, stage - *South Pacific*-[11]

Leslie Woods - Actress - Radio-[2]

Richard Yaffe - Writer-[2]

Adding in the people already featured in this book, you will come to a total of 151, nearly all of whom were unjustly accused. A great many of those citations had absolutely no foundation in fact, and truth be known, the introduction of *Red Channels* said as much. You will note that some of those victims were presented with as few as one item, while other's lists go on and on. Some of the reasoning behind the piling-on for a few of them could be traced to the personal vindictiveness of the *Red Channels* producers. Even the accusations that were indeed true could usually stem from motives that had nothing whatever to do with subversion or Communism. Many of the organizations listed, despite their questionable connections, also did some good and valuable work.

The list covered many people beyond performers, writers, producers, and directors. There are quite a few news people, a lawyer, and even a former head of the Federal Communications Commission.

This proves simply that the folks at *Red Channels* were equal opportunity purveyors of scurrilous misinformation.

BOOK THREE
The Beginning of the End

Chapter Thirty-Nine
John Henry Faulk
Part One: The Filing

While I realize that Mr. John Henry Faulk was not one of the 151 people listed in *Red Channels*, I feel that it is imperative to include him in this publication because his libel suit against Aware, Inc., Vincent Hartnett, and Laurence A. Johnson was an important step toward the final demise of the blacklist in the Arts. His case was not quite so simple; it stretched over more than six years from the time the suit was filed until the jury in the proceedings rendered their final landmark decision.

John was born into old southern wealth in Austin, Texas. He grew up in a Victorian mansion called "Green Pastures." After his elementary and high school education, he attended the University of Texas in Austin, where he eventually earned a Master's Degree in Folklore. His thesis for his degree was titled "Ten Negro Sermons," which demonstrated his early and lifelong devotion to civil rights. He then taught a course on the English language at the same University. By doing so, he was able to hone his skills as a public speaker.

He later worked as a broadcaster at WCBS radio in New York City. His program was an hour-long, five days a week format, on which he explored and told stories based in his knowledge of down-home literature and word-of-mouth folklore passed down through the generations that pre-dated his time. His show was well-received by his audience, and more importantly, his many sponsors.

John had been performing on his series for several years when his troubles began. He had noticed that the New York Local AFTRA union was infested with many people who were also members of Aware, Inc., including most of the ruling committee of thirty-five. He became one of the sponsors of a proposition excoriating those with Aware, Inc. for not taking any action when one or more of the union members were accused without proof of being un-American due to ties with the Communist Party USA. That proposition passed with an overwhelming majority vote.

John then took it one step further. Since the ruling committee had been controlled for years by Aware, Inc. people, he decided to do something about the situation because it was getting more intolerable. He decided to organize a slate of candidates to run for positions on the Board of Directors in the next election in order to clear the air and get the union back on track. They were fronted by John, Charles Collingwood, and Orson Bean. In that election, their group, called the "Middle-of the-Roaders," swept into control of the local, at least for a short time. They won twenty-seven of the thirty-five seats on the Board. They wrested the reins from the old guard, most of whom were also part and parcel of Aware, Inc. Charles became President of the local, Orson was first Vice President, and John was second Vice President.

This proved to be too much for Bud Collyer and his cohorts to tolerate. Bud had been the head man for several terms until the uprising took him out. They decided to strike back. Since John had been the main instigator of the revolt, he became their principal target for revenge. On February 10, 1956, Aware, Inc. issued a bulletin sent to all of the membership titled "Aware Publication 16," which presented the following seven unproven allegations, very much in the style of *Red Channels:*

According to the *Daily Worker* on April 26, 1946, 'John Faulk' was to appear at Club 65, 13 Astor Place, N. Y. C.—a favorite cite of pro-Communist affairs.

According to the *Daily Worker* on April 17, 1947, 'Johnny Faulk' was to appear as an entertainer at the opening of Headline Cabaret, sponsored by Stage for Action (Officially designated a Communist front) The late Philip Loeb was billed as emcee.

According to the *Daily Worker* on April 5, 1948, 'John Faulk' contributed cabaret material to "Showtime for Wallace," reviews staged by the Progressive Citizens of America (Officially designated a Communist front) in support of Henry A. Wallace's candidacy for the presidency of the U. S. Although Wallace was the officially endorsed candidate of the Communist Party USA, by no means all of his supporters were Communists or pro-Communists. What is in question here is support of any candidate given through a Communist front setup.

A program dated April 25, 1946 named "John Faulk" as a scheduled entertainer (with identified Communist Earl Robinson and two non-Communists) under the auspices of the Independent Citizens Committee of the Arts, Sciences and Professions (Officially designated a Communist front, and predecessor of the Progressive Citizens of America)

Volume 3, Nos. 1 & 2 of the Bulletin of People's Songs (Officially designated a Communist front) named Faulk as one who had sent greetings to People's Songs on its second anniversary.

"Johnny Faulk" was listed in a circular as an entertainer or speaker (with Paul Robeson and two others) to appear at "Spotlight on Wallace" to be held in room 200 of the Jefferson School of Social Sciences on February 16, 1948. The Jefferson School has been found by the federal government to be what is the official training school of the Communist conspiracy in New York.

"John H. Faulk" was a U. S. sponsor of the American Continental Congress for Peace, staged in Mexico City, September 5-10, 1949, as shown by the official call. The Congress was later designated by the HUAC as "another phase in the Communist world peace campaign, aimed at consolidating anti-American forces throughout the western hemisphere".[1]

The bulletin went on to try to also ruin Orson Bean and Charles Collingwood to a somewhat lesser degree. Charles wrote a letter to the HUAC in response to answer their attack on Middle-of-the-Road administration. He received a totally unsatisfactory reply from Frank Tavenner, counsel for the committee. It said, in part, "There is not only no blacklist at all, but some of the named individuals have found it easy to secure employment." He added, "It is significant to note that the election of the Middlers has been greeted enthusiastically by the Communist party."[2]

Did you notice the wording of that statement? How could it be—if there was no blacklist—that he could refer to "some of those listed?"

The walls of John's broadcasting house were beginning to crumble. He took a copy of the *Aware Publication 16* to show it to Sam Slade, his direct boss at CBS and also Carl Ward, then General Manager at WCBS. He wanted to get their opinion about where he stood and more importantly, what their take on it was. After reading it, they both assured him that his status had not changed. He would remain a popular feature on their station. Sam had been a long-standing friend so John put his trust in what Sam said.

During July and a part of August 1956, John took his family to Jamaica for a long-anticipated vacation. While he was away, not only did the walls crumble but the roof fell in on his world, when CBS sent a letter to Gerald Dickler, John's business manager and close friend, telling him that their contract with John would not be renewed after his current thirteen-week run. Of course, John did not learn of their decision until he returned. As it turned out, CBS's reasons for his dismissal were bogus. They carefully avoided the real issue.

John proceeded to call on his fellow Middle-of-the-Roaders seeking support. The results were mixed, at best. Some of them were staunchly on his side, while others were running scared.

John decided that his best route to pursue was to go after the principals causing his trouble—Aware, Inc., Vincent Hartnett, and Laurence Johnson the infamous Syracuse grocer. While thinking about attorneys he wanted to represent him, Louis Nizer, the acclaimed New York trial lawyer, immediately came to mind. Lou had successfully fought his way through some very high profile cases. He was the right man for the job, if it could be arranged.

John made an appointment with Lou. When he arrived for his first meeting with the renowned defender of civil rights, he was greeted warmly. After listening intently to his tale of woe, and then scanning the documentation that John had brought along, Lou said that he would take the case and they would win. He expressed no doubts as to the final outcome. He also warned John that it would be neither fast nor easy.

When John happily related his good news to his friends, they informed him that he was forgetting something rather important: the small matter of the retainer that would be required in order to get the ball rolling. They told him that a man like Lou, whose standing in the legal community was impeccable, would want $50,000-$100,000 up front.

Feeling discouraged, John confronted Lou with this information. Lou laughed and told him that his colleagues were somewhat misinformed; however, he would need $20,000 to get started. He explained that that amount would be needed to cover basic court costs and that not one penny of it would line the pockets of his associates or his own. Even that amount far exceeded John's resources. He was only able to raise about $2,500 from his own bank accounts and some loans from friends.

Then a wonderful thing happened. Ed Murrow, upon hearing of John's dilemma, asked him to come to his office at CBS. When they met, Ed told John that he would gladly cover the balance he needed, not as a loan, but as a contribution to the cause. Ed was willing to do anything he could to stop the insidious blacklist.

In late 1956, legal action began in the chambers of the Supreme Court of the City and County of New York. At that time, Justice Saul Streit upheld the validity of the claim, the first step in a long and arduous process that would drag on until 1962. Even then, the ordeal would not really be 'over.'

Chapter Forty
John Henry Faulk
Part Two: The Pre-trial

After filing the libel suit and getting the approval of Justice Streit to go to trial, there was still much to be done before the proceedings could move forward. On top of the normal delays, Louis Nizer, *et al*, had to contend with constant roadblocks and delays thrown in their path by the defense.

This presented John with overwhelming problems. He could no longer work in his own field. He did have a few offers, but they mysteriously disappeared into thin air; perhaps not so mysteriously, considering the atmosphere at that time. He got a call from Bill Schwarz at WCCO in Minneapolis suggesting that he had the perfect job for him in the Twin Cities. Bill had, at one time, been the director on one of John's shows at WCBS before he moved on to the head honcho position at WCCO. At about the same time, John was offered by Joe Hyman, a Broadway producer, a role in his new play, *Fair Game*.

John went to Minnesota to negotiate the terms of his new contract with his would-be employer. In the meantime, Joe told him John that he would wait until John got back to get his decision about doing the play.

As luck would have it, the WCCO offer was rescinded at the last minute, and when John returned to New York, he was told that the role in the play had been recast. The reasons given for all of this were anything but satisfying, but he knew the real truth was that his potential benefactors had been gotten to.

He ran into a similar scenario with Wendell Campbell at KFRC in San Francisco. Once again, just when all was looking good, the job offer went up in smoke.

Without any income, John's situation went from bad to worse. The only way he and his family could survive was by borrowing funds from his friends. Even that well was bound to run dry. He swore out an affidavit declaring his innocence, which could be passed on to prospective employers, but the affidavit produced negligible results.

Adding more salt to his wounds, he was subpoenaed to appear at the HUAC hearings on June 6, 1958. Lou, using all of his legalistic legerdemain, managed to get a postponement and ultimately a full revocation of that demand. Until the subpoena was rescinded, it was just one more brick in John's house of pain.

After many delays over legal nuances, it finally became time to begin the Examination Before Trial (EBT) of all of the principals in the case on both sides of the issue. The first one was begun on June 5, 1958 in the offices of Lou Nizer with attorneys for the plaintiff, those for the defendants, and a court stenographer in attendance.

The first defendant to testify was Vincent Hartnett. He was represented by his attorney, Godfrey Schmidt.

At the outset, Vincent displayed a great deal of confidence and arrogance about his position, but it did not take very long for Lou to destroy that facade. For the first few minutes, the whole affair consisted of simple questions about Vincent's background. This relaxed him even more. Then, in an offhand manner, Vincent said, "I would remind you, Mr. Nizer, I am not on the witness stand, and you're not a District Attorney."

The climate in the room turned to ice. Lou took off the kid gloves, looked coldly at Vincent, and responded, "Do I understand, sir, you presume to instruct me in the conduct of this examination? Are you, sir? How dare you impudently speak of District Attorneys and witnesses! You, sir, who have sat as judge, jury, prosecuting attorney and executioner on the lives and careers of hundreds of loyal, innocent victims! You, sir, who have drawn the noose of starvation around the neck of that innocent man sitting there, seeking to starve his children and ruin his reputation. You dare, sir, to instruct me in the conduct of this case?"

Vincent and Godfrey were stunned. They had not expected such a vehement reply. Vincent tried to act nonchalant, but when he sought to puff on his big cigar, he mistakenly stuck it in his left ear instead of his mouth. After that, he began to give answers to all of the questions posed quietly and succinctly.

Lou extracted many names of those active at Aware, Inc., who were trying to put John down. He also quizzed Vincent at length about other celebrities they had victimized and the fees Aware, Inc. had collected with a promise to help clear them of all charges. Those clearances did little or no good for many of them.

By the time the first stage of Vincent's EBT was concluded on June 16, he and Godfrey had given up the fight. They said they would be willing to sign any statement asked of them. However, Lou had yet to prove malice on Vincent's part, so his ordeal was not over. Lou intended to leave no stone unturned while he had the chance.

Assuming that it was virtually over, John was elated. Then Lou burst his bubble. That this was merely the first step along the path of a long trek.

A couple of days later, Paul Martinson, one of Lou's associates, called John to inform him that Godfrey had withdrawn from the case and that the new attorney would be Roy Cohn. Roy had once been Joe McCarthy's lead henchman. Roy then told them that he would be overseas for a couple of months, so the continuation of Hartnett's EBT would have to be postponed until at least October.

In spite of all the finagling that the defense could muster, that the first EBT was completed in early 1960. Then they began to examine Paul Milton, an officer of Aware, Inc. Paul was taken over many of the same rocky roads that Vincent had been subjected to.

When that EMT was finished, they started in on Laurence Johnson, one of the primary defendants and a key witness to what had been transpiring. He proved to be almost impossible to interview with complete satisfaction. By that time, he was showing his advanced age and his health was rapidly deteriorating. His stock answer to almost every question was that he could not recollect.

He was presented with documentation to jog his memory, but even then he was not cooperative.

Lou assured John that Johnson's tactics would not hinder their case. On the contrary, they would only help in the long run.

John spent much of the time back in Austin, Texas, where he had built a rather unsuccessful advertising agency to try to earn some much needed income. He arrived back in New York on August 24, 1961 for his own EBT, after which a trial date was to be set.

John's EBT was conducted in Cohn's sumptuous office overlooking the East River. The inquisitor was Thomas Bolan, one of Cohn's partners. Bolan would be the person who would be with the case until its completion in June of 1962. On his side of the ledger John had Paul Martinson and George Berger, another of Lou's associates, who was thoroughly familiar with every aspect of the suit. They, along with Lou, would also be present throughout the proceedings in court. The EBT progressed smoothly, and Paul brought out the many commendations that John had received for community service in the course of his career.

After completing his testimony, John returned to his family in Austin to await further news. On March 16, 1962, he got a call from Paul informing him that the trial had been set to begin on April 3, 1962. At last, the big show was about to begin, or at least, they all thought so.

Chapter Forty-One
John Henry Faulk
Part Three: The Trial

John Faulk's trial had been set for April 3, 1962, in room 252 of the New York Supreme Court Building with Justice Abraham Geller presiding. At the very last moment, Thomas Bolan, who would be conducting the defense, proclaimed that he had to go to Egypt to aid one of his other clients. He asked for yet another delay of undetermined length. Justice Geller granted his wish, but would not allow more than two weeks for Bolan to tend to his other business. The trial date was reset for April 23, 1962.

John assumed that this last little delay would give him a short respite to relax, but Lou Nizer thought of the delay as a great opportunity to get better prepared for what was yet to come. He, his associates, and John began an intense period of going over every detail that would or could come up during the trial. These sessions sometimes lasted until three in the morning and resumed early the next day. This sort of scheduling continued until the final decision was reached, with only a couple of brief breaks in the action.

They would have to show the existence of a blacklist, something that was often denied by studio executives and ad agencies. They would have to show how it affected John and others, and show how the defendants were largely responsible for it. They would have to establish the amount of damages they sought. This figure would be based, not only on John's lost income, but also on the destruction of his good name in the industry. In the course of doing this, they would likewise have to demonstrate how the reputations of others in radio and television had been trashed.

A simple case it was not.

The jury selection was begun on April 20, 1962, and was completed without serious delays. A panel of twelve plus two alternates were sworn in, and the trial began.

The first event on the agenda took place on the morning of April 23, 1962, with Lou Nizer's opening remarks to the jury. His reputation for oratory had preceded him. The chambers were packed with interested observers. Lou did not disappoint them. He said, in part, "Who are the defendants in this case? One of them is Vincent Hartnett. We will show you about Mr. Hartnett's career. He was a man who earned some fifty to seventy-five dollars a week in radio in some script department. Then he was out of work for a considerable time, but then he fell upon the idea which brought him a great deal of prosperity. That was the idea of collecting data; becoming a so-called consultant on radio artists and television artists, and informing the radio companies, the sponsors, the people who advertised, or the agents who placed these programs, informing them of the records of those artists; the so-called records, and their affiliation with questionable causes. He was the principal author of *Red Channels*, a book which made these listings of people on the air. He thereafter continued this work, charging sponsors five dollars a throw, to put it bluntly, to investigate somebody.

"He would decide if a certain performer was a good American, what his alleged record was, and we will show you how that worked. If a name came back after a couple of weeks; if the same actor had a second show on radio or television, why, then Mr. Hartnett charged less. He charged $2. For original performers it was $5 to check, and in some cases $20, and if it was a little more important for some reason, $50. We will show you that these payments were made to him, and that a man who had earned $50 to $75 a week was earning $26,000 a year collecting these payments as an alleged consultant Let me call your attention to one other thing we will prove. Aware, Inc. is not an organization that has any authority from the government of the United States. It is a private organization. So, Aware, Inc. has no standing except as a private individual, with Mr. Hartnett cashing in.

"Second, we will show you that Mr. Laurence A. Johnson has not been designated. He is self-appointed and self-anointed. He has no authority of any governmental agency to pass upon the lives of American citizens, economically, patriotically, or in any other way."[1]

He then went through the accusations that had been made against his client, one by one. He clearly explained away each and every one of them. He discussed, at length, the tactics that had been employed by the defendants and added that the American Legion post in Syracuse might also have been named as a co-defendant, because they were a large part of the problem at hand.

He went on to say, "What we have brought, for the first time so far as I know, is an issue before this court whether an American court of justice is going to approve the kind of blacklisting that went on in this case for all artists, and which John Henry Faulk makes a test of in this case, and we are going to bring other evidence to you as to how this operated on famous artists.

"What we are bringing to this court is a question as to whether private organizations, or as I would call them, vigilantes, can exist in this nation, when we have a court of law by which we can obtain relief."[2]

Lou then dwelled for a time on the damages that they claimed and how they arrived at the figure they were going to suggest.

In Lou's conclusion, he spoke of some of the witnesses that would be called:

"I plead with you particularly to observe Mr. Hartnett when the time comes for him to take the stand, and Mr. Laurence A. Johnson when the time comes for him to take the stand. I plead with you to watch them closely and listen to their answers and to observe their mannerisms, and see who it was, as we charged, intimidating the television industry. I want you to follow their answers closely. I plead with you in this particular case to take particular note of Mr. Hartnett and Mr. Johnson under oath and under cross-examination, and when you do I have no doubt that, in what we consider a great cause, justice will be done not only for the plaintiff, but for a great American cause, as well."[3]

At this point, the court adjourned for a lunch break. During the break, more than half of the attendees left and did not return, which had less to do with the trial and more with the interest in Lou Nizer.

When the proceedings resumed, Thomas Bolan began his opening remarks by explaining his version that the defendants were a simple formality. He then attempted to explain their side of the question before the court. In part, he said, "Now, before discussing the complaint, I would like to speak just a few words on the backgrounds of the individual defendants. Before I can do that, too, I would like to say that my duty is rather a solemn one, because this is not an ordinary case where one party is seeking to get money from another party.

"The plaintiff, John Henry Faulk, in support of his complaint, has charged that the defendants have conspired against him. He has libeled the defendants, and Mr. Nizer did not bring this out. He has libeled them as extortionists, as racketeers, and as intimidators—as terrorists.

"So therefore, in this case, there is more than money involved as far as my clients are concerned. Their reputations are at stake, and in the case of Aware, its powerful existence is at stake.

"Now, the charges that I have read to you, or mentioned to you, are surely all very serious. It is a very serious charge to call someone an extortionist or a racketeer, but I assure you that those charges, like the other charges in the complaint, are absolutely without foundation.

"As to the background of the individuals, first of all, Aware, Inc. is a New York corporation. It describes itself as an organization to combat the Communist conspiracy in the entertainment and communication fields. Among its dedicated purposes are to disseminate information and material concerning the Communist Party, the Communist fronts, and similar areas.

"It is a non-profit organization. None of its officers receive any salary or any other remuneration. Mr. Hartnett is vice-president of Aware, Inc., and is one of its founders. Mr. Hartnett is an expert and a specialist in the field of Communism and the Communist Party front groups. He spent many years of study, read many articles, has written many articles, and has accumulated enormous files on the workings of the Communist Party, and the Communist front groups, in particular.

"In the course of time, many organizations and groups requested Mr. Hartnett to do special work into the backgrounds of prospective actors or entertainers in radio and television and other related fields.

"Those people, the producers or sponsors, did not want to take the risk of hiring somebody who either had been identified as a member of the Communist Party or who has a significant record of affiliation with organizations closely tied in with the Communist Party."[4]

Bolan went on in closing to describe Laurence Johnson in equally glowing terms. "We will show that beyond any doubt, too, Mr. Faulk's earnings were not affected by anything that Aware did and nobody of the defendants, Aware, Johnson or Hartnett, or anybody else, ever went to any of Faulk's sponsors to request that he be terminated. Nobody in any of the defendants ever collected one cent for the activities with respect to Mr. Faulk, and we will prove that beyond any doubt."[5]

The next morning, with the opening statements out of the way, the plaintiff's case began. The first witness called by Lou was, as expected, John. They spent that whole day and the next establishing his reputation and celebrity. In order to do this, Lou introduced reams of material from CBS and other sources praising his client's abilities. They also meticulously went over the many awards John had received for his constant service to the community.

After two days of intensive interrogation about these matters, Lou asked for, and was granted, permission from Justice Geller to interrupt John's testimony in order to bring on well-known radio and television producer David Susskind as a witness, because Susskind had travel commitments and could only be heard at that time. Bolan raised multiple objections, saying that he was not prepared for this unexpected turn of events, but he was repeatedly overruled.

The press was deeply into the trial. Murray Kempton, an old friend of both the plaintiff and his attorney, wrote in the *New York*

Post noon edition on the second day of John's testimony, "Judge Abraham Geller's courtroom was crowded yesterday, as it is likely to be for the next six weeks, because Louis Nizer will be practicing surgery there. Nizer, of course, was the main attraction; but, once there, it was surprising how glad many of the spectators were to see John Henry Faulk again."[6]

On Friday morning, April 27, 1962, David Susskind's credentials were substantiated. Then, Lou got into the meat of the subject at hand and began questioning David about a program called *Appointment with Adventure*.

David replied, "*Appointment with Adventure* was a half-hour dramatic program conceived by my company and sold to Young & Rubicam on behalf of the Lorillard Company, and was on, I believe, in March of 1955, Sunday nights, 10 p.m., and stayed for fifty weeks."

Lou said, "Mr. Susskind, I have read passages from that program, and you have already told us that you were the packager, the producer of that program for the Lorillard Company. Is that right?"

"Yes, sir, we created that program. We sold it to Young & Rubicam for Lorillard, and I personally produced that program."

"When you say you 'sold it' to Young & Rubicam, that was the advertising agency that represented the sponsor, Lorillard. Is that the sequence of it?"

"Yes, sir."

Lou continued. "Did you, when you suggested various actors and actresses and even the names of technicians or the director, did you submit those names to anyone?"

Bolan objected, but he was overruled.

David answered, "Yes, sir. I had to submit the names of everybody on every show in every category to an executive of Young & Rubicam, and nobody could be engaged by me finally or a deal consummated before a clearance or acceptance came back from Young & Rubicam."

"Did that acceptance deal with the quality of the actor or the technician or the director?"

Bolan objected and was sustained.

Lou then asked, "When you submitted those names, what was the purpose of submission?"

Bolan again objected, but was overruled.

David answered, "When I sold the program to the ad agency, Young & Rubicam, for Lorillard cigarettes, the condition of the sale was that all names of all personnel in all categories were to be submitted for political clearance by Young & Rubicam, and nobody was hired until they approved and said, 'All right, hire this person'."

Lou asked, "How long did it take before the approval or disproval came back?"

Bolan objected and was overruled.

David replied, "It generally took forty-eight hours. I was told that I should always anticipate a forty-eight hour delay on the approval or rejection of any name."

"Can you estimate how many names on this one program over the year that it ran that you submitted in this way for political approval?"

Bolan objected again and was overruled again.

David said, "I must have submitted over the period of time about 5,000 names."

"Can you give us the estimate of how many of the names that you submitted came back rejected?"

David replied, "I would guess approximately one-third, maybe a little higher."

"Can you indicate who you spoke to, Mr. Susskind?"

"The executive in charge of this particular program for Lorillard was David Levy."

"Tell us what was said."

"I said to Mr. Levy that it was extraordinarily difficult to find the right actors for the right parts, the right writers for the right scripts, and the right directors for the right stories; that his restrictions were making the program almost unworkable and impossible artistically, and that I could not accept responsibility for the steady deterioration of the program when the practice was in vogue. I said, 'If you reject somebody, let me get that somebody and ask him. In many cases I know these people and they are fine people and I know they are acceptable. You only say no or yes to me about them, but you never give me any substantiation.' He said, 'I can't give you any. I deplore the practice as much as you do. We're caught in a trap. I have no alternative'."

"Did you also submit the names of children on this program?"

"Even children."

"Will you give us an illustration or instance on this program where it occurred for a child?"

"Once, we required the services of a seven- or eight-year-old girl actress. It was a backbreaking assignment to find a child who could act well enough to be on a professional program coast to coast. We finally found a child, an American child, eight years old, female. I put her name in along with some other names. She came back unacceptable, politically unreliable."[7]

David Susskind proved believable because, as a respected radio and television producer, he was very familiar with the workings of the blacklist.

When Bolan strenuously objected to this line of questioning, Lou cited page 847 of Vincent's EBT where he was specifically asked why he checked on children. He responded that it was because they had left-leaning parents or that some children were politically savvy at a young age.

Before beginning his cross-examination, Bolan moved for a mistrial, stating that David Susskind's testimony was inflammatory. Justice Geller denied him his wish.

When the proceedings resumed after a break for lunch, Bolan asked David, "Did you ever have any discussion with these people as to what was meant by political rejection or political approval?"

David responded, "I endeavored over and over again to find out what the charges were so that I could investigate or apprise the actor and give him the opportunity to face the accusation and discover whether it was true, and, if it was true, whether it was sufficient to bar him from employment. This opportunity was never granted me by the agencies or firms or anybody else who made the final determination."

Bolan asked, "Do you have any idea that these charges related to Communist Party membership or Communist Party front group membership?"

"I know of specific instances where I do know things about the charges. In the case of a particular actress, she was unemployable because her husband was deemed to have pro-Communist organization sympathy. She herself was clear and clean politically."[8]

A little later, Bolan asked David what he meant by blacklisting, if it had anything to do with preventing an artist to perform due to Communist tendencies.

David responded, "I don't know the theory of blacklisting except that it is a private vigilantism to keep people off television."[9]

While David Susskind's testimony did not relate directly to John, it did serve a very important purpose by clearly demonstrating the viciousness of the blacklist and proving its existence.

Next on the agenda was John's return to the stand to complete what had begun several days earlier. His direct examination took nearly two weeks due to the constant legal bickering between the lawyers on both side of the issue. Many times, there were long side-bar conferences with the judge out of ear-shot of the jury. Some of the disputes had to be settled in the judge's chambers, but eventually they got through it all.

Lou Nizer concluded his questioning and turned John over to Bolan for his cross examination. Bolan made every effort to discredit Faulk's abilities as a performer. He spent an inordinate amount of time trying to show that John was nothing more than a disc jockey.

Bolan asked, "Were you a disc jockey at CBS?"

John answered, "I didn't regard myself as one, nor did CBS regard me as one."

"Did the profession regard you as a disc jockey?"

"I don't know how to answer that. Never was I included as a disc jockey in the common parlance."

"Do you have any aversion to being described as a disc jockey?"

"Not in the least, sir."

"That is an answer. You said before that you were not regarded as a disc jockey in the profession."

"I was not."

"Weren't you a member of the Fresh Air Disc Jockey Committee for the *Herald Tribune* Fresh Air Fund at one time?"

"That is perfectly correct, sir."

"Haven't you always been referred to in reviews as a disc jockey?"

"No, I was not."

"Have you ever been referred to in reviews as a disc jockey?"

"I don't remember any specific instance, but in all likelihood I have been."

"I ask you the question, have you ever been referred to in reviews as a disc jockey?"

John replied, "The reason I said that in all likelihood is that at the time my contract was signed they did not know how to describe me, describe the kind of program I was going to do, because I was employed primarily for the kind of stories and comments that I made. It was understood that I know nothing about music. A disc jockey is an authority on music."[10]

Bolan obviously was not getting anywhere with his line of inquiry, which had absolutely nothing to do with the suit. A little later, he took a different tact, still attempting to denigrate John. "Did you ever hear the term, Professional Texan?"

John answered, "Yes indeed."

"Did you ever hear it in reference to you?"

"I think I have, yes."

"What does that term mean?"

"I think in one instance, someone writing a review of me—and I don't recall who it was because it stung. It was very uncomplimentary, as far as I was concerned. It means that one is pompous and inflated and goes about boasting of Texas being the biggest and the best and the finest, and that the sun rises and sets there; that the first law of gravity was passed by the Texas legislature."

Justice Geller then asked, "Aren't the Texans proud of being the biggest and the best?"

John said, "I'm infinitely proud. I'm trying to characterize a pompous humbug who gives Texas a black eye. By the way, it's one of the points I made quite frequently on my program; of these Texas oil men who say that they could buy Russia and then lease it back to Khrushchev; that sort of thing."

Bolan questioned, "Isn't it part of your act as a disc jockey; as a person from Texas, to underplay your intelligence?"

"It certainly is not. It's far from it. I referred frequently to my lectures at Yale University. I quoted Shakespeare quite frequently and John Milton quite frequently on the air. I do it on a folk level, that is true, but that is very different from conducting myself like a country bumpkin. I have a very wide audience among university people, Princeton and Columbia Universities."[11]

Bolan tried several other ways to discredit John, but with little or no success. He finally gave up.

That afternoon when they were leaving court, Lou commented, "Bolan used McCarthy tactics. That will cost him dearly. He just ran the judgment up another million dollars."

John returned to Austin to be with his family over the weekend. When he came back to New York, he was feeling refreshed and ready for more. He knew the best was yet to come.

On Monday morning, Lou called on Charles Collingwood to take the stand. Charles was a devastating witness for the plaintiff. Lou spent considerable time quizzing him about the whole situation at the New York local of AFTRA and the reasoning behind the formation of the Middle-of-the-Road group to take control away from the hands of the Aware, Inc. people that had been running it for several years. When the election was concluded, Charles took the presidency from Bud Collyer.

After getting this information into the record, Lou moved on to the most salient issue, the blacklist. "What is the employment practice with respect to an artist who becomes involved in a controversy with respect to his loyalty?"

Collingwood said, "Well, it really depends, Mr. Nizer, on how much guts the sponsor has, the network and the station, whether they have enough guts to stand up to the pressures which are brought against them, or whether they don't. During the time of which we are speaking, in most cases, they didn't have the guts. Quite often, performers were denied employment when it later turned out the charges against them were unfounded. Therefore, it would appear to be pretty clear that the actual guilt or innocence was not the controlling factor in the decisions that were made. There were instances in which an actor, either because he was well-connected or for some other reason was brought before one of these persons charged by an organization for whom he worked for clearing people. He was brought before them to explain. This was by no means the universal practice. He was not usually informed of the source of the charges if they had not been made public."[12]

In his cross-examination of Collingwood, Bolan somewhat foolishly pressed the issue. He asked him about what organizations other than Aware were involved in such practices. "I am not sure of the whole spectrum, but there were people who organized themselves and presented information. There were letters from the American Legion and other groups referring to performers. There was an apparatus of pressure upon the network and the stations relating to their performers. The principal one from the point of view of the union, which was my immediate concern, was Aware, which had become an issue within the union. That there were others, I have reason to believe, although, I can't identify them for you."[13]

Other groups doing similar work were not relevant to the proceedings, though there were many of them.

There was a crucial time element involved with actor Tony Randall, who was scheduled to be the next witness, and who was committed to depart for Greece the following morning to appear in a motion picture there. The members of John's team were worried that Collingwood's cross examination would effectively not allow enough time for even a brief appearance by Tony. As it turned out, Bolan was taking a beating from Collingwood, so he decided to stop questioning him, which left the entire afternoon, after the lunch recess to hear from Tony Randall.

Tony's testimony was short but powerful. Lou had not planned to do a long interview so the time allotted worked out to perfection. His main intention was to have the jury hear what Tony had to say about AFTRA and his work for the Middle-of-the-Road group. Tony spoke of how he wanted to hide under a rock until the proclamation condemning Aware, Inc. was passed. He stated that this was a common attitude among members at that time.

Aware, Inc. had given them reasons to be fearful. They wielded that kind of power.

Bolan's cross examination was quick and ineffectual. He was still feeling a bit snake-bitten.

The next day, Lou called Tony Murray, a surprise witness—at least in the minds of the defendants—an Account Executive for the Grey Advertising Agency. One of Tony's accounts was Pabst Brewing, one of John Faulk's sponsor. Until that time, the attorneys for the defense had denied that Laurence Johnson had played any role in John's blacklisting. Tony proved them wrong.

Lou began, "In March 1956, did you receive a communication from one Laurence Johnson?"

Tony answered, "Yes, I did."

"Did you, when you met Mr. Johnson, subsequently refer to the telephone conversation?"

"I did."

"Did Mr. Johnson, when you met him, identify himself as Laurence Johnson, the man who called you?"

"Yes, he did."

"Will you tell us please, on the first occasion when he telephoned you, what he said and what you said to him?"

"On the first occasion when I spoke to Mr. Johnson by telephone, he did not telephone me, I telephoned him in response to a message I received in my office saying that Mr. Johnson had called me while I was out of my office and would I call him at his hotel."

"Which you did?"

"I did, sir."

"All right, will you tell us of the conversation?"

"First, Mr. Johnson identified himself as Larry Johnson of Syracuse. He said that he owned several supermarkets and had influence over a number of others in central New York State. He gave me an indication of the total gross volume of food business that was done in the area and it was most impressive. It ran into the millions. He said that he felt that it was a disgrace that our company was using a Communist, John Henry Faulk, to advertise its products. I replied that I had no such knowledge about Mr. Faulk.

He said, 'You had better get in line because a lot of people along Madison Avenue are getting in line and the display space that the Pabst Brewing Company has in the stores that I either own or control was hard-won space.' I said that I could not accept a telephone implication of that kind. I felt there were legal ways of establishing whether or not Mr. Faulk was a Communist and that I had no intention of firing or recommending the firing of a man who was a first class salesman for our product. Then he said, 'How would you like it if your client were to receive a letter from an American Legion post up here?' I said that I was a veteran myself and I could not believe that the American Legion would lend itself to what I considered to be an obvious blackmail attempt. He said, 'Well, you will find out'."

"What did you do immediately after the call?"

"I went to my superior, Mr. Dalsimer. Mr. Dalsimer said to me, 'This could be very serious. You had better get on it fast and do something about it.' I called the hotel and asked to talk to Mr. Johnson. There was no answer in his room. I got into a cab and went to Mr. Johnson's hotel. I picked up the house phone and rang his room. Again there was no answer. I asked the desk clerk to help me find Mr. Johnson. The clerk pointed him out standing in the lobby. I went over and introduced myself. Johnson said, 'After the way you spoke to me, I want nothing further to do with you.' He turned and walked out of the hotel."

Lou questioned further. "After your conversation with Mr. Johnson, did your client receive a letter from an American Legion post in Syracuse?"

Tony replied, "They did."

"Was there attached to the letter a bulletin from Aware, Inc.? [The one accusing Faulk, Collingwood, and Orson Bean.]

"There was."[14]

When Bolan tried to minimize the damage, he failed to shake Tony from his memories of what had occurred, and he gave up rather quickly.

There were many more witnesses called before Lou rested his case, including actress Kim Hunter. She was at first very apprehensive when asked to testify because she too had been blacklisted. She had gone through a terrible browbeating by Vincent Hartnett before giving in to his pressure and sending out some self-deprecating telegrams to try to clear her name.

When CBS asked Vincent to produce information on Kim, he said he would do it for a fee of $200, not his usual $5. She ran into similar problems with ABC. She ultimately decided to tell the whole story in open court because she wanted to help others who had had similar experiences. Her tale did immense damage to the defense in the eyes of the jury.

Lou called on Himan Brown, who had produced and directed such well-known radio series as *The Thin Man, Bulldog Drummond*, and a host of others. His accounts of his dealings with Vincent and Laurence Johnson made tremendous impact. In the end, Brown admitted to a personal hatred of Vincent.

Some of the others that Lou called on were Peter Hill—the President of Kaster-Hilton Advertising; Mark Goodson—President of Goodson-Todman Productions; Actor Gary Moore, a member of the Middle-of-the Road slate, who testified to John's patriotism and his talent. Lou also made a strong case that demonstrated all that John Faulk was losing by being unemployable.

These and several others told mostly the same story, each from their own perspective.

Bolan did his best to try to negate what had been said, but he failed.

When the plaintiff rested, it was time to hear from the defense. The direct testimony of the various defense witnesses did not go much better for Bolan. He seemed to be setting trap after trap for himself by asking the wrong questions at the right times giving Lou some unbelievable openings.

For example, Bolan first set up for a fall Paul Milton, former President of Aware, Inc., by painting him into a corner. Bolan brought up the AFTRA situation, and soon wished he had not done so. "You stated that Aware's membership at one point was 350 members. Is that correct?"

Paul replied, "Yes."

"Where there some members of Aware who were members of the American Federation of Radio and Television Artists?"

"Yes, there were."

"And at its peak of 350 members, approximately how many members were members of AFTRA?"

"I would say 75 to 100."[15]

Bolan's unwise direction simply demonstrated the huge influence Aware, Inc. had over the New York chapter of AFTRA in those days. A little later, Bolan asked Paul to describe Vincent Hartnett's qualifications as a researcher. Lou Nizer rose and adamantly objected to the question. This called for another conference with Justice Geller out of the earshot of the jury. Bolan pleaded, "I'm entitled to show that the Board of Directors of Aware had considered Hartnett's reputation to be one of the finest as a researcher and that they were confidently relying on the material he supplied."[16]

To this, Lou shot back, "In other words, Milton can say that he relied on Hartnett, and Hartnett can say that he relied on Milton, and this is internal reliance testimony on reputation, and Milton is going to say that Hartnett had a good reputation as a researcher. Do you think that this is the reliable proof that is submitted by courts with respect to libels?"[7]

Justice Geller sustained Lou's objection.

During their evening meeting after the day's direct testimony was completed, John expressed his fear that Paul Milton may have come across looking too good in spite of the mistakes that had been made.

The next morning, Lou proceeded to allay those trepidations. He attacked Paul tooth and nail, from every possible angle, and soon turned the man's smugness to jelly. He pointed out several instances where Paul had taken an entirely different stance from the words he had spoken during his sworn EBT prior to the trial. Lou showed no mercy while picking Paul apart. By the time Paul left the stand, he was looking more like a witness for the plaintiff than for the defense.

Vincent Hartnett was next. He was intended to be a star witness. Tom Bolan treated him with kid gloves trying to avoid controversy as much as he could.

Once again, Lou Nizer, a master of his craft, managed to turn nearly every statement made by Vincent against him. Not one word ever escaped Lou's ears. Vincent was also a victim of his own EBT. His only response upon being presented with the proof of his two-faced approach to the truth was that it had been a long time since the EBT and his recollections were not perfect. Of course, that was no excuse for his apparent perjury at either one time or the other.

Others were called upon with nearly the same results. One very important person who did not appear was Laurence Johnson. Johnson had been seriously ill for some time. He said his doctors would not want him to face the pressures of an open court. This point was argued by Lou, who then had his own doctors examine Laurence. They deemed him fit enough to appear, but it all proved to be of no avail. Laurence did not show up.

After tying up some loose ends with character witnesses and such, the opposing attorneys offered their summations.

Chapter Forty-Two
John Henry Faulk
Part Four: Summation & Verdict

Before the summations could begin, Justice Geller issued some final instructions to the members of the jury. He stated that all issues which were not supported by evidence must be dismissed. He said that the two affirmative defenses—mainly truth and fair comment—were stricken because the defendants had presented no evidence that would establish the truth of their charges against the plaintiff; and the defendants had not proved that their libel had been provoked. He added, "This leaves as the affirmative defense of the defendants, Aware, Inc. and Hartnett, the partial defense of reliance on sources, which goes to mitigation of punitive damages. These defendants offered no direct proof of truth, but did present evidence of alleged reliance on sources, mostly in the form of documents which were not admitted for the truth of their content. So, listen carefully to both counsels. Reject what you consider to be unfounded."

By making these charges to the jury, Justice Geller effectively cut off most of what Bolan might say.

As he began, Bolan asked, "Why has this case lasted so long? It is probably a record for a libel case in New York County. The answer is simple. Because the plaintiff, at the outset, knew he was not going to be able to prove his case. Had he confined this case to Mr. Faulk and the defendants, we would have been out of here several weeks ago. Why was somebody like Tony Randall, the movie actor, brought in here before you to testify? Did he know Mr. Faulk? Did he have anything to do with Exhibit 41 (Aware's bulletin 16) or any of the issues in the case?"[1]

Bolan was wrong on two fronts. First, Tony and John knew each other quite well. Second—perhaps more importantly—the suit was not brought solely on behalf of John Henry Faulk but was also meant to take up arms against the whole concept of blacklisting and those who had been victimized by the practice.

Then, a little later, Bolan went off the deep end into a sea of fallacy. He proceeded to call John nothing more than an arrogant liar. "Mr. Faulk has deliberately lied to you on numerous occasions in this case on matters of great importance. There are so many lies that it is hard to list them all. I will cite you nine or ten for a start".[2]

Bolan rambled on and on with his line of continued libel. During the lunch break, Lou repeated to John something he had said on an earlier date, this time with a slightly different twist. "That viciousness is going to cost Bolan dearly. I'm really surprised he would take that route. I would have thought he would have been smarter than that. He's done his case no good with that violent attack." He added, "Don't listen today. Let it go in one ear and out the other. Prepare to listen tomorrow."

After lunch, Bolan returned to the very same train of thought. "This is another hoax which the plaintiff is seeking to perpetrate. From the start of his career he has been primarily a disc jockey, nothing else. His ability, or lack of ability, was well known in the industry. He has ranked third of fourth among radio disc jockeys in New York."[3]

There was his disc jockey reference again. Radio ratings were based mainly on a performer's time slot and how he did against his competition for audiences, not about classifications. John was not a disc jockey, and his job title had absolutely nothing to do with his case.

Finally, Bolan got around to the issue of blacklisting. "The plaintiff seeks to put the blame on the defendants for what he calls blacklisting, but he is dead wrong. It is the American public that does not want identified Communist Party members on its radio and television programs. It does not want people who invoke the Fifth Amendment concerning Communism on its programs. It does not want people with records of Communist-front affiliations that have never been repudiated on their programs.

"And since the public does not want it, the sponsors don't want it. Experts, such as Mr. Hartnett, in the field, were employed. He knows the workings of the Communist Party. The defendants here are not without support. You have seen from Exhibit 41 that the House Un-American Activities Committee backs the activities of the defendants. There has been testimony by Mr. Collingwood that the Catholic War Veterans, the Jewish War Veterans and the American Legion, branches of those organizations, support the defendants. Mr. Collingwood described it as part of the blacklisting apparatus."[4]

When he was finished with his all day rant, Bolan had apparently done little to boost his case. He had used every vindictive bone in his body to denigrate his opponents instead of making a strong argument to support the defense of his clients. This sort of dialogue did not pack the punch it might have a few years earlier. By 1962, the public had caught on to that kind of rhetoric to a large degree.

The following morning, Lou Nizer took center stage. The courtroom was again packed and extra seats had been added to accommodate the overflow. He began, "This is a case by John Henry Faulk against these defendants, but certain cases involve extraordinary principals. There are, in the history of litigation, just a few of these, sometimes only one in a generation. I stand here with a very deep sense of responsibility because I have upon me the burden of presenting this case to you. For six years we have waited for this day, six years! We have worked during those six years day and night. You see the exhibits, the documents, the unraveling of which was very difficult to prove in a courtroom under oath; and so, we too have been under stress. It has been a great responsibility, which we take very earnestly and you ought to have, I hope, the satisfaction that your work, whatever it be when this case is over, will have significance in the history of litigation nationally, and I hope, internationally. The last day was a bitter day, because we would have thought that, after everything that had happened in this courtroom, there could have been a different position taken by the defendants. I would expect them to defend themselves, but they didn't have to spill their malice and hate in this courtroom until I felt that I was neck-deep in mud.

"When a man has no generosity in his heart he has a real heart disease, and I think the defendants, yesterday, demonstrated the malice with which this case, from the first moment, has been steeped.

"Here we were with this learned court, whose research and learning on the complicated question of libel and law have awed us all, instructing you that the defenses of truth were stricken out of this case. They couldn't plead the truth because there wasn't a shred of evidence to show there was any truth.

"Don't you think it would have been the decent thing under the circumstances for the defendants to take the usual, proper position for a defendant, 'I was wrong; I am sorry?' But no, even under those circumstances, they came into this court and called my client a liar for testifying his rights.

"I admire Mr. Faulk for keeping silent under that attack, because I had to grip my seat. At the last moment we were libeled again.

"In the first place, there is no issue of Communism in this case. John Henry Faulk, from the first moment he could understand and breathe, has been anti-Communist, and no one has proved otherwise. The issue is not Communism at all. It is private vigilantism, and the only time Mr. Bolan came near to touching the issue in this case is when he told you yesterday all about the Fifth Amendment fellows. He said, 'If a fellow takes the Fifth Amendment, haven't we the right, when I want to employ a man, to take it into consideration?' Why, you don't need the Fifth Amendment. I, as an individual, can refuse to hire anybody because I don't like the color of his tie. I can refuse to hire anybody because I don't like his speech or I don't like the way he dresses. This is my privilege as an American, but that isn't blacklisting. That doesn't mean that I send around a list to all employers that this man will go to.

"And the question is not whether somebody should have the right to reject a man who took the Fifth Amendment. The question is whether Mr. Hartnett can send around a list to all the agencies and sponsors and say, "If you use this man we're going to see to it that you get pressure from the American Legion, Post

41, and the Veterans Action Committee, and thus, by concerted conspiracy, hit a man behind his back and deprive him of his livelihood. Mr. Faulk never faced any accuser. The only way we have had a chance is by waiting six years to come into this courtroom and struggle through every witness, objection after objection, and then we were maligned for coming into an American court. We were told we're liars."[6]

During his two-day summation, Lou Nizer repeatedly hammered on that last sentence by showing how the defendants were the liars, not his client. He went to great lengths to show how the defendants had attempted to deceive the court by altering what they had said in their EBTs.

He reestablished the reasoning behind the appearance of each and every witness for the plaintiff. He also asked that the amount of the damages awarded should be separately leveled on each defendant individually.

Throughout his long oration, Lou never lost the attention of the observers that packed the courtroom, and more importantly, of those twelve people in the jury box in whose hands rested the final outcome of the case. His presentation was forceful, unrelenting, and at times, dramatic. He never let up on the accelerator once he got started.

In conclusion he said, "I will not go on with the rest of the terrible story of this man's ordeal, but I now place his life in your hands. I place his wife's life and his three children's lives in your hands, very literally, because this man's reputation is either going to be restored by a verdict that will ring to the world, or he will be besmirched all over again. I leave to your hands the doing of full justice, and if you do that, ladies and gentlemen, you can sleep well because God will be awake. Thank you."[7]

During the last day of the summations, something totally unexpected occurred when Justice Geller called Lou Nizer and Thomas Bolan into his chambers to inform them that Laurence Johnson had passed away. In his efforts to avoid being called to testify, Johnson checked into a motel in the Bronx, where he was discovered dead from a barbiturate overdose. To be fair to

Johnson, the overdose might have been purely accidental. He was a very sick man at the time, so it could have been simply a bad miscalculation on his part.

To keep this information from the jury, and not to influence their decision, Justice Geller told the attorneys that the panel would be sequestered for the night to prevent them from reading news stories or hearing them from other media.

The next morning, Justice Geller issued his final instructions to the jury before beginning their deliberations. "The good reputation of a person has always been regarded as a cherished possession among the people of a civilized community. A conspiracy is an agreement or understanding between two or more persons, which may include a membership corporation, to do an illegal act. A libel is an illegal act."[8]

Justice Geller went on to explain what was meant by damages. "Compensatory damages are intended to compensate a plaintiff for all the damage he has suffered, that is, to make him whole. The damages awarded must be based upon the injury to his reputation and in his profession. He is entitled to be compensated for the mental anguish, mortification and humiliation which you find and believe he experienced in his public and private life. Punitive damages are intended to protect the community and to vindicate public decency. Malice would include the notion of hostility or intent to injure. You may consider, if you deem it indicative of malice, any testimony given by either of the defendants in this case."[9]

Justice Geller also reminded the jury that the defendant's partial defense on reliance had no effect on compensatory damages, but there could be a mitigation of punitive damages if the defendants had shown great care; accuracy and truth in the use of information on which they relied. He added that none of the organizations described as Communist-fronts were officially so designated.

What he did with that statement in effect was to rule out Bolan's entire case. All that was left to the jury was to determine the amount of the damages. Another important factor was that this case required only ten jurors to agree. The verdict did not have to be unanimous.

At 5:35 p.m., the panel was sent to the jury room.

A little after 9:30 p.m., they were brought back to the courtroom because they had sent a message to Justice Geller that they wanted to ask if they could award more damages than the plaintiff had asked for. Justice Geller told them that it was entirely up to them, and sent them back to finish their work.

At 11:40 p.m., they filed back in to render the decision reached by eleven of the twelve.

The Foreman replied, "We, the jury, have arrived at our decision in favor of Mr. Faulk. We have awarded the plaintiff, Mr. Faulk, compensatory damages in the sum of $1 million against Aware, Inc., Mr. Vincent Hartnett, and the estate of the late Mr. Laurence Johnson. We have also awarded the plaintiff, Mr. Faulk, punitive damages in the sum of $1,250,000 against Aware, Inc. and $1,250,000 against Mr. Hartnett."[10]

Because he was deceased, Laurence could not be held liable for punitive damages.

After six years, the case finally concluded. The awards exceeded the amounts that had been requested. In fact, the total of $3,500,000 was the largest granted by a New York court up to that time in a libel case.

However, the libel case was still not really over.

CHAPTER FORTY-THREE
John Henry Faulk
Part Five: The Aftermath

The verdict in the libel suit filed by John Henry Faulk against Aware, Inc., Vincent Hartnett, and Laurence Johnson was rendered just before midnight on June 28, 1962. The original filing date in the New York Supreme Court was in 1957, but the work needed to put it together began in 1956. As we have seen, the actual trial started on April 23, 1962 after the jury selection process which took place on April 20, 1962.

On the morning after the conclusion of the more than six-year ordeal, the *New York Times* ran a very complimentary editorial titled, "The Faulk Verdict." Among other comments, it said:

> "The libel verdict should have a healthy effect in curing the excesses of the super patriots who sometimes show no more concern for the rights of individuals than the Communists they denounce. The case should assist in establishing a judicial delimitation on the lengths to which private groups, arrogating to themselves the mantle of public protector against subversion, can go in blacklisting and defaming their fellow citizens. We do nothing to strengthen democracy if Americanism is distorted into a device for undermining the freedom the Constitution guarantees to every American."[1]

You would assume that six years would have been enough, but it was not. A request for a rehearing was filed by Aware, Inc. and Vincent Hartnett at the New York Supreme Court Appellate Division. That arm of the judicial system came down with an even stronger acclamation on the original case on October 1, 1963. They found:

"The proof in support of the plaintiff's case was overwhelming. He conclusively established that the defendants planned to destroy his professional career through the use of libelous publications directed to the places where they would do him the most harm. He proved that they succeeded in doing so. The proof established that the libelous statements were not made recklessly, but that they were made deliberately. The acts of the defendants were proven to be as malicious as they were vicious. The defendants were not content merely with publishing the libelous statements complained of knowing that injury to the plaintiff must follow such publications. They pursued the plaintiff with the libel, making sure that its poison would be injected into the wellspring of his professional and economic existence. They did so with deadly effect. He was professionally destroyed."[2]

Once more, Vincent Hartnett appealed only to be struck down by a 6-0 decision in 1964.

One detrimental thing that the appeals court did do was to lower the total of the awards to $550,000, still a considerable sum.

When it came time to collect, there were additional complications. By then, Aware, Inc. was nearly non-existent. Secondly, Vincent was bankrupt, and third, the Laurence Johnson estate was much smaller than had been estimated. After paying off some debts he had accrued and the legal fees, the end result was that John Faulk realized only approximately $175,000, a long way from $3.5 million.

His libel suit accomplished quite a lot. John found work again after a six year drought. The case hammered one of the final nails into the coffin of the blacklist, clearing the road for others, as well as for John. While it did not completely finish the practice, it went a long way toward that end.

We should be eternally grateful to John for having the intestinal fortitude to face up to some of the perpetrators of crimes against our own people.

I can only add, "Well done, John!"

If you want to know the complete story of this trial, I suggest that you read John Faulk's book, *Fear on Trial*. You can also get many details of the proceedings of the case in Louis Nizer's book, *The Jury Returns*.

Chapter Forty-Four
Afterword
The Story of *The Front*

There are many ways to fight back at injustice, even after the fact. One of them is by presenting some of the information on the big screen. There have been several movies made on the subject of the blacklist, but none of them truly hit the nail on the head. However, Walter Bernstein's *The Front* (1976) went a long way toward informing the public about what had occurred during that stormy period in our national history. As you read earlier in this book, the last minute rewrite actually occurred once during Walter Bernstein's career.

The Front made use of several of the people who knew firsthand about the red-baiters running rampant during the 1950s. While some critics panned it for not going far enough, it did make some strong statements about those events.

The Front was the story of a down-on-his-luck restaurant cashier and small-time bookie, Howard Prince, played by Woody Allen, who is approached by his long-time friend, Alfred Miller, played by Michael Murphy, a blacklisted TV writer, to be his front. Miller can no longer get employment due to his blacklisting so he needs someone to present his scripts to producers under his own name. The plan works well for a while, with a few glitches along the way, one of them when Howard is asked to make some last minute changes in a script on the same day the program is to air. How he overcomes the problem is fun to watch. The plan works so well that before long he fronts four writers instead of just Miller.

During the process, Howard meets Florence Barrett, played by Andrea Marcovicci, a script supervisor for the network. She admires Howard for his creative ability and soon they become romantically involved. The network soon becomes the target of the witch-hunters because they cannot find any background information about this new rising star from the writing world. Things get a little murky after that. Unfortunately, the producer of the show in question, Phil Sussman, played by Herschel Bernardi, is all too willing to go along with the probe and will do nothing about it even though he says that he is strongly against what is going on.

One of the primary characters in the scenario is the narrator for the series, Hecky Brown, played by Zero Mostel. He is also being closely watched because of his alleged Communist activities. As a result, he is let go by his employers and forced to try to find another way to earn a living. He attempts to return to super club stand-up comedy and is thwarted, as well. In one case, he is offered only a fraction of what he has been accustomed to getting in that venue. In fact, when it comes time for him to be paid, he receives only a small portion of what he had been promised. Of course, he goes ballistic.

Hecky has been offered a spurious deal by the self-appointed guard dogs of our political conscience. If he befriends Howard and does a little snooping into his history, he, might just get off the hook. This never happens because Hecky and Howard bond in some strange way. They are totally different personalities. The bonding seems to be unlikely, but it happens.

In the end, Hecky becomes thoroughly despondent and throws himself out of a hotel window to end his troubles.

While all of this was going on Florence decides she has had enough of the hypocrisy. She leaves her high-paying job and begins publishing an anti-red-baiting newsletter of her own because she cannot stand by and watch the events affect those close to her. When she asks Howard to assist her in the project, he refuses. He has grown accustomed to his new-found financial security.

Eventually, after Hecky's funeral, Howard changes his mind. He is called to testify at the HUAC hearings. This and Hecky's unfortunate demise make his decision an easy choice. He comes clean with Florence, tells her he is a fraud. He also tells her that he knows how to handle the committee. He will not take the Fifth. He will simply side-step their questions. He knows that all that they really want is to get him to name names that they already have, including poor Hecky Brown. He refuses to comply and tells them in no uncertain terms to find another boy. He is cited for contempt and is sent off to jail to the cheers of an admiring crowd at the train station.

The casting was interesting because Zero and Walter Bernstein were both close friends of Philip Loeb, who ended his own life under similar but real-life circumstances. The rest of the cast and the crew were carefully selected, making use of several previous victims of the blacklist, including director Martin Ritt, a blacklistee. One of the writers Howard fronts for is played by Joshua Shelley, a blacklistee. The TV producer is played by Herschel Bernardi, a blacklistee. Screenwriter Walter Bernstein, Zero Mostel, and Lloyd Gough, also one of the writers Howard fronted for, were all actually listed in *Red Channels*. The incident at the Cascade super club was very similar to what had actually happened Zero.

George Santayana said, "Those who cannot remember the past are condemned to repeat it."

Be ever aware and alert, my friends. We create history every day that we live. I leave you with one more quote to contemplate that I believe to be apropos to the overall subject of this book. Eleanor Roosevelt said, "Yesterday is history, tomorrow is a mystery, and today is a gift, that's why they call it the present." Think about it!

Source Notes

Chapter Two — The Publication

(1) American Business Consultants. *Red Channels: The Report on Communist Influence in Radio and Television* — p. 9

(2) Cogley, David. *Report on Blacklisting: II, Radio-Television* — p. 10

Chapter Three — Kirkpatrick, Bierly and Keenan

(1) *Counterattack* — 7/2/50
(2) Miller, Merle. *The Judges and the Judged* — p. 99
(3) Ibid — p. 100
(4) *Report on Blacklisting* — p. 7
(5) *The Judges and the Judged* — p. 91
(6) *Newsweek* — 6/9/50
(7) *The Judges and the Judged* — p. 91
(8) Ibid — p. 62
(9) Ibid — p. 98

Chapter Four — Laurence A. Johnson

(1) Barnouw, Eric. *The Golden Web: A History of Broadcasting in the United States, 1933-1953* — p. 275
(2) Ibid — p. 275
(3) Ibid.–.p. 275
(4) *Report on Blacklisting* — p. 100-1
(5) Ibid — p. 104
(6) Ibid — p. 105
(7) Ibid — p. 106
(8) Ibid — p. 106
(9) *The Judges and the Judged* — p. 62

Chapter Five — Hartnett, McNamara & Aware, Inc.

(1) *Report on Blacklisting* — p. 135
(2) Caute, David. *The Great Fear: The Anti-Communist Purge under Truman and Eisenhower* — p. 524
(3) *Report on Blacklisting* — p. 130

Chapter Six — The Fronts

(1) *Red Channels* — p. 190
(2) *The Great Fear* — p. 95
(3) Ibid — p. 95
(4) Ibid — p. 95
(5) Ibid — p. 95
(6) *Red Channels* — p. 173
(7) The **Fifth Amendment** of the U.S. Constitution provides, "No person shall be held to answer for a capital, or otherwise infamous crime, unless on a presentment or indictment of a grand jury, except in cases arising in the land or naval forces, or in the militia, when in actual service in time of war or public danger; nor shall any person be subject for the same offense to be twice put in jeopardy of life or limb; nor shall be compelled in any criminal case to be a witness against himself, nor be deprived of life, liberty, or property, without due process of law; nor shall private property be taken for public use, without just compensation."
(8) Ibid — p. 176
(9) *The Great Fear* — p. 614
(10) *Red Channels* — p. 182
(11) *The Great Fear* — p. 614
(12) *Red Channels* — p. 175-6
(13) Ibid — p. 202

Chapter Seven — Clearance

(1) *Report on Blacklisting* — 89-91 (Interpolation)
(2) Navasky, Victor S. *Naming Names* — p. 103-4
(3) Ibid — p. 106

Chapter Eight — Loyalty Oaths

(1) *The Judges and the Judged* — p. 187
(2) Ibid — p. 189-90
(3) Sperber, A. M. *Murrow: His Life and Times* — p. 361

(4) Ibid — p. 361
(5) Ibid — p. 195-6

Chapter Nine — Friendlies

(1) Vaughn, Robert. *Only Victims: A Story of Show Business Blacklisting* — p. 160
(2) *The Great Fear* — p. 499
(3) *Only Victims* — p. 257
(4) Ibid — p. 252
(5) Buhle, Paul and McGilligan, Patrick. *Tender Comrades: A Backstory of the Hollywood Blacklist* — p. 47
(6) Ibid — p. 215
(7) Ibid — p. 486
(8) Ibid — p. 578
(9) Ibid — p. 564

Citations-Cobb-*Red Channels* — p. 37-38

(10) *Naming Names* — p. 270
(11) Bigsby, Christopher. *Arthur Miller: 1915-1962* — p. 435
(12) *Naming Names* — p. 271

Chapter Ten — HUAC

(1) Whitfield, Stephen J. *The Culture of the Cold War*
(2) Bentley, Eric. *Thirty Years of Treason: Excerpts from Hearings before the House Committee on Anti-American Activities—1938-1965* — p. 955
(3) Ibid — p. 956
(4) Ibid — p. 956
(5) Ibid — p. 956
(6) Ibid — p. 956
(7) Ibid — p. 956
(8) Wikipedia: article on Jack Tenney

Chapter Eleven — Jean Muir

Citations — *Red Channels* — p. 113-114

(1) Wikipedia: article on Jean Muir
(2) Everitt, David. *A Shadow of Red: Communism and the Blacklist in Radio and Television* — p. 53-4
(3) Ibid — p. 54
(4) Ibid — p. 69

Chapter Twelve — Ireene Wicker

Citations — *Red Channels* — p. 158

(1) Dunning, John. *On the Air: The Encyclopedia of Old-Time Radio* — p. 618
(2) *Report on Blacklisting* — p. 32
(3) Ibid — p. 33
(4) Author interview with A. M. Sperber — 6/18/86

Chapter Thirteen—Philip Loeb

Citations — *Red Channels* — p. 101-102

(1) Brown, Jared — *Zero Mostel — A Biography* — p. 119
(2) Ibid — p. 120
(3) *Naming Names* — p. 341

Chapter Fourteen — Walter Bernstein

Citations — *Red Channels* — p. 17-18
No Notes

Chapter Fifteen — Zero Mostel

Citations — *Red Channels* — p. 113

(1) *Zero Mostel — A Biography* — p. 97
(2) Ibid — p. 128
(3) Ibid — p. 128
(4) Ibid — p. 130
(5) Ibid — p. 130-1
(6) Ibid — p. 131

Chapter Sixteen — Pete Seeger

Citations — *Red Channels* — p. 130-131

(1) Dunaway, David King — *How Can I Keep from Singing? — The Ballad of Pete Seeger* — p. 229
(2) Ibid — p. 161
(3) Ibid — p. 212
(4) Ibid — p. 212-13
(5) Ibid — p. 213-14
(6) *Only Victims* — p. 201
(7) *How Can I Keep from Singing?* — p. 216
(8) Ibid — p. 218
(9) Ibid — p. 427

Chapter Seventeen — Millard Lampell

Citations — *Red Channels* — p. 95-97

(1) *New York Times* obit — 10/4/97
(2) *A Shadow of Red* — p. 60

(3) *How Can I Keep from Singing?* – p. 84
(4) Ibid – p. 151
(5) Ibid – p. 88
(6) *A Shadow of Red* – p. 206
(7) *How Can I Keep from Singing?* – p. 112
(8) *Arthur Miller* – p. 567

Chapter Eighteen – Marc Blitzstein
Citations – *Red Channels* – p. 20-23
(1) Gordon, Eric A. – *Mark the Music – The Life and Work of Marc Blitzstein* – p. 196
(2) Ibid – p. 205
(3) Ibid – p. 455
(4) Ibid – p. 455
(5) Ibid – p. 455
(6) *New York Herald-Times*-Eric Salztman – 1/23/64

Chapter Nineteen – Artie Shaw
Citations – *Red Channels* – p. 132-133
(1) Nolan, Tom – *Three Chords for Beauty's Sake – The Life of Artie Shaw* – p. 275
(2) Ibid – p. 277
(3) Ibid – p. 277
(4) Ibid – p. 278
(5) *Only Victims* – p. 181
(6) Ibid – p. 182

Chapter Twenty – Hazel Scott
Citations – *Red Channels* – p. 129-130
(1) Chilton, Karen – *Hazel Scott – The Pioneering Journey of Jazz Pianist from Café Society to Hollywood to HUAC* – p. 144
(2) Ibid – p. 143
(3) Ibid – p. 143
(4) Ibid – p. 145
(5) Ibid – p. 146-7
(6) Ibid – p. 147
(7) Ibid – p. 144
(8) Ibid – p. 193

Chapter Twenty-One – Lena Horne
Citations – *Red Channels* – p. 79-80
No notes

Chapter Twenty-Two – Leonard Bernstein
Citations – *Red Channels* – p. 16-17
(1) Seldes, Barry – *Leonard Bernstein – The Political Life of an American Musician* – p. 70

Chapter Twenty-Three – William N. Robson
Citations – *Red Channels* – p. 123-124
(1) Author interview – 9/7/86
(2) Ibid

Chapter Twenty-Four – Norman Corwin
Citations – *Red Channels* – p. 41-43
(1) Bannerman, R. Leroy – *On a Note of Triumph – Norman Corwin and the Golden Years of Radio* – p. 219-20
(2) Ibid – p. 220
(3) *The Judges and the Judged* – p. 105-6
(4) Corwin, Norman – *Overkill and Megalove* – p. 76-7

Chapter Twenty-Five – Arthur Miller
Citations – *Red Channels* – p. 110-112
(1) Bigsby, Christopher. *Arthur Miller: 1915-1962* – p. 410
(2) Ibid – p. 210
(3) Ibid – p. 550
(4) Ibid – p. 559
(5) Ibid – p. 562
(6) Ibid – p. 561
(7) Ibid – p. 597-8

Chapter Twenty-Six – Dorothy Parker
Citations – *Red Channels* – p. 115-116
(1) Keats, John. *You Might as Well Live: The Life and Times of Dorothy Parker* – p. 223-4
(2) Goodman, Walter. *The Committee: The Extraordinary Career of the House Committee on Un-American Activities* – p. 107-8
(3) Plaque outside NAACP headquarters in Baltimore

Chapter Twenty-Seven — Lillian Hellman

Citations — Red Channels — p. 75-77

(1) Speech at American Booksellers Association — 1/9/40
(2) Reply to Governor Lehman — 10/41
(3) Letter to Lehman — 11/41
(4) Article for Screen Writer magazine — 11/47
(5) Only Victims — p. 163-4
(6) HUAC Testimony — 5/21/52

Chapter Twenty-Eight — Dashiell Hammett

Citations — Red Channels — p. 71

(1) Layman, Richard. *Shadow Man: The Life of Dashiell Hammett* — p. 248-9
(2) Ibid — p. 260
(3) Ibid — p. 226-7

Chapter Twenty-Nine — Henry Morgan

Citations — Red Channels — p. 113

(1) Morgan, Henry. *Here's Morgan! The Original BAD BOY of Broadcasting* — p. 200
(2) Ibid — p. 205-6
(3) Ibid — p. 158

Chapter Thirty — Howard Duff

Citations — Red Channels — p. 51-52

(1) Hill, Jason. *Life in the Past Lane—Volume Three: A Look into Media History through the Eyes of Those Who Made It* Author Interview — 5/23/86
(2) *Thirty Years of Treason* — p. 304
(3) Ibid — p. 306-7

Chapter Thirty-One — Lionel Stander

Citations — Red Channels — p. 139

(1) Only Victims — p. 186
(2) Ibid — p. 186-8
(3) HUAC Testimony — 5/6/53
(4) Ibid

Chapter Thirty-Two — Marsha Hunt

Citations — Red Channels — p. 85

(1) *Tender Comrades* — p. 318-19
(2) Ibid — p. 320
(3) Ibid — p. 321
(4) Ibid — p. 323
(5) Ibid — p. 323-4
(6) Ibid — p. 325

Chapter Thirty-Three — Jose Ferrer

Citations — Red Channels — p. 54-55

(1) *The Great Fear* — p. 507
(2) Ibid — p. 99
(3) *Only Victims* — p. 147-8
(4) Ibid — p. 148-9
(5) Ibid — p. 149-50

Chapter Thirty-Four — John Garfield

Citations — Red Channels — p. 58-60

(1) Swindell, Larry. *Body and Soul: The Story of John Garfield* — p. 243
(2) Ibid — p. 243-4
(3) Ibid — p. 244
(4) Ibid — p. 244-5
(5) Ibid — p. 246
(6) *Only Victims* — p. 141-3
(7) Ibid — p. 143
(8) Bernstein, Walter. *Inside Out: A Memoir of the Blacklist* — p. 199

Chapter Thirty-Five — Orson Welles

Citations — Red Channels — p. 155-157

(1) Thomson, David. *Rosebud: The Story of Orson Welles* — p. 53
(2) Callow, Simon and Welles, Orson. *Orson Welles, Volume One: The Road to Xanadu* — p. 249
(3) Ibid — p. 249
(4) Ibid — p. 249
(5) Flanagan, Hallie. *Arena: The History of the Federal Theatre* — p. 336
(6) *Rosebud* — p. 81
(7) *Xanadu* — p. 557
(8) Ibid — p. 557-8

Chapter Thirty-Six — Edward G. Robinson

Citations — Red Channels — p. 122-123

(1) Robinson, Edward G. and Spigelgass, Leonard. *All My Yesterdays: An Autobiograph* — p. 252

(2) Ibid – p. 253
(3) Ibid – p. 242-3
(4) *Only Victims* – p. 164-5
(5) *All My Yesterdays* – p. 264
(6) Ibid – p. 244-5

Chapter Thirty-Seven – Langston Hughes

Citations – *Red Channels* – p. 82-84

(1) *New York Times* obit – 5/23/67
(2) *The Nation* – 6/19/26
(3) Hughes, Langston (author), Rampersad, Arnold (Editor). *The Collected Poems of Langston Hughes* – p. 165
(4) Ibid – p. 195
(5) Ibid – p. 291
(6) Ibid – p. 572
(7) Testimony for Permanent Subcommittee on Investigations – U.S. GPO – p. 988
(8) *Naming Names* – p. 192-3
(9) Hughes Statement – 1953
(10) *The Collected Poems of Langston Hughes* – p. 453

Chapter Thirty-Eight – The Others

List from *Red Channels*

Chapter Thirty-Nine – John Henry Faulk – The Filing

(1) Faulk, John Henry. *Fear on Trial* – p. 18
(2) Ibid – p. 19

Chapter Forty – The Pre-Trial

No Notes

Chapter Forty-One – The Trial

(1) *Fear on Trial* – 156-7
(2) Ibid – p. 158
(3) Ibid – p. 158
(4) Ibid – p. 160-2
(5) Ibid – p. 164
(6) Ibid – p. 170
(7) Ibid – p. 173-9
(8) Ibid – p. 181
(9) Ibid – p. 182

(10) Ibid – p. 188-90
(11) Ibid – p. 190-1
(12) Ibid – p. 208-9
(13) Ibid – p. 210
(14) Ibid – p. 216-18
(15) Ibid – p. 271
(16) Ibid – p. 272
(17) Ibid – p. 272

Chapter Forty-Two – John Henry Faulk – Summation & Verdict

(1) *Fear on Trial* – p. 367-8
(2) Ibid – p. 368
(3) Ibid – p. 370
(4) Ibid – p. 371
(5) Ibid – p. 373
(6) Ibid – p. 373-5
(7) Ibid – p. 385
(8) Ibid – p. 387
(9) Ibid – p. 387-8
(10) Ibid – p. 390

Chapter Forty-Three – The Aftermath

(1) *Fear on Trial* – p. 392-3
(2) Ibid – p. 395-6

Bibliography

American Business Consultants. *Red Channels: The Report on Communist Influence in Radio and Television.* New York: Counterattack, 1950.

Bannerman, R. Leroy. *On a Note of Triumph: Norman Corwin and the Golden Years of Radio.* New York: Lyle Stuart, 1986.

Barnouw, Eric. *The Golden Web: A History of Broadcasting in the United States, 1933-1953.* New York: Oxford Press, 1968.

Barth, Alan. *The Loyalty of Free Men.* New York: Viking Press, 1951.

Bentley, Eric. *Thirty Years of Treason: Excerpts from Hearings before the House Committee on Anti-American Activities—1938-1965.* New York: Thunder's Mouth Press/Nation Books, 1971.

Bernstein, Walter. *Inside Out: A Memoir of the Blacklist.* New York: Da Capo Press, 2000.

Bigsby, Christopher. *Arthur Miller: 1915-1962.* Massachusetts: Harvard University Press, 2009.

Brady, Kathleen. *Lucille: The Life of Lucille Ball.* New York: Hyperion, 1994.

Brown, Jared. *Zero Mostel: A Biography.* New York: Atheneum, 1989.

Buhle, Paul and Wagner, Dave. *Blacklisted: The Film Lover's Guide to the Hollywood Blacklist.* New York: Palgrove-McMillan, 2002.

Buhle, Paul and McGilligan, Patrick. *Tender Comrades: A Backstory of the Hollywood Blacklist.* New York: St. Martin's Press, 1997.

Callow, Simon and Welles, Orson. *Orson Welles, Volume One: The Road to Xanadu.* New York: Viking Press, 1995.

Caute, David. *The Great Fear: The Anti-Communist Purge under Truman and Eisenhower.* New York: Simon and Schuster, 1975.

Chilton, Karen. *Hazel Scott: The Pioneering Journey of a Jazz Pianist, from Café Society to Hollywood to HUAC.* Ann Arbor, Michigan: University of Michigan Press, 2008.

Cogley, David. *Report on Blacklisting: II, Radio-Television.* New York: Arno Press/New York Times, 1972.

Corwin, Norman. *Trivializing America: The Triumph of Mediocrity.* Secaucus, New Jersey: Lyle Stuart, 1986.

Corwin, Norman. *Overkill and Megalove.* New York: World Publishing Company, 1963.

Donati, William. *Ida Lupino: A Biography.* Lexington, Kentucky: University Press of Kentucky, 1996.

Dunaway, David King. *How Can I Keep From Singing?: The Ballad of Pete Seeger.* New York: Villard Books, 2008.

Dunning, John. *On the Air: The Encyclopedia of Old-Time Radio.* New York: Oxford University Press, 1995.

Dyrector, Stanley. *Shedding Light on the Hollywood Blacklist: Conversations with Participants.* Albany, Georgia: Bear Manor Media, 2013.

Everitt, David. *A Shadow of Red: Communism and the Blacklist in Radio and Television.* Chicago: Ivan R. Dee, 2007.

Faulk, John Henry. *Fear on Trial.* New York: Simon and Schuster, Inc., 2007.

Flanagan, Hallie. *Arena: The History of the Federal Theatre.* New York: Limelight Edition, 1940.

Gavin, James. *Stormy Weather: The Life of Lena Horne.* New York: Atria, 2009.

Gentry, Curt. *J. Edgar Hoover: The Man and His Secrets*. New York: W. W. Norton and Company, 1991.

Goodman, Walter. *The Committee: The Extraordinary Career of the House Committee on Un-American Activities*. New York: Farrar, Straus and Giroux, 1968.

Gordon, Bernard. *Hollywood Exile, or How I Learned to Love the Blacklist*. Austin, Texas: University of Texas Press, 1989.

Gordon, Eric. *Mark the Music: The Life and Work of Marc Blitzstein*. New York: St. Martin's Press, 1989.

Hamilton, James. *The Power to Probe: A Study of Congressional Investigations*. New York: Random House, 1976.

Haskins, James and Benson, Kathleen. *Lena: A Personal and Professional Biography of Lena Horne*. New York: Stein and Day, 1984.

Haygood, Wil. *King of the Cats: The Life and Times of Adam Clayton Powell, Jr.* New York: Harper-Collins, 1993.

Hellman, Lillian. *An Unfinished Woman: A Memoir*. Boston: Little, Brown and Company, 1999.

Hellman, Lillian. *Pentimento*. Boston: Little, Brown and Company, 1973.

Hellman, Lillian. *Scoundrel Time*. Boston: Little, Brown and Company, 1976.

Hill, Jason. *Life in the Past Lane—Volume One: A Look into Media History through the Eyes of Those Who Made It*. Albany, Georgia: Bear Manor Media, 2013.

Hill, Jason. *Life in the Past Lane—Volume Two: A Look into Media History through the Eyes of Those Who Made It*. Albany, Georgia: Bear Manor Media, 2015.

Hill, Jason. *Life in the Past Lane—Volume Three: A Look into Media History through the Eyes of Those Who Made It*. Albany, Georgia: Bear Manor Media, 2015.

Hughes, Langston (author), Rampersad, Arnold (Editor). *The Collected Poems of Langston Hughes*. New York: Vintage Books, 1995.

Horne, Lena and Schickel, Richard. *Lena*. New York: Doubleday and Company, 1965.

Houseman, John. *Unfinished Business: Memoirs: 1902-1988*. New York: Applause Theatre Books, 1989.

Hunt, Marsha. *The Way We Wore: Styles of the 1930s and '40s and Our World Since Then*. Fallbrook, California: Fallbrook Publishers, Ltd., 1993.

Keats, John. *You Might as Well Live: The Life and Times of Dorothy Parker*. New York: Simon and Schuster, 1970.

Keyes, Evelyn. *Scarlett O'Hara's Younger Sister: My Lively Life In and Out of Hollywood*. New York: Fawcett Crest Books, 1977.

Keyes, Evelyn. *I'll Think About That Tomorrow*. New York: Penguin Books, 1991.

Layman, Richard. *Shadow Man: The Life of Dashiell Hammett*. New York: Harcourt, Brace, Jovanovich, 1981.

Meredith, Burgess. *So Far, So Good: A Memoir*. New York: Little, Brown and Company, 1994.

Miller, Merle. *The Judges and the Judged*. New York: Doubleday and Company, Inc., 1952.

Morgan, Henry. *Here's Morgan! The Original BAD BOY of Broadcasting*. New York: Barricade Books, 1994.

Morris, George. *John Garfield. An Illustrated History of Movies*. New York: A Jove Publications, 1977.

Navasky, Victor S. *Naming Names*. New York: Viking Press, 1980.

Nizer, Louis. *The Jury Returns*. New York: Doubleday and Company, 1966.

Nolan, Tom. *Three Chords for Beauty's Sake: The Life of Artie Shaw*. New York: W. W. Norton and Company, 2010.

Paper, Lewis J. *Empire: William S. Paley and the Making of CBS*. New York: St. Martin's Press, 1987.

Peyser, Joan. *Bernstein: A Biography*. New York: Beech Tree Books, 1987.

Rampersad, Arnold. *The Life of Langston Hughes: Volume II: 1941-1967, I Dream a World*. New York: Oxford University Press, 2002.

Rampersad, Arnold (Editor), Hughes, Langston (author). *The Collected Poems of Langston Hughes*. New York: Vintage Books, 1995.

Robinson, Edward G. and Spigelgass, Leonard. *All My Yesterdays: An Autobiography*. New York: Hawthorne Books, 1973.

Schrecker, Ellen. *Many are the Crimes: McCarthyism in America*. Princeton, New Jersey: Princeton University Press, 1998.

Seldes, Barry. *Leonard Bernstein: The Political Life of an American Musician*. Berkley, California: University of California Press, 2009.

Sperber, A. M. *Murrow: His Life and Times*. New York: Freundlich Books, 1986.

Swindell, Larry. *Body and Soul: The Story of John Garfield*. New York: William Morrow and Company, 1975.

Thomson, David. *Rosebud: The Story of Orson Welles*. New York: Alfred A. Knopf, 1996.

Whitfield, Stephen J. *The Culture of the Cold War*. Baltimore, Maryland: John Hopkins University Press, 1996.

Vaughn, Robert. *Only Victims: A Story of Show Business Blacklisting*. New York: G. P. Putnam's Sons, 1972.

Index

Abbott & Costello, 17
Abernathy, Ralph, 77
Ackerman, Harry, 123
Adler, Larry, 222
Adler, Luther, 222
Adler, Stella, 222
Allen, Steve, 99
Allen, Woody, 268
Alma Long Scott All Girl Jazz Band, 104
Andersen, Hans Christian, 53
Anthony, Earl C., 36
Arens, Richard, 136, 138
Armstrong, Louis, 108
Astor, Mary, 158
Atwater, Edith, 222
Aumack, Charlotte, 36
Auslander, Dr. Jacob, 25
Avery, Andrew aka Sam Horn, 8
Aware Publication, 16, 233, 235, 258
Baarslag, Karl H. W., 165
Bacall, Lauren, 179
Ball, Lucille, 27
Barrymore, Ethyl, 27
Barth, Alan, 38
Bauman, Paul, 65
Bay, Howard, 222
Bean, Orson, 233, 234, 254
Bedin, Ezio, 108
Beethoven, Ludwig von, 54, 75, 97, 120
Bell, Ralph, 222
Benchley, Robert, 142
Bennett, Joan, 27
Berg, Gertrude, 59
Berger, George, 240
Berkeley, Martin, 39-40, 154, 165
Bernardi, Herschel, 269, 270
Bernstein, Leonard, 27, 93, 97, 100, 105, 115-120

Bernstein, Walter, 40-41, 60, 62-67, 72, 197, 268, 270
Bessie, Mike, 38
Biberman, Herbert, 195, 196
Bierly, Ken, x, 7, 9, 10, 32
Black, Ivan, 69
Blankfort, Michael, 223
Blitzstein, Marc, 89-97, 116, 117
Blomberg, J. Edward, 223
Boardman, True, 223
Bogart, Humphrey, 158, 168, 179
Bolan, Thomas, 240, 262
Bond, Ward, 39
Bonner, Herbert, 45
Bookman, Sidney, 27
Brand, Millen, 223
Brand, Oscar, 223
Brando, Marlon, 192
Brewer, Roy, 189
Brooks, Mel, 69
Brooks, Richard, 27
Browder, Earl, 5
Brown, Himan, 223, 255
Brown, Jared, 73
Brown, John, 223
Broz, Josep (Marshall Tito), 63
Buchanan, Eleanor Johnson, 15-17
Buchman, Sidney, 88
Buchner, Georg, 203
Burrows, Abe, 223
Butler, Hugo, 195
Café Society, 69, 105, 112
Calhern, Louis, 27
Calloway, Cab, 111
Campbell, Wendell, 237
Cantor, Eddie, 27
Carey, Joseph, 44
Carnovsky, Morris, 223

Carrington, John, 45
Case, Francis, 45
Caspery, Vera, 223
Cerf, Bennett, 27
Chekov, Anton, 167
Cherveny, John, 26
Chess, Stephen, 50
Chodorov, Edward, 223
Chodorov, Jerome, 27
Christians, Mady, 223
Clardy, Kit, 45, 101, 102
Clark, Tom, 29
Clegg, Hugh, 17
Clurman, Harold, 195
Cobb, Lee J., 41-42, 72
Cohn, Harry, 172
Cohn, Roy, 160-161, 219, 220, 239, 240
Collingwood, Charles, 233, 234, 251-252, 254, 260
Collins, Richard, 28
Collyer, Bud, 251, 233
Connelly, Marc, 223
Conniff, Frank, 100
Copeland, Aaron, 117, 119, 223
Corwin, Al, 127
Corwin, Emil, 127
Corwin, Norman, 86, 126-130
Cotton Club, 111
Cotton, Joseph, 27
Coward, Noel, 167
Cox, James, 121
Cronyn, Hume, 88
Crosby, Bing, 123
Crosby, John, 54
Crowninshield, Frank, 142
Dann, Michael, 51
DaSilva, Howard, 27, 188, 202, 223
Dassin, Jules, 41
Davis, Benjamin J., Jr., 54-55, 106, 113, 185, 186, 188
Davis, Bette, 158

Dean, James, 192
DeKoven, Roger, 223
DeMille, Agnes, 27
DeMille, Cecil B., 36
Dempsey, John, 44
Dewey, Tom, 65
Dickens, Charles, 2
Dickler, Gerald, 235
Dickstein, Samuel, 43-44
Dies, Martin, 44, 144, 201-202
Dixon, Dean, 223
Dolan, Jose, 157, 161
Douglas, Kirk, 27
Douglas, Melvin, 27
Downes, Olin, 223
Doyle, Clyde, 45, 71-72, 101
Drake, Alfred, 223
Draper, Paul, 223
Duff, Howard, 167, 171
Dunne, Philip, 179, 181
Dunne, Steve, 171
Durbin, Deanna, 27
Durr, Clifford J., 224
Dyer-Bennett, Richard, 224
Eagle, S. P. (Sam Spiegel), 168
Ellington, Duke, 111
Ernst, Morris, 38
Fadiman, Clifton, 27
Faulk, John Henry, 23. 232-266
Ferrer, Jose, 45, 183-189, 193
File 13-Volume 1, 19
File 13-Volume 2, 19, 164
Fineschriber, William, 38
Fish, Hamilton, III, 43
Fiske, Harrison Grey, 201
Fitch, Louise, 224
Flanagan, Halle, 201-202
Fonda, Henry, 27
Ford, Henry, 86
Fortas, Abe, 185
Franco, Francisco, 119, 148, 217

Frazier, James, Jr., 45
Freedman, David, 55
Gabel, Martin, 224
Gaeth, Arthur, 224
Gailmor, William S., 224
Gang, Martin, 22, 34
Gardner, Ava, 27
Garfield, John, 27, 45, 112, 178, 190-198
Garrett, Betty, 112
Garrison, Lloyd, 220
Gaynor, Leonard, 127
Geer, Will, 188, 224
Geller, Abraham, 241, 245, 246, 248, 250, 255, 256, 258, 262-264
Gerrard, James W., 36
Gilbert, Ronnie, 75
Gilford, Jack, 224
Gillespie, Dizzy, 108
Glazer, Tom, 224
Goddard, Paulette, 27
Goodman, Benny, 27, 99
Goodson, Mark, 255
Gordon, Ruth, 224
Gough, Lloyd, 224
Gould, Jack, 22, 23, 51
Gould, Morton, 224
Graham, Shirley, 224
Gramercy 5, 100
Grauer, Ben, 224
Grayson, Mitchell, 224
Greene, Felix, 125
Greenstreet, Sidney, 158
Grenell, Horace, 224
Grimm Brothers, 10, 53
Guthrie, Woody, 64, 75, 84
Hagen, Uta, 27, 224
Hahn, Paul M., 14
Haley, Arthur, 44
Hall, George, 79
Hammer, Armand, 56
Hammer, Victor, 56

Hammerstein, Oscar, III., 38
Hammett, Dashiell, 155, 156-162, 168, 169, 170
Harburg, E. Y. (Yip), 224
Harding, Warren G., 121
Harrison, Burr, 45, 106, 107
Hart, Moss, 27
Hartnett, Vincent, x, 4, 18-23, 128, 163-164, 232, 235, 238-239, 242-245, 248, 255, 260, 261, 264, 265-266
Hayes, Lee, 75, 84
Hayton, Lennie, 113, 114
Hearst, William Randolph, 203-205
Hebert, F. Edward, 45
Hecht, Ben, 27
Hecht, Harold, 27
Heflin, Van, 27
Heller, Robert, 224
Hellerman, Freddy, 75
Hellman, Lillian, 45, 105, 146-155, 160, 168
Hemingway, Ernest, 143, 149
Henley, Paul, 26
Hepburn, Katherine, 27
Hiken, Nat, 224
Hobart, Rose, 225
Hodges, Johnny, 108
Holden, William, 27
Holiday, Billy, 225
Holiday, Judy, 225
Holmgren, Roderick B., 225
Hoover, J. Edgar, 5, 10, 11, 95, 119, 139, 209
Hopkins, Harry, 201
Horn, Sam aka Andrew Avery, 8
Horne, Edna, 110
Horne, Lena, 105, 109-114
Horne, Teddy, 110
Horton, Zilphia, 77
Houseman, John, 92, 93, 117, 200-201, 202, 203, 205
Hughes, Howard, 203
Hughes, Langston, 212-221
Hunt, Marsha, 178-182

Hunter, Kim, 254-255
Hurwitz, Leo, 225
Huston, John, 27, 178, 181
Huston, Walter, 27
Hyman, Joe, 237
Irving, Charles, 225
Ives, Burl, 225
Jackson, Donald, 45, 46, 70, 101, 102, 136, 185, 187-188, 196-197
Jaffe, Sam, 225
Janney, Leon, 225
Jerome, V. J., 153
Johnson, Laurence A., xi, 13-17, 67, 123, 232, 235, 239-240, 243, 245, 253-255, 257, 262-265
Josephson, Barney, 69, 105, 106
Judd, Morris, 26
Julian, Joe, 225
Kahn, Gordon, 28
Kanin, Garson, 225
Kaye, Danny, 179
Kazan, Elia, 40, 41, 42
Keane, George, 225
Kearney, Bernard, 179
Keenan, Jack, x, 7, 12, 32
Keith, Donna, 225
Kelton, Pert, 225
Kempton, Murray, 245
Kendrick, Alexander, 225
Keyes, Evelyn, 102-103, 179
Khrushchev, Nikita, 250
King, Dr. Martin Luther, Jr., 108, 144
Kipling, Rudyard, 53
Kirkpatrick, Theodore, x, 7, 30, 32, 50, 54-55
Klein, Adelaide, 225
Knight, Felix, 225
Knopf, Alfred, 158
Koch, Howard, 28, 33, 203, 225
Kohlberg, Alfred, 7, 50
Koussevitzky, Serge, 117
Kraber, Tony, 225

Kramer, Stanley, 180
LaGuardia, Fiorello, 158
Lambertson, William, 58
Lampell, Millard, 75, 82-88
Lancaster, Burt, 27
Landon, Alf, 5
Lang, Fritz, 27
Langston, Mary Patterson, 214
LaTouche, John, 225
Laurents, Arthur, 225
Lawrence, Jerome, 86
Lawson, John Howard, 153, 170
Layman, Richard, 157
Ledbetter, Huddie William (Lead Belly), 75
Lee, Canada, 27
Lee, Gypsy Rose, 225
Lee, Madeline, 226
Lee, Robert E., 86
Lehman, Herbert, 149
Lev, Ray, 226, 247
Levy, Dave, 22
Lewis Elliott, 203
Lewis, Bill, 122
Lie, Trygve, 8
Loeb, Philip H., 45, 57-61, 233, 270
Logan, Ella, 225
Lomax, Alan, 226
Long, Avon,
Lord, Phillips H., 18
Lorre, Peter, 27, 158
Losey, Joe, 36, 226
Lovell, Glen, 180-182
Loy, Myrna, 27, 158
Lupino, Ida, 171
Lyon, Cecil, 108
Lyon, Peter, 108, 226
MacLeish, Archibald, 122, 200
MacMahon, Aline, 226
Madden, Owney, 111
Magana, Manuel, 25
Mankiewicz, Joe, 36, 203, 204

Mann, Paul, 226
March, Fredric, 112
Marcovicci, Andrea, 268
Margo, 226
Martinson, Paul, 239, 240
Marx, Groucho, 27
Marx, Karl, 158
Mason, Noah, 44
McCarthy, Joseph, x, 2, 46, 160, 169, 200, 219, 239
McCormack, John, 43
McCormick, Myron, 226
McCormick, Robert R., 203
McCullough, Hester, xi, 50
McDowell, John, 45
McGrath, J. Howard, 11
McGrath, Paul, 226
McNamara, Frank, x, 18
McSweeney, John, 45
Menjou, Adolph, 39
Meredith, Burgess, 226
Michelangelo, 54
Milestone, Lewis, 28
Miller, Arthur, 45, 132-139
Milton, John, 251
Milton, Paul, x, 23, 239, 255-256
Mitropoulos, Dimitri, 117
Monroe, Marilyn, 135
Montgomery, Robert, 39
Moore, Gary, 255
Moore, Sam, 66
Morgan, Henry, 163-166
Morros, Boris, 118
Mostel, Kate, 60
Mostel, Zero, 45, 60, 68-73, 105, 269-270
Moulder, Morgan, 45, 185
Muir, Jean, 48-52
Mundt, Karl, 45
Mundy, Meg, 226
Muni, Paul, 200
Murphy, Michael, 268

Murray, Lynn, 226
Murray, Tony, 253-254
Murrow, Edward R., 37, 38, 56, 236
Myers, Ben, 226
Nichols, Lou, 10
Nixon, Richard, 45, 119
Nizer, Louis, 235-266
Odets, Clifford, 192
Overman, Lee, 43
Oxnam, Bishop G. Bromley, 8, 25
Paley, Bill, 5, 38, 118, 123, 124
Parker, Dorothy, 140-145, 155
Parks, Larry, 112
Parsons, Louella, 204
Patri, Dr. Angelo, 192
Peck, Gregory, 27
Perl, Arnold, 226
Peterson, J. Harden, 45
Peyser, Joan, 116, 120
Pichel, Irving, 28
Pious, Minerva, 226
Piston, Walter, 116
Plain Talk, 7, 32
Polansky. Abe, 27, 41
Ponti, Carlo, 66
Potter, Charles, 45
Powell, Jr., Adam Clayton, 106
Powell, William, 158
Powers, Stefanie, 173
Pulitzer, Joseph, 203
Pyle, Ernie, 51
Radulovich, Milo, 56
Randall, Tony, 252, 258
Rankin, John, 25, 44, 45
Raphaelson, Sam, 226
Reagan, Ronald, 184
Ream, Joseph H., 37
Reiner, Fritz, 116
Reis, Bernard, 226
Revere, Anne, 27, 226
Ritt, Martin, 41, 270

Roberts, Kenneth, 227
Roberts, Marguerite, 41
Robeson, Paul, 64, 105, 112, 119, 189, 193, 234
Robespierre, Maximilien, 203
Robinson, Earl, 86, 227, 234
Robinson, Edward G., 27, 45, 112, 200, 206-211
Robson, William N., 121-125, 169
Rockefeller, Nelson, 79, 105
Rodzinski, Arthur, 117
Rome, Harold, 227
Roosevelt, Eleanor, 84, 105, 113, 123, 143, 180, 185, 270
Roosevelt, Franklin D., 3, 5, 28, 57, 84, 143, 201, 218
Rosenthal, Jean, 93
Rossen, Robert, 28
Rosten, Norman, 128, 227
Royle, Selena, 227
Ruskin, Coby, 227
Ryan, Robert, 27
Ryan, Sylvester, 159, 160
Salt, Waldo, 28
Salzman, Eric, 97
Santayana, George, viii, 270
Saypol, Irving, 159
Schiller, Friedrich, 120
Schmidt, Godfrey, 238, 239
Schultz, Rabbi Benjamin, 50
Schwarz, Bill, 237
Scott, Hazel, 45, 104-108, 110, 112
Seaton, Irene, 56
Seeger, Pete, 27, 45, 64-65, 74-81, 84, 85
Seeger, Toshi, 65, 75, 77
Sergio, Lisa, 227
Shakespeare, William, 167, 251
Shaw, Artie, 27, 45, 98-103, 176
Shaw, Irwin, 27, 227
Shayon, Robert Lewis, 227
Shelley, Joshua, 270
Shepherd, Anne, 227
Sherer, Gordon, 45, 46, 78, 79, 80, 101
Sherwood, Robert, 142
Shirer, William L., 227
Shostakovich, Dmitri, 119
Silber, Irwin, 77
Siloti, Alexander, 91
Simonov, Konstantin, 193
Sinatra, Frank, 27, 112
Sissle, Noble, 112
Slade, Sam, 235
Sloane, Allan, 227
Smith, Howard K., 227
Sondergaard, Gale, 227
Sondergaard, Hester, 227
Sorenson, Max H., 5
Spellman, Francis Cardinal, 7
Spier, William, 168
St. John, Robert, 227
Stackovich, Tony, 25
Stalin, Joseph 'Joe', 170, 203
Stander, Lionel, 44, 45, 172-177
Stanislavsky, Constantin, 192
Stanton, Frank, 123, 124
Starnes, Joe, 44
Steele, Johannes, 227
Stewart, Donald Ogden, 144
Stewart, Paul, 227
Stokes, Alvin William, 112
Stookey, (Noel) Paul, 76
Streit, Saul, 136, 237
Stripling, Robert, 44, 45
Stritch, Samuel Cardinal, 7
Sullivan, Elliot, 227
Susskind, David, 22, 245-249
Sweets, William, 19, 228
Tamiris, Helen, 228
Tarantino, Jimmy, 170
Tavenner, Frank, 45, 46, 78, 79, 101, 153, 185-186, 193-194, 195, 196, 234
Tenney, Jack, 46, 112, 185
Thomas, J. Parnell, 44, 45, 185
Thompson, Kay, 168

Todd, Betty, 228
Tone, Franchot, 27
Travers, Mary, 76
Trotsky, Leon, 203
Truman, Harry, 11, 44
Trumbo, Dalton, 170
Untermeyer, Louis, 228
Vail, Richard, 45
Vaughn, Hilda, 228
Velde, Harold, 45, 46, 102, 173-176
Verdi, Giuseppe, 54
Voorhis, Jerry, 44
Wagner, Oscar, 104
Wagner, Robert, 173
Wallace, Henry A., 233, 234, 246
Walsh, J, Raymond, 228
Walter, Francis, 45, 78, 79, 106, 153, 154, 155, 185, 208, 210
Wanamaker, Sam, 228
Ward, Carol, 235
Ward, Theodore, 228
Warner, Jack, 40
Washington, Fredi, 228
Wayne, John, 39
We, the Underground, 11
Webster, Margaret, 228
Welles, Orson, 27, 92, 93, 117, 199-205
Wells, H. G., 203
White, E. B., 35, 38
White, Josh, 228
White, Walter, 124
Whitman, Walt, 80
Wicker, Ireene, 53-56
Wicker, Walter Charles, 56
Wicker, Jr., Walter Charles, 55
Wilde, Cornell, 27
Wilder, Billy, 27
Wilder, Gene, 68-69
Willis, Edwin, 45
Windsor, Kathleen, 100
Winkler, Betty, 228

Wolfson, Martin, 228
Wood, John, 45, 57, 106, 151, 152-153, 154, 185
Woods, Leslie, 228
Wren, Jack, x, 32, 33, 164, 165, 166
Wyler, William, 27, 179, 181
Yaffe, Richard, 228
Yarrow, Peter, 76
Young, Robert, 17, 27

www.ingramcontent.com/pod-product-compliance
Lightning Source LLC
Chambersburg PA
CBHW060555230426
43670CB00011B/1834